Exiles: A Prisoner's Daily Devotional is true to the Word of God and challenges, convicts, informs, and encourages readers in their walk with Christ. Each of the three authors uses their own style of writing as a vehicle to drive the reader to the place God has designed for us all. *Exiles* gives the liberated Christian prisoner a battle cry of triumph for each day.

– Jesse A., serving life

Knowing Terry, Jason, and Johnny, I am aware of the effort, time, and care put into developing this daily devotional for prisoners. Inside you will find the cares and concerns of three men of God standing firmly in the midst of their most trying experiences. In times of trial, struggle, and even the purging of God, this devotional will serve to inspire, encourage, and guide you through those most trying times of *your* exile.

– Frank W., serving life

Countless daily devotions are produced every year, but *Exiles: A Prisoner's Daily Devotional* is unique because it is written for prisoners by prisoners. The writers draw from their personal experiences in prison, expressing them through the lens of Scripture, to aide other prisoners in their quest and struggle to live for God.

– Mike W., serving life

Exiles will assist believers along the path of discipleship and instruct them on faithfulness in prison life, while enriching them with good theology packed inside of short daily devotionals.

– Jarrett H., serving 60 years

Who better to communicate the heart of God to prisoners than fellow prisoners who've been transformed by the love of Christ? Solley, Karch, and Blevins capture the essence of a prisoner's daily struggles and lift readers out of deep personal introspection into a focused, growing knowledge of God. *Exiles* evokes changed thoughts that lead to right actions as each day's readings build faith in the One who brings us all out of exile into His welcoming arms.

Exiles: A Prisoner's Daily Devotional is a profound work from the soul of an incarcerated Christian, husband, and father. Terry Solley's walk with Christ while he has been incarcerated is a testimony to the power of a changed heart—something only God can do. He skillfully weaves his life experience with his understanding of what Christ has gifted and called him to be. His dependence on Christ for his daily strength is borne out in this 365 day devotional guide, one that will definitely relate to the individual currently behind bars. There's no greater credibility than hearing from one who has lived what he is testifying about. Terry Solley does just that in this exceptional devotional guide. I highly recommend it.

I find this resource—written by and for prisoners—fills a great need for solid material in this unique environment. To meet men and women in this setting exactly where they are at with the clear Word of God, which is the only source of strength and promise, is something that will serve the kingdom of Christ in immeasurable ways.

Exiles is a beautiful testimony to the grace and to the power of the word of God. In this daily devotional, the authors guide the reader into the riches of the scripture. Writing from the experience of knowing first-hand the grace of Christ, Johnny Blevins applies the truths of Scripture to the unique circumstances of incarceration. The glory of the gospel and of the Savior comes shining through in each of the 365 devotions. I heartily recommend *Exiles* and personally look forward to seeing how Christ will use this wonderful work.

Exiles is a source of spiritual strength to anyone whose faith has ever been tested. Terry Solley, Jason Karch, and Johnny Blevins know what it is like to walk through fire and not be set ablaze. This devotional is a testimony to God's impeccable credibility.

– John D. Wilsey, Ph.D., Southeastern Baptist Theological Seminary
Assistant Professor of History and Christian Apologetics,
Southwestern Baptist Theological Seminary

Exiles is a book of Christian devotions written by three men who embraced their gift of faith in Jesus Christ while in prison. Combined, they have already been in prison for 51 years. Two of them have life sentences, and one has a 35-year sentence. They have written this outstanding devotional book from their ongoing confinement behind bars but with the freedom they have in Christ. If you are reading this book while in prison, this devotional was written for you by those who are there with you. Each page teaches you something new about how life in prison does not have to be the same old game. No matter who you are or where you are, you can read *Exiles* and learn more about Jesus Christ, his care for the prisoner, and the transformative power of his gospel. This devotional book will point you to Jesus Christ like no devotional book I have ever read.

–Brenna M. Norwood, Ph.D., The Southern Baptist Theological Seminary
The Heart of Texas Foundation

A Prisoner's Daily Devotional

But seek the welfare of the city where I have sent you into exile, and pray to the LORD on its behalf, for in its welfare you will find your welfare. –Jeremiah 29:7

Johnny Blevins, Jason Karch, and Terry Solley

THE HEART OF TEXAS FOUNDATION PRESS

HEARTOFTEXASFOUNDATION.ORG

Exiles
© Copyright 2015 by From East to West Ministries

Third Edition, 2017.

The Heart of Texas Foundation Press
Bellville, Texas

The Heart of Texas Foundation Press exists to publish resources that proclaim the good news of Jesus Christ. www.HeartofTexasFoundation.org

For inquiries, write to:
The Heart of Texas Foundation
Post Office Box 110
Bellville, TX 77418
press@heartoftexasfoundation.org

ISBN-13: 9780692506653
ISBN: 0692506659

Subject Heading: Bible. Christian. Devotional. Prison.

Managing Editor: Brenna M. Norwood
Cover Design: Nan E. Donahoe

Printed in the United States of America

Available on Amazon in paperback and Kindle.

FOREWORD

Many devotionals have been written throughout history, some have been written by prisoners. Some of those prisoners were suffering for the gospel while others were serving time for committing crimes. *Exiles: A Prisoner's Daily Devotional* is written for those who have been convicted of crimes by men who understand that life as much as any.

I am blessed to see this work come to fruition and to know the men who crafted it. It is our hope that these devotional thoughts resonate with men and women serving time in such a way as to give them real hope—not a false hope in parole, personal freedom, healing, or any of the pitfalls put before the eyes of desperate people, but a true hope in the person and work of Jesus Christ as He steps down into their cell.

Sometimes the devotional for the day might be at a slightly higher reading level than some are used to. Take this as a challenge. Prison, in spite of its many hardships, is the ideal place to expand your mind. I went to prison while still in high school and began my real education and spiritual journey while serving time. I earned a GED, several vocational trades, and an associate's degree. After making parole, I finished a bachelor's degree. In the spring of 2015, I graduated with the master of divinity from Southwestern Baptist Theological Seminary. The men who wrote the devotional you hold are on the same journey; though in my estimation, they have a firmer grasp of the Christian walk than I do.

Think about this counsel: Do not read each devotional as merely a routine or ritual, but as wisdom, rooted in Scripture, meant to transform your life and give you a firm foundation. It is also our hope that you would share these words with others. Only the good news of Jesus

Christ can make the penitentiary a better place. Remember, contrary to what the penitentiary would have you believe, there are no Lone Ranger Christians. *Exiles* is an example of three prisoners sharing what Christ has done for them with you. You cannot keep what Christ has done for you to yourself.

Brandon Warren, M.Div.
Administrative Assistant,
Darrington Undergraduate Program,
Southwestern Baptist Theological Seminary &
Founder, Enlightened Prisoner Project

ACKNOWLEDGMENTS

N o endeavor like this begins or ends without God's hand guiding it along, and it is to Him we are eternally thankful; not only for what He has done to each of our lives but for what He continues to do through them. May He receive the glory and praise and honor forever. Amen.

We also thank Grove Norwood and The Heart of Texas Foundation for helping to take tragedy and turn it into triumph. Grove Norwood has been an inspiration to all of us, and the Heart of Texas Foundation's tireless support affords us the opportunity to pursue projects which would otherwise never see the light of day.

We offer a special thanks to Brandon Warren, our professor, counselor, and friend, whose dedication to helping men in prison find their hope in Jesus Christ is a shining example of how prison ministry can and should be conducted. We proudly support his Enlightened Prisoner Project which gives those behind bars an opportunity to broaden their horizons with a gospel-centered education.

Our gratitude also extends to all the faculty of Southwestern Baptist Theological Seminary–Darrington Campus. The challenge of teaching prisoners in such a dark environment takes enormous amounts of courage and patience; we greatly appreciate your faithfulness to God's call.

Additionally, we are indebted to each one of our many editors. Thanks go out especially to Brenna Norwood, Managing Editor, who resolutely and meticulously kept our voice, and to Steve Norwood, who sailed the manuscript safely to harbor with a watchful and tireless grammatical eye so that *Exiles* could sail safely and effectually through the minds and hearts and souls of those who would read it; and to Jill Hogue, Sarah Dean, Robert Franz, Brandon Brewer, and all the others who so diligently assisted in putting the commas in all the right places.

Furthermore, Terry Solley and Johnny Blevins would like to thank our two beautiful daughters, Brittney CheyAnne Solley and Madison Taylor Blevins, for loving and believing in us despite our absence. We also owe a deep debt of gratitude to the wonderful women raising our precious little angels. Thank you to Tasha and Natali for being such wonderful mothers and for ensuring that our children never forget how much we love them. Likewise, Jason Karch would like to acknowledge an unpayable debt of gratitude to Me-maw (Helen Isbell) and thank her for being a constant source of support and strength for all we have set our hands to do.

Finally, our warmest and most heartfelt thanks go out to our mothers, Sandra Lofton, Sharla Karch, and Valerie Vaughan. We thank our patient and compassionate mothers for enduring all the rebellious son-induced headaches over the years and for suffering through a lifetime of heartache. This devotional is as much the fruit of our mothers who refused to quit as it is our labor to write. "Moms, we love you."

This book is dedicated to

Grove Norwood, founder of The Heart of Texas Foundation, who has touched each of our lives in a very special way, and without whom none of this would have been possible.

And in memory of

Charles "Chuck" Colson (1931–2013), founder of Prison Fellowship, whose life was devoted to leading the exiles home to the foot of the cross of Jesus Christ.

TABLE OF ABBREVIATIONS
BOOKS OF THE BIBLE

THE OLD TESTAMENT

Genesis........Gen	Ezra ....Ezra	Daniel .....Dan
Exodus.......Exod	Nehemiah ....Neh	Hosea......Hosea
Leviticus......Lev	Esther........Esth	Joel.........Joel
Numbers .....Num	Job ....Job	Amos ......Amos
Deuteronomy .Deut	Psalms ....Ps	Obadiah....Obad
Joshua ....Josh	Proverbs......Prov	Jonah ......Jonah
Judges ....Judg	Ecclesiastes ...Eccl	Micah......Mic
Ruth.........Ruth	Song of	Nahum.....Nah
1 Samuel .....1 Sam	Solomon .....Song	Habakkuk ..Hab
2 Samuel .....2 Sam	of Sol	Zephaniah ..Zeph
1 Kings.......1 Kgs	Isaiah ....Isa	Haggai .....Hag
2 Kings.......2 Kgs	Jeremiah .....Jer	Zechariah...Zech
1 Chronicles ..1 Chr	Lamentations..Lam	Malachi ....Mal
2 Chronicles ..2 Chr	Ezekiel ....Ezek	

THE NEW TESTAMENT

Matthew........Matt	1 Timothy .....1 Tim
Mark...........Mark	2 Timothy .....2 Tim
Luke ....Luke	Titus.........Titus
John...........John	Philemon......Phl
Acts...........Acts	Hebrews.......Heb
Romans ....Rom	James ....Jas
1 Corinthians....1 Cor	1 Peter ....1 Pet
2 Corinthians....2 Cor	2 Peter ....2 Pet
Galatians ....Gal	1 John ....1 John
Ephesians.......Eph	2 John ....2 John
Philippians......Phil	3 John ....3 John
Colossians ......Col	Jude ....Jude
1 Thessalonians..1 Thess	Revelation .....Rev
2 Thessalonians..2 Thess	

INTRODUCTION

E very writing project is birthed somewhere; this work is no exception. *Exiles: A Prisoner's Daily Devotional* was birthed in a 9' x 5'
prison cell during one of the most difficult periods of my life. I had recently been accepted to attend the Southwestern Baptist Theological
Seminary–Darrington Campus, the first seminary inside of a Texas
prison, and had great expectations for my future. I was answering the
call of God, and from this point on, life was going to consist of one
blessing after another. However, within a few short months, my world
was turned upside-down. My wife of many years left me and my father
was diagnosed with terminal lung cancer and died shortly thereafter.
As I struggled with losing two of the most important people in my life
at the same time, I sought solace in the Word of God and in my daily
devotional time with the Lord. During this dark and trying period,
God placed a burden in my heart to write a daily devotional for prisoners that spoke to situations unique to being incarcerated.

No writing project is ever done single-handedly. As I faced the
enormous task ahead of me, I knew I could not accomplish writing
Exiles alone. I also knew there was no one I would rather have join me
in this endeavor than my best friend, Jason Karch. He is a godly man I
respect greatly and whose life is a living example of how a man can be
transformed by the power of the gospel of Jesus Christ. I would not be
where I am today in my spiritual maturity had it not been for the patience, kindness, and love Jason has shown me. Then there is Johnny
Blevins, who graciously stepped in when Jason and I needed a little
reinforcement. I have only known Johnny for three years, but in that
time I have seen him grow and blossom into a man I know God will

use greatly. He is a great encouragement and an even greater friend. I could not ask for two better co-authors than these men with whom God has blessed me.

At the time of publication, Karch, Blevins, and I will have a combined forty-eight calendar years of prison time done. There is nothing about prison life we have not experienced. The devotional you hold in your hand is the product of two years of wrestling through those experiences and applying God's Word to them. As we have written these devotions, we have grown in our faith and trust in God. Our hope for you is that as you read them, you will do likewise.

In addition to the daily devotionals, each day includes a reading guide that will lead you through the entire Bible once and the Psalms and New Testament a second time throughout the year. These Bible readings are taken from Robert Murray M'Cheyne's, *Daily Bible Reading Guide*. We have also included an appendix consisting of special devotions and conclude with a topical index. Each of the special devotions are written for holidays that do not fall on the same day each year and for the unique occasions prisoners are faced with at some point during their incarceration.

If, while reading anything in this devotional, you ask yourself what you must do to be saved, please see the next page titled, "The Good News," for the answer.

We understand there is nothing more intimate in the Christian life than personal devotion time with God. We thank you for giving us the opportunity to share in that time with you. May God's Word keep you, comfort you, and guide you through your period of exile.

In Exile,
Terry Solley

THE GOOD NEWS

T he authors have compiled this devotional with the hopes of comforting and encouraging our brothers and sisters in Christ, and particularly, to remind the church behind bars that our true hope exists only in Jesus Christ. However, we do realize and acknowledge that there may be those reading this who have not accepted Jesus as Lord and Savior. To those we say, if you are reading this, it is not too late. There is no pretension and will be no excuse: all humans are sinners and without excuse before God (Rom 3:23). Consequently, all those outside of Christ will be judged and eternally condemned for their sin—sin that has separated us from God.

The bad news is that sinners can do nothing on their own to change God's judgment against them. If you have begun to understand your need for reconciliation with God and you have a broken and contrite heart because of the way you have sinned against God (Ps 51), then God has provided a way for you to be forgiven and reconciled to Him: "For the wages of sin is death, but the free gift of God is eternal life in Christ Jesus our Lord" (Rom 6:23). The good news is, because of His love, God sent His Son, Jesus Christ to die for our sins: "but God shows his love for us in that while we were still sinners, Christ died for us" (Rom 5:8).

Having understood your sinfulness before God and recognized your need to be reconciled to Him, do you acknowledge that Jesus has indeed accomplished your forgiveness and reconciliation? If so, then all that is left for you is to entrust yourself to Him: "because, if you confess with your mouth that Jesus is Lord and believe in your heart that God raised Him from the dead, you will be saved. For with the heart one believes and is justified [made right with God], and with the mouth one confesses and is saved" (Rom 10:9–10).

We realize that some people are unsure how to pray. If you find yourself struggling over how to come to God with your sins, simply talk to Him. The conversation can be as simple as:

Heavenly Father, I understand that I am a sinner and recognize that I need to be reconciled to You. I believe that You sent Your Son, Jesus, to die for my sins and that He was raised from the dead so that sinners like myself could be reconciled to You. I confess this to You now and ask that You would forgive me of my sins and restore to me a right relationship to You. Save me, Father. I ask this in Jesus' name. Amen.

NEW BEGINNINGS

*"Therefore, if anyone is in Christ, he is a new creation.
The old has passed away; behold, the new has come."*
2 CORINTHIANS 5:17

Life is about new beginnings. Each turn of the calendar constantly brings that to our attention. One year is gone and a new one takes its place. For those of us incarcerated, the turn of the calendar from one year to another really does not mean much. It is just another day incarcerated, living in conditions we are not designed to live in and separated from our loved ones. Sometimes, with a sense of sadness or indifference, we mark another year off our calendars and keep on trucking.

However, when I think about the old year passing away and the new year beginning—about the new replacing the old—I cannot help but recall Paul's words in 2 Corinthians 5:17, "Therefore if any man be in Christ, he is a new creation. The old has passed away; behold, the new has come." Like the old year that has passed away and the new year that has taken its place, in Christ, our old self has passed away and the new self has taken its place. The newness that we have in Christ is so much more than simply putting another mark on a calendar and going on with our lives. It is something that transforms our lives every single day—something we can rejoice about from one day to the next.

As this new calendar year begins, let us look to Christ and rejoice in what He has done for us. As new creatures in Him, we can know and live as though every day is a new beginning. –Solley

Morning: Gen 1; Matt 1 — *Evening:* Ezra 1; Acts 1

BLACK DAYS

*"You have caused my beloved and my friend to shun
me; my companions have become darkness."*
PSALM 88:18

In the 1990s the band, Sound Garden, released their hit song, "Black Days." The chorus of the song was, "I fell on black days, black days, black days." The experience of incarceration feels like falling on black days. Initially, friends and family may stay in contact, but visits and letters are not enough to mitigate against the sense of isolation and alienation that comes with being in prison. As time goes on, friends fade away, and in some instances, family does, too.

In Psalm 88, the psalmist understands this. He knows black days. The last line of the psalm can also be translated, "darkness has become my *only* companion." Reading this strikes close to the reality of prison. Surrounded by people there is still the sense of alienation and loneliness. Looking closely at the psalm, it is addressing God. The psalmist recognizes God's sovereignty and unashamedly pours out his heart to the One he is sure is there. At the point where beloved and friends have shunned him and his companions are darkness—even when he is fallen on black days—he speaks to God. Not only does he speak to God, he does so with a level of intimacy and illustrates his closeness to God who has not abandoned him.

Even when incarceration feels like falling on black days, remember that God is there, and we can pour our hearts out to Him who hears. –Karch

Morning: Gen 2; Matt 2 — *Evening:* Ezra 2; Acts 2

START PRAYING

*"But seek the welfare of the city where I have sent
you into exile, and pray to the LORD on its behalf,
for in its welfare you will find your welfare."*
JEREMIAH 29:7

In 1995, transformation began to take place inside the Louisiana State Penitentiary at Angola—one of America's bloodiest prisons. The prisoners there were blessed by a godly warden, Burl Cain, who felt responsible not just for their correction and safety, but also for their souls. Led by God, Warden Cain established the first accredited seminary inside a prison. Then something phenomenal took place: the men of Angola began to pray, not merely for themselves and their families, but for the prison where they lived. Two decades later, Angola is one of the safest prisons in the world and a glaring example of what the Lord will do when people, incarcerated, begin to seek His face for the prosperity of their place of exile.

As God commanded the Israelites to do during their seventy-year captivity in Babylon, and as the prisoners of Angola mirrored, we must seek the welfare of the "city" where we have been exiled. We must pray for the prisons where we live. When those of us inside these walls begin to pray, the impossible becomes possible: lives are transformed, men are saved, and prison culture is radically changed. If you want to see those around you saved, start praying. If you want to see the violence decline, start praying. If you want to see parents restored to their children, start praying. If you want to see the officers' attitudes toward prisoners change, start praying. If you want to see God do the impossible right where you are, start praying!

What happened at Angola can happen in any prison. All it takes are men and women who are bold enough to start praying. So, what are you waiting for? Start praying. –Solley

Morning: Gen 3; Matt 3 — *Evening:* Ezra 3; Acts 3

A MOTHER'S BURDEN

*"Honor your father and your mother, that your days may be
long in the land that the LORD your God is giving you."*
Exodus 20:12

Children have been the main source of their mothers' suffering since the first child Cain was born. Eve, the mother of all living, bore her first child in pain because of her part in the fall (Gen 3:16). However, her burden reached far beyond labor pain. It wasn't long before Eve experienced the sorrow many of our own mothers have felt. She lost one son as a victim of crime, and another was exiled for committing the crime. Eve was the mother of both a crime victim and a criminal. She bore the burden of losing both her sons to senselessness.

Many of us never had a father in the house, leaving mom to pull double duty. While our mothers weren't perfect, I doubt we would deny the unconditional love they had for us. My own mother worked multiple jobs to keep a roof over my head and food on the table, all while putting herself through nursing school. Yet, she still found a way to be at all of my ball games. I dare say our mothers sacrificed much on our behalf.

God commands us to honor our parents, but how do we do that after a lifetime of rebellion and heartache? A good way to start is by acknowledging the pain we've caused them and seeking their forgiveness. Despite past mistakes, begin a new relationship with your mother—one that's grounded in respect and consideration. "A wise son makes a glad father but a foolish man despises his mother" (Prov 15:20). Remember, the consequences of our sins have wide-reaching, painful effects, especially for our mothers.

Today, make it a point to lighten your mother's burden; begin treating her with love and respect in appreciation for all she's done for you. –Blevins

Morning: Gen 4; Matt 4 — *Evening:* Ezra 4; Acts 4

SOLD OUT

*"but my righteous one shall live by faith, and if he
shrinks back, my soul has no pleasure in him."*
HEBREWS 10:38

T he text quoted here is an allusion to Habakkuk 2:4. It is also
quoted in both Romans 1:17 and Galatians 3:11. Nevertheless,
while Habakkuk's statement is utilized these three times in the New
Testament, it does not dissolve the complexity of what it means to *live
by faith.*

We have to think, whatever complexities are involved in living by
faith, the Christian faith bears on every aspect of our lives. We are
placed in a position where everything is examined in light of Christ.
If this is not the case, then we have to question what kind of faith we
really have. Christ calls us to a saving faith that commits us to an entire
way of life. Many theologians distinguish the faith of those who confess only with their mouths from those who are actually committed to
following and living for Christ. There is a shift from the kind of life
we once led to the new life Christ has called us to live. We become
committed—sold out, as we live by faith—a faith that creates in us a
sense of power, passion, danger, and mystery and adds a new dynamic
to everyday living that those who do not live by faith can never know.

The self-examining question each of us must ask is: What kind
of faith do we have? Do we shrink back from the total commitment
Jesus has called us to and displease the Lord? Do we actually live by
faith? While all the nuances of what it means to live by faith may not
be immediately clear, we can tell the Lord we desire that commitment and we want to live by faith. Tell Him you want to be sold out
to Him. –Karch

Morning: Gen 5; Matt 5 — *Evening:* Ezra 5; Acts 5

THE TRUE MARK

"Beloved, never avenge yourselves, but leave it to the wrath of God,
for it is written, 'Vengeance is mine, I will repay, says the Lord.'"
ROMANS 12:19

How many times have you driven yourself crazy contemplating revenge because someone has wronged you? Maybe it was a friend or family member who turned their back on you, a girlfriend or even a spouse who disappeared as soon as the police slapped the cuffs on you. What about the person who disrespected you and thinks he got away with it, or your fall-partner who sang like Tweety Bird in the court room? Whoever it may have been, you likely rehearsed over and over in your mind exactly how you were going to make them pay for what they have done to you.

One of the most difficult things for us to do is let go of a wrong someone has done to us. We want revenge, and we want them to suffer the consequences of their actions. However, is this attitude the true mark of a Christian? Of course not. As Paul writes in his letter to the church of Rome, the *true* mark of a Christian is to never seek revenge for wrongs suffered, but to leave it to the wrath of God—a noble concept. Yet, Paul takes it one step further; he instructs believers to return good to their enemies for the evil they have suffered (v. 21), meaning more than simply "letting go and letting God." Paul is declaring that we, as Christians, must go out of our way to show the same love and mercy God has shown us to those who have wronged us.

Yes, our natural inclination is to get even. Yet, seeking revenge only continues the cycle of evil, and evil can only be overcome with good. As believers, let's bear the true mark of a Christian and leave vengeance to the Lord. –Solley

Morning: Gen 6; Matt 6 — *Evening:* Ezra 6; Acts 6

THE CHRISTIAN CONUNDRUM

*"And those who belong to Christ Jesus have crucified
the flesh with its passions and desires."*
GALATIANS 5:24

I t was supposed to be a piece of cake. It was supposed to be easy, right? Why then, now that I am a Christian, does it seem so hard to live according to God's Word? I thought Christians were weak-willed pushovers who took the easy road in life. Little did I know the call to this life entailed a life-long struggle. When we come to Christ by grace through faith we are set free from the bondage of sin, but much like the Galatians found out, falling back into old sinful habits is all too easy.

Paul exhorts the Galatians to "walk by the Spirit" so they will not carry out those sinful deeds of the flesh (v. 16). But *how* is one supposed to walk by the Spirit? That's the Christian conundrum. Paul expresses this very same concern in Romans 7:14–25: "For the good that I want, I do not do, but I practice the very evil that I do not want" (v. 19). It's all kinds of confusing, but I think Jesus gives us a big hint when He tells His disciples they must deny themselves, and take up their cross daily and follow Him (Luke 9:23).

Unfortunately, many of us, much like the Galatians, believe we can obtain righteousness on our good merit or by living according to the Law. However, although our flesh has been dealt a death-blow, we must still rely on the Holy Spirit to help us overcome the continuous struggle of our new life. It's the Spirit working in us that produces the fruit of love, joy, peace, patience, kindness, goodness, faithfulness, gentleness, and self-control (Gal 5:22–23). We must choose to embrace this new life and stop letting the struggle between the flesh and the Spirit confuse us. –Blevins

Morning: Gen 7; Matt 7 — *Evening:* Ezra 7; Acts 7

OLD SCHOOL

"Thus says the LORD: 'Stand by the roads, and look,
and ask for the ancient paths, where the good way is;
and walk in it, and find rest for your souls . . ."
JEREMIAH 6:16

Most times we are caught up within one of two extremes where, on the one hand we constantly desire something new, and on the other hand we always reminisce about how things used to be back in the game. In prison, we are always on the lookout for the newest trend, the newest commissary item, or the newest legislation that affects parole requirements. On the other hand, we are always bemoaning the fact that things are not the way they used to be—when people who get on our nerves or act in disrespectful ways would not have gotten away with half of all of the things they get away with now.

In one sense, seeking the old school way is a good thing. Scripture tells us that there is an ancient path which is good—a path we can walk in that not only transcends all others, but meets our needs in a way that others cannot. Through this old school way of things, we meet Jesus in a way that no novelty can ever mirror or match. This is particularly important when understood in context of our spiritual and devotional practices.

Next time we are tempted to become caught up within one of those extremes, we can kick it old school in a new way, seeking the old path with Jesus, the Lamb, who was slain from the foundation of the world (Rev 13:8). This is how we find rest for our souls. –Karch

Morning: Gen 8; Matt 8 — *Evening*: Ezra 8; Acts 8

A FUTURE AND A HOPE

"For I know the plans I have for you, declares the LORD, plans
for welfare and not for evil, to give you a future and a hope."
JEREMIAH 29:11

S hortly after the Texas Court of Criminal Appeals affirmed my conviction, I received a copy of the court's opinion from my attorney's secretary. As I sat on my bunk reading the paperwork, a sense of
despair overwhelmed me—my life seemed dark and hopeless. I was in
administrative segregation, once again, and struggling with the guilt I
felt for leaving my wife and daughter alone, for failing as a husband
and a father. To make matters worse, I was only a few years into a long
prison sentence, and the only chance I had at freedom—of being
home with my family—was just shot down.

Yet, along with the court's opinion was a personal letter from my attorney's secretary. With her condolences and encouragement, she sent
me a copy of an exposition on Jeremiah 29:11. In one of the darkest
moments of my life, when it felt like all hope was gone, God sent me
hope. I have read this verse hundreds of times since then, and every
time I read it, Jeremiah's words speak peace to my soul.

Though this promise is given to the people of Israel during their
captivity, it is a comforting reminder that no matter what state we find
ourselves in, God has a plan and a purpose for our lives because we
are His—a plan of wholeness and not of evil, a plan to give us a future
and a hope. Just as God did not forget the people of Israel during their
captivity, He has not forgotten us during ours. We are His and He loves
us. Today, know that God has a plan and a purpose for your life. Let
Jeremiah's words comfort your heart. –Solley

Morning: Gen 9, 10; Matt 9 — *Evening:* Ezra 9; Acts 9

PICKING FLOWERS

*"My eyes are awake before the watches of the night,
that I may meditate on your promise."*
PSALM 119:148

In the middle ages, monks kept a little notebook called *florilegium*. The main purpose of these little notebooks was to write reflections gleaned from meditations on Scripture. The Latin word can denote "picking flowers." These little notebooks provide us with a wealth of spiritual material for understanding how these believers viewed, understood, and applied the Word of God to their lives.

For these monks, the routine life of the monastery could easily become monotonous as they did the same things each day at the same times. In the same way, the routine of prison life is monotonous, and it is easy to allow ourselves to settle into the habit of incorporating this same monotony to all aspects of life. It is almost natural. However, this should not be the case when it comes to reading and meditating on Scripture. Doing so should always be a new experience. We should expect the Scriptures to have something to say to us each day and those flowers that we pick to become treasures we store in our hearts for difficult times. The reflections left behind by various monks throughout the centuries prove that the Scriptures were alive and new to them each day.

As we meditate on the Word of God, contemplate the full ramifications of His promises for us, and hide those things within our hearts, these meditations become the "flowers" we have picked along the way. When you meditate on the Scriptures each day, pray for and search out those flowers that you can store in your own heart—you may even write them down in your own florilegium. –Karch

Morning: Gen 11; Matt 10 — *Evening:* Ezra 10; Acts 10

WHEN NO ONE'S LOOKING

"They have turned aside quickly out of the
way that I commanded them."
EXODUS 32:8A

In today's climate of relativistic worldviews, it's hard to find people who are consistent in their core values and who do not change whenever the wind blows in the opposite direction. Where are those who hold firm to what they believe, even in the face of adversity?

When Moses left to go up on the mountain to receive the tablets of stone, Aaron was left in charge of Israel. However, Aaron wavered in the face of pressure from those who were tired of waiting on Moses' return and who demanded gods they could see and touch. They needed something tangible to worship, not some distant, invisible God. So what was Aaron to do? You'd expect, after witnessing the mighty miracles God had performed, he would've stayed true. But alas, with Moses out of sight and Israel screaming for new gods, Aaron caved. A golden calf was built, and the consequences were severe.

Whether we know it or not, we're being watched all the time. Prison is a culture of consistency, so when Christians talk and walk one way around their brothers but act differently around everyone else, it's obvious. Most people would call them hypocrites, and it's one of the biggest excuses guys give for ignoring the gospel call.

Don't be a Christian who acts like an angel on Sunday but lives like the devil the rest of the week. Don't give in to the crowds of people calling for you to ignore the God you know to be true. And don't think for one second you can get away with being a hypocrite because you think no one's looking; you're only fooling yourself. –Blevins

Morning: Gen 12; Matt 11 — *Evening:* Neh 1; Acts 11

FILTHY RAGS

*"We have all become like one who is unclean, and all
our righteous deeds are like a polluted garment."*
ISAIAH 64:6A

I was frustrated. I had waited for what seemed like an hour in the
long, hot line at showers for clean clothes. After I showered and
went to dress, I discovered that the boxers I had been given looked like
a filthy rag someone had used to clean the floor. They were covered in
stains and had what appeared to be gray specks of paint all over them.
Plus, there was a mysterious dark brown streak right on the back. I seriously doubted they had even been washed. There was absolutely no
way I was putting on those boxers. Angry and frustrated, I got back in
the long line, *again,* to exchange the filthy rag I held in my hand.

I had been standing in line for a couple of minutes when it suddenly dawned on me. In our sinful states, we are just like those dirty
boxers. The prophet Isaiah tells us that all our righteousness is like
a polluted garment. In other words, the best we have to offer, all the
so-called "good" we do in life, is nothing but filthy rags in God's sight.
There is nothing good in us or about us. We are stained, we are filthy,
and we are unrighteous. However, it was in this state that God chose to
send His son to die for us. God took the filthy rags we once were and
washed them clean by the precious blood of His son, Jesus.

This gives us even more reason to thank God for the grace He has
given us in Christ who is our wisdom, righteousness, sanctification,
and redemption (1 Cor 1:30). –Solley

Morning: Gen 13; Matt 12— *Evening:* Neh 2; Acts 12

WHERE YOU GOIN'?

*"Follow the pattern of the sound words that you have heard
from me, in the faith and love that are in Christ Jesus."*
2 TIMOTHY 1:13

In Lewis Carroll's classic story, *Alice in Wonderland*, there is an early interaction between Alice and the Cheshire cat. Alice is at a point where she is wondering which way she ought to go. Noticing the Cheshire cat up in a tree, she says to him, "I just wanted to ask you which way I ought to go." The cat responds, "Well, that depends, on where you want to get to." Alice responds, "Oh, it really doesn't matter." At this the cat replies, "Then, it really doesn't matter, which way you go."

Oftentimes, we too easily lose sight of where it is we ought to be going as we live out the Christian life inside prison. The everyday routine makes it seem as if we are actually going nowhere, and we adopt an attitude where it is hard to care. As believers in Christ, we have been commissioned with a direction. Paul realized this, and understanding the way in which complacency easily besets believers, he instructs Timothy to *follow the pattern of the sound words.* Today we have these sound words throughout Scripture, and the idea of following the way we find there indicates we have a definite direction we should be going. We pursue this direction *in the faith and love that are in Jesus.*

When you find yourself at a point like Alice where you don't know which way you ought to go, seek direction in the Scriptures. When you find your direction, don't hesitate to follow it, and in doing so, ensure that it is representative of the faith and love that are in Jesus. –Karch

Morning: Gen 14; Matt 13 — *Evening:* Neh 3; Acts 13

PARENTING FROM PRISON

*"There are six things that the LORD hates, seven that are an
abomination to him: haughty eyes, a lying tongue, and hands
that shed innocent blood, a heart that devises wicked plans,
feet that make haste to run to evil, a false witness who breathes
out lies, and one who sows discord among brothers."*
PROVERBS 6:16–19

As I looked down into her tear-filled eyes, my heart broke. I knew
chastening my daughter for lying was the right thing to do, but
I did not want to spend the short, two hours in visitation as a discipli-
narian. I cherished these times with my little girl, and having to be the
"bad guy" left a sour taste in my mouth. Yet, I knew that as her father
and as a man of God, I had to bite the bullet and correct her.

Even as incarcerated parents, sowing seeds of righteousness in the
lives of our children is still something we are called to do no matter
how difficult it may be. Making the effort to be a positive influence
and build a strong moral foundation in your children should be the
goal of every incarcerated parent. Yes, parenting from prison can be
extremely difficult for many reasons, including limited access to our
children. But letters, phone calls, and visitation are all designed to
provide us with communication to our loved ones, and we, as parents,
have a responsibility to utilize them to the fullest extent possible when
given the opportunity.

Additionally, God has given us the ultimate parenting tool—the
Bible. The book of Proverbs is packed full of godly instruction for those
looking to teach their children right from wrong. Are you using every
avenue available to parent your child in the ways of the Lord? –Blevins

Morning: Gen 15; Matt 14 — *Evening:* Neh 4; Acts 14

BLESS HIS NAME

"Bless the LORD, O my soul, and all that is
within me, bless his holy name!"
Psalm 103:1

I t is easy to get so caught up in life and focused on the negativity around us that we forget how blessed we really are—even in prison. Sure, we are surrounded by concrete and razor wire, confined to cells as small as your average bathroom, and every aspect of our lives is micromanaged by someone other than ourselves; yet, our immediate circumstances pale in comparison to the big picture. They pale in comparison to who God is, what He has done for us, and how much He has blessed us.

Look at the truth of it. We are convicted felons: the worst of the worst, the outcasts of society. Many believe we are worthless and unredeemable—just lock them up and throw away the key! Yet, the psalmist says God forgives all of our iniquities, heals all our diseases, redeems our lives from the pit, crowns us with steadfast love and mercy, and satisfies us with good so that our youth is renewed like an eagle (Ps. 103:3–5). God is talking about us—people who have placed their faith and trust in Jesus Christ. You see, while many in society are busy condemning us, God has already forgiven us and redeemed us by the blood of His son. When we understand all God has done for us, we cannot help but to feel blessed and to bless God with all that is in us.

Read Psalm 103 today and meditate on how much God has done for you. Certainly, like the psalmist, we should feel compelled to cry out, "Bless the LORD, O my soul, and all that is within me, bless his holy name!" –Solley

Morning: Gen 16; Matt 15 — *Evening:* Neh 5; Acts 15

"I" KANT

*"For I do not understand my own actions. For I do not
do what I want, but I do the very thing I hate."*
ROMANS 7:15

R omans 7 is one of the most controversial portions of the New
Testament. Is Paul speaking of the period while he was a Pharisee
and struggled with upholding the law, or is he speaking in the present
tense as a believer who still cannot overcome sin in his life? These are
the kinds of questions the text forces us to ask.

The legacy of the German idealist Immanuel Kant has levied tremendous influence on theology since the 18th century. One of his main
arguments is that moral behavior is discernible through reason alone.
Through the "categorical imperative" people know what they ought to
do; the problem is the everyday experiences of people prove they cannot do what they ought to do. This is the quandary Paul is bemoaning
in Romans 7. For Kant, realizing that people can't do what they ought
to do in a universal and perfect way, it is Christianity that provides an
avenue through which moral power is gleaned to perform the categorical imperative. This is exactly how Paul concludes the chapter.

In any case, as questions are continually asked of the text in an attempt to get to the bottom of what Paul is writing about, a small devotional will not solve the complexities presented there. However, what
you and I can be sure of, even when we do not understand our own
actions and we feel as if we cannot win the battle, we can conclude with
Paul that we will be delivered from the struggle through our Lord and
Savior Jesus Christ. –Karch

Morning: Gen 17; Matt 16 — *Evening*: Neh 6; Acts 16

GUARD YOUR SOUL

"Thorns and snares are in the way of the crooked;
whoever guards his soul will keep far from them."
PROVERBS 22:5

When I first entered the Texas prison system at the age of eighteen, I was very young and naïve. As many of us have done, I quickly migrated to those who seemed to have one thing in common with me—the color of their skin. I soon became caught up in the prison lifestyle of hate and violence, running with crowds I should not have been running with, and doing things I knew in my heart were wrong. I became *the* crook among the crooked, and I ran into many thorns and snares along the way. I would end up doing most of my first sentence of fifteen years, spending years in administrative segregation (solitary confinement), and living with the effects of my past indiscretions for a very long time.

I discovered at a young age that it is easy to be attracted to those who seem to be thriving and prospering in this environment: the hustler, the gangster, the con artist, the convict, and the crook. Yet, Solomon, in all of his wisdom, warns us about these types of individuals: "Thorns and snares are in the way of the crooked, yet whoever guards his soul will keep far from them." This is sound advice for anyone residing within prison walls. If adhered to, as I learned the hard way, it will save a lot of trouble and heartache down the road.

As we walk these halls, we must guard our souls on a daily basis because it is so easy to become entangled and snared in the thorns that lie in the path of the crooked. –Solley

Morning: Gen 18; Matt 17 — *Evening:* Neh 7; Acts 17

BLOOD IN-BLOOD OUT

"For the life of the flesh is in the blood, and I have given it for you on the altar to make atonement for your souls, . . ."
LEVITICUS 17:11

The majority of people in prison have either seen or heard of the movie, *Blood In, Blood Out.* The basic connections between gangs and prison portrayed in the movie emerge in a very real sense within the confines of any American prison. For anybody who has ever been incarcerated in an American prison, those connections are hard to miss. Whether a person is, or has been, involved with a gang does not undermine an understanding of what those connections imply—everybody believes in something. As a result, we understand to some degree what it means to bleed for what we believe.

In light of this verse from Leviticus (which reads like a sacrificial and priestly code of honor), we can see the Lord's devotion to redeem the original goodness of humanity made in His image. Jesus took on human flesh and gave Himself as a sacrifice so that our atonement could be won.

As we understand the concept of blood in-blood out, and know what it is God has done for us in Jesus Christ, we can appreciate His dedication to those who believe in Him—His devotion to us as it is displayed in His blood on the altar of the cross. May we honor Him in that with each breath we take. –Karch

Morning: Gen 19; Matt 18 — *Evening:* Neh 8; Acts 18

WHERE YOU ARE NOW

"About midnight Paul and Silas were praying and singing hymns to God, and the prisoners were listening to them."
ACTS 16:25

How many times have you thought to yourself, "I can't wait until I get out. I'm going to do all kinds of great things in Jesus' name?" I know I still catch myself planning all the good things I'm going to do when I leave prison. I suppose after doing so much wrong in my life, the fact I even have a desire to do the right things is a testament to God working in me. But why do I need to postpone such things until I get out?

Paul and Silas were imprisoned unjustly by city officials in Philippi, but they did not let that stop them from praising God and spreading the gospel. Paul and Silas weren't concerned about where they had been or where they were going, it was all about where they were that moment. With their eyes firmly fixed on God, they lifted up their voices in praise and literally brought down the house. They even shared the gospel with one of their jailers. What a remarkable attitude!

Thinking about your future is a good thing. Planning ahead is definitely beneficial, but don't put off until tomorrow what is within your ability to do today. God is calling you to join Him today in His work, and He has provided you with all the tools necessary to get the job done. Prayerfully ask God to show you what needs to be done here and now, and be ready to enter the door He opens. Because it's not about where you have been or where you are going, it's about where you are now. –Blevins

Morning: Gen 20; Matt 19 — *Evening:* Neh 9; Acts 19

BROKEN

*"The sacrifices of God are a broken spirit; a broken and
contrite heart, O God, you will not despise."*
PSALM 51:17

There was a point in my life when I fell hard. I broke all of the promises I made to God, my wife, and myself. As a direct result of breaking those promises, I returned to prison and lost myself in a world full of guilt, shame, and deep regret. I was so ashamed of failing God and my family that I could not even pray. I felt I did not deserve to pray or to be forgiven by God. I felt the *only* thing I deserved was to suffer for what I had done. My heart and spirit were broken.

One night, when the world seemed to press in on my shoulders, I lay on my bunk with my sheet over my head. As the tears streamed down my face, I whispered silently to God, "I am sorry. I am sorry." I had nothing to offer God but a broken spirit and a contrite heart. That night was the beginning of a long healing process for me that is still taking place today.

For years, I lived in a world of guilt and shame because I did not understand that God loves us despite our failures and our flaws. Since then, I have discovered that when we do fall, and we will, when we turn to God with a broken spirit and contrite heart, He will not despise us nor will He turn us away. God will forgive us and heal the part of us that has been broken.

Maybe your guilt and shame have kept you from asking God for forgiveness. If so, know that God is a forgiving God who loves you and desires for you to come to Him so He can heal *your* broken spirit and contrite heart. –Solley

Morning: Gen 21; Matt 20 — *Evening:* Neh 10; Acts 20

ONE OF US

"Elijah was a man with a nature like ours, and he prayed fervently that it might not rain, and for three years and six months it did not rain on the earth."
JAMES 5:17

E lijah, the great prophet, challenged the tyrannical rule of Ahab and his wicked queen Jezebel. In reading his story and seeing how he lands in the New Testament several places, we cannot help but to be impressed with such a man of God. Imagine what it would have been like to kick it with Elijah.

James says something here that arrests our attention: "Elijah was a man with a *nature like ours."* What? How can we compare such a great man of God with ourselves, knowing our own natures? Looking into our hearts we can easily feel as if men like Elijah were made of a different kind of material—cut out of an entirely different cloth. Yet, James says Elijah was one of us. No different. The thing that makes him stand out is that he *prayed fervently.* That is the key to whatever greatness Elijah seemed to possess. Apart from praying in this way, Elijah was no different than any one of us.

Remember that we are no different than the great men of faith. Men like Elijah were one of us in every sense. In order for us to aspire to mirror their faith, we too must always pray fervently, looking in hope to the risen Christ who stands ready to hear us and answer our prayers. –Karch

Morning: Gen 22; Matt 21 — *Evening:* Neh 11; Acts 21

SNAP DECISIONS

"Immediately they left the boat and their father and followed him."
MATTHEW 4:22

Most of the worst decisions we made in our lives were ones we did not think through, we just *did*. No thought or careful consideration played any part in our choice; we just rushed right in headfirst. In contrast to that, decisions where much thought took place usually produced a better outcome.

That is what is so confounding about the calling of the disciples. When Jesus made the invitation, there was no strategic planning session or tribal counsel. The disciples simply left everything to follow him. Not only did they decide to leave, they parted ways with everyone and everything they knew. So the decision was not only quickly made, it was costly. However, unlike the thoughtless decisions that led most of us into trouble, their decision was the best one they ever made.

How are we supposed to respond when we receive the invitation to follow Jesus? Do we take our time weighing the pros and cons, all the while continuing to live our lives the same way? Or do we dive in headfirst, dropping everything to experience that life-changing relationship? Can you make such a radical choice? Can you leave it all in a heartbeat? Can you make the most important snap decision of your life? The invitation has been given. What are you waiting for? Follow Jesus. –Blevins

Morning: Gen 23; Matt 22 — *Evening:* Neh 12; Acts 22

GOD'S WILL?

"Father, if you are willing, remove this cup from me.
Nevertheless, not my will, but yours, be done."
LUKE 22:42

I believe the will of God plays a vital role in our incarceration. This is difficult to see if we only look at our situations from our limited perspectives. It is only when we allow our thoughts to transcend beyond the here and now that we can see God's divine will playing a part in where we find ourselves today.

Case in point: we could easily be dead. There have been many times in our lives when death was waiting around the corner, yet God intervened. He chose to spare our lives and allow us to live. With this in proper perspective, what if coming to prison was the way God chose to save our lives? If this is the case, should we not thank God that, unlike many, we woke up this morning—in prison?

How about another thought? Prison is the place it took to bring many of us to the realization that without Christ, we are nothing. It is where we began to see our depravity and our need for not just a Savior, but a Lord. Prison is the place where God took the dirty lumps of clay we once were and began molding them and shaping them into the people He desires us to be.

Do I believe that God placed us in prison? No, we put ourselves here. However, that does not limit God in what He can do. God so often takes the messes we make out of our lives and turns them into messages. He looks far beyond our limited vision and sees His overall purpose. So, let God be God. And, as Christ prayed in the garden of Gethsemane, let His will be done. –Solley

Morning: Gen 24; Matt 23 — *Evening:* Neh 13; Acts 23

THE RACE

*"Have we not all one Father? Has not one God
created us? Why then are we faithless to one another,
profaning the covenant of our fathers?"*
MALACHI 2:10

Malachi marks the end of the prophetic voice to Israel until the coming of John the Baptist a little over four centuries later. There were several tendencies Israel developed that created the potential for disaster. One of these was a pseudo-racial difference between the Northern and Southern Kingdoms. Even after the Babylonian and Assyrian captivities, they still treated one another with disdain. This faithlessness toward one another is a profanation of the covenant God made with them as a whole.

One fundamental problem pronounced inside prison more than any other place is that of racism. Men separate themselves along so-called racial lines. This arbitrary separation is no different than that of the Northern and Southern Kingdoms in Malachi's day. These differences are always, at bottom, false. Modern genetics demonstrate the *sameness* of all human beings. This leads us to ask the question Malachi asks: "Have we not all one Father?" If all human beings are created by God and can be traced to the present through a single familial bond back to Adam and Eve, then any racial distinction is both false and wrong. We are all members of the human race.

For those of us in prison who are aware of this, the impetus is on us to transcend the lies of the world—to form strong bonds with brothers and sisters across these pseudo-racial lines. Furthermore, we are to extend the hand of fellowship as the family of God and the body of Christ. Seek out somebody today with whom you can generate this kind of fellowship and bond. –Karch

Morning: Gen 25; Matt 24 — *Evening:* Esth 1; Acts 24

A SERVANT'S HEART

"If I then, your Lord and Teacher, have washed your feet, you also ought to wash one another's feet. For I have given you an example,"
JOHN 13:14–15A

J esus knew His time with His disciples was growing short. In one of His last moments with His followers, Christ did something that would leave behind a humbling legacy for them to follow. He removed His outer garments, tied a towel around His waist, filled a basin with water, and washed His disciples' feet. Their Lord and Teacher became a humble servant, a living example for all to follow.

It is very easy to want others to serve us, but it is very difficult for us to humble ourselves in order to serve others, especially in the type of environment we live in where humbleness is viewed by many as weakness. Yet, in washing His disciples' feet, Jesus revealed to us the type of heart He wanted His followers to have—not a heart that lorded over others who they were, but a servant's heart—a heart of humble service to others. When I think about this, I am forced to ask myself some penetrating questions: What type of heart do I have? Am I willing to humble myself and serve those around me, or do I always want others to serve me? Do I have the heart of a humble servant, or is it stubborn and self-seeking? The answers to these questions will reveal who I truly am as a professed disciple of Jesus Christ. Am I Christ-like, or do I just like Christ?

Today, I encourage you to search your own heart, and if it reveals to you an answer you do not like, may you have the courage to follow Jesus' humble example of servitude. –Solley

Morning: Gen 26; Matt 25 — *Evening:* Esth 2; Acts 25

TAKE AND READ

"O you who dwell in the gardens, with companions
listening for your voice; let me hear it."
SONG OF SOLOMON 8:13

O ne of the most famous conversion stories in Christian history, second only to the apostle Paul's, is that of Aurelius Augustine. In his spiritual autobiography *Confessions,* he tells of being in a garden with his friend when he hears a voice instructing him to "take and read." The only book in the vicinity was a Bible, and he opened it and read from Romans. The rest, as they say, is history.

While prison is a long way from the comforts and quietude of a garden, we do often find ourselves like Augustine with a need to hear from the Lord. As we understand the importance of hearing from Him, we long to hear what He has to say to us. We need to hear Him speak to our situation so that we may be comforted, encouraged, and strengthened. In a very basic way, we need to know He is with us and hears us. Inasmuch as we acknowledge both intellectually, we often need to have them confirmed existentially.

Anytime we find ourselves surrounded by the general chaos of prison, either alone in our need to hear from the Lord or in the company of those who are together listening for His voice, we can garner inspiration from Augustine's experience. When needing to hear from the Lord, he was instructed to take and read; and in opening the book of Romans, the Lord spoke to him through the Scriptures. Augustine spent the rest of his life hearing the voice of the Lord from the pages of the Bible. So any time we find ourselves needing to hear from Him, all we need to do is take and read. –Karch

Morning: Gen 27; Matt 26 — *Evening:* Esth 3; Acts 26

GOOD DEEDS?

*"For, being ignorant of the righteousness of God, and seeking to
establish their own, they did not submit to God's righteousness."*
ROMANS 10:3

G iving out shots of coffee, feeding a hungry neighbor, and staying
out of trouble all seem like righteous acts. Outwardly, it would
appear like you are doing your godly service, but the question you
need to ask yourself is, "Why?" These things are all good to do, but if
you are trying to earn some sort of favor with God by doing them, you
might want to think again.

In Romans 10, Paul talks about desiring salvation for the Jews. He
is concerned because although they considered themselves righteous
by living according to the Law, salvation still eluded them. You may be
wondering, "Well, how would Paul know if they were saved or not?"
Because Paul knew that the only way to be saved was through faith
in Jesus Christ. The Jews, despite all their good deeds, refused to acknowledge Jesus as the Messiah. They could not fathom a God who
offers salvation based on His grace, and not on their merit.

Righteous behavior, while good and preferable to unholy living,
can never earn you a ticket to heaven. If the Jews, God's chosen people,
can't make it without faith in Christ, what makes you think you can?
Even on our best day, without the righteousness of Christ, all our good
deeds are as filthy rags before God (Isa 64:6). If you are unfamiliar
with this basic principle of God's redemptive message, read through
Romans 10, especially verses 9 and 10. Remember that outward acts of
kindness are good, but they can never compare to the work of grace
coming through faith in Jesus Christ. –Blevins

Morning: Gen 28; Matt 27 — *Evening:* Esth 4; Acts 27

SIMPLE FAITH

*"Truly, I say to you, unless you turn and become like
children, you will never enter the kingdom of heaven."*
MATTHEW 18:3

Not long ago, I was facilitating a Bible study in the dayroom on Monday nights. About twenty men were broken up into several small groups that, at the end of each evening, would come together in one big group to pray. This particular night, one of the brothers asked if he could pray. Because of many scars from self-inflicted wounds on his head and wrists that attest to some very deep emotional and mental problems, most people in prison deem him a psych-patient. The truth is his mentality is very childlike. Yet one thing is certain, he loves the Lord. Not in any way eloquent or articulate, he prayed a simple prayer. Over and over he kept saying with heartfelt sincerity, "I love you, God, and I thank you, Father. I love you, God, and I thank you, Father."

Many other Christians looked down upon this brother and talked about him because of his mental state. Ironically, he taught us all a valuable lesson that night. He showed us firsthand that there is no need to come to God with pious sounding petitions or articulate and eloquent words. Jesus said, "Unless you turn and become like children, you will never enter the kingdom of heaven." When we come to God, we must come to Him baring our hearts. We must come with simple faith, the faith of a child, knowing God is our Father and He hears us.

Sometimes, like this brother demonstrated, we have to put everything aside, and in childlike faith, pray a simple prayer, "I love you, God, and I thank you, Father." –Solley

Morning: Gen 29; Matt 28 — *Evening:* Esth 5; Acts 28

CROSSED OUT

*"But now, if you will forgive their sin—but if not, please
blot me out of your book that you have written."*
EXODUS 32:32

N obody likes to get "crossed out." Many of us have seen lives lost,
people hurt, and reputations destroyed from somebody getting
crossed out. It is never a good thing, and I cannot recall anybody vol-
unteering explicitly to get crossed out.

In Exodus, Moses was on Mt. Sinai receiving the Ten Commandments
when the Lord alerted him to what was taking place at the foot of the
mountain. Moses immediately interceded for the people. As Moses
came down the mountain and witnessed for himself the severity of the
situation, and after a long night of getting things back under control,
Moses goes back to the Lord and intercedes again—this time with a
new emphasis. He not only asked the Lord to forgive the people but
asked that he be crossed out if the Lord cannot forgive them. Likewise,
Paul was willing to forgo his own salvation to see his people saved (Rom
9:3). There is no greater love than this (John 15:13).

As Christians, we are often ready to intercede for someone who has
fallen into sin just like Moses interceded for Israel. However, how serious are we when we intercede for somebody? Is our love to the point
where we can ask the Lord, "If you don't forgive and restore them
Lord, cross me out, too!"? –Karch

Morning: Gen 30; Mark 1 — *Evening:* Esth 6; Rom 1

STOP CRYING; START PRAYING

*"First of all, then, I urge that supplications, prayers, intercessions,
and thanksgivings be made for all people . . . that we may lead
a peaceful and quiet life, godly and dignified in every way."*
1 TIMOTHY 2:1–2

Ever since county jail, I've heard guys talk about the coming changes in sentencing laws. These are mostly men with lengthy sentences, who desperately cling to the hope of one day returning to the world. They sit around and complain about the way things are and speculate on how things will be. They are terrified by the possibility that prison may be the end of the road for them. That is a hard pill to swallow, especially if you don't have the hope of eternal life in Christ. It is no wonder guys keep up with legislative sessions and election years, hoping and wishing the right person will be elected and "set the captives free." But is that realistic? Is that what Scripture teaches us to do?

Early Christians faced persecution of unimaginable proportions. Burned, tortured, fed to wild animals, they did not have time to sit around and wait for laws to change or new rulers to come to power. Their need for change was immediate. So what does Paul instruct them to do? Pray! Pray! Pray! Likewise, we are not to sit around whining and complaining about how things are and hoping they get better; we are to go to the throne and petition God Almighty. What do we pray? We pray not for new rulers, but for those we already have. Pray that God will stir their spirits and give them a heart for prisoners. Pray that they realize the men in prison are not the enemy, but that sin and Satan are. We pray for God's will to be done on earth as it is in heaven.

When incarcerated men and women stop crying about their situation, and begin praying for people in authority, real meaningful change will take place. –Blevins

Morning: Gen 31; Mark 2 — Evening: Esth 7; Rom 2

MORNING-TIME BLUES

*"Satisfy us in the morning with your steadfast love,
that we may rejoice and be glad all our days."*
PSALM 90:14

Some mornings in prison seem unbearable—mornings where you wake up, take one look around at all of the concrete and steel surrounding you, and say to yourself, "There has to be more to life than this." I cannot count how many of those mornings I have had during my incarceration—times when I lay in my bunk dreading getting up and facing the loneliness and frustration of another day. I would eventually force myself to get out of bed, only to mope around feeling sorry for myself.

Yet, I learned a simple trick that makes the morning-time blues disappear. When I have those type of mornings now, I lie there with the sheet pulled over my head, ignore everyone and everything around me, and silently thank God for all of the good things He has given me: my hope in Christ, His love, my daughter, my family, my friends, my health, my sanity, and so much more. As I begin listing the things God has blessed me with, my mood starts to change. I am quickly reminded that no matter how tough life may seem, I am blessed. Before I know it, my entire mood has transformed. I am up, the hot pot is plugged in, and I am ready to face another day—thankful for all God has given me.

On the days when you experience the morning-time blues, try something new. Instead of focusing on all of the negative things in your life, focus on all the good things God has done for you. When you begin your day by thinking about how blessed you really are, you can't help but to have a little pep in your step. –Solley

Morning: Gen 32; Mark 3 — *Evening:* Esth 8; Rom 3

TAKEN FOR GRANTED

"And the people complained in the hearing of the LORD about their misfortunes, and when the LORD heard it, his anger was kindled . . ."
NUMBERS 11:1

E very day someone is born, and every day someone dies. But the other day, as I was reading my cellmate's hometown obituary page, I noticed something unusual. There was a picture of two baby footprints, and next to them was a single date for both birth and death. Then I snapped, "This baby died in the delivery room." I dwelt on this unpleasant fact of life and realized that this living soul spent months developing only to be taken before ever having spent any time in this world. The life we all take for granted every day was here and gone in less than twenty-four hours for that child.

The Israelites were very much the disgruntled freed slaves the Bible portrays them to be. Having been delivered from four hundred years of brutal slave labor, they were finally free. But that just wasn't good enough. Moses was guiding God's chosen people toward a new life and a new land, but the Israelites couldn't stop complaining or taking for granted the life of freedom God had given them. And God heard every last word.

Dissatisfaction often comes when our focus turns from what we have to what we don't have. In prison we complain about a lot of things we don't have, but have you considered the very breath you just took? Not everyone enjoyed waking up this morning. And, like that new born baby I read about, not everyone even made it out of the delivery room. God has blessed us beyond measure with the very life we are now living. Isn't it time to stop taking it for granted and start being grateful? –Blevins

Morning: Gen 33; Mark 4 — *Evening:* Esth 9, 10; Rom 4

JESUS LOVES ME

"but God shows his love for us in that while we
were yet sinners, Christ died for us."
ROMANS 5:8

I recall reading where, during an interview, Karl Barth was asked to identify the most profound theological thought he had ever turned over in his mind. Without hesitation he replied, "That Jesus loves me." Even as a Christian, Barth's response crystalized the entire framework of Christianity for me. My understanding of the gospel transcended into that final realm of religious attainment. I finally understood (on a very small scale) the enormity of what Jesus had done for me and His overarching motives for suffering in the way He did—for *me*.

What Barth said affected me so much that my head still swims when I run across statements in Scripture like the text for today which displays and defines Christ's love for us. The ramifications of the truth of those things are very literally life transforming. For me, it is brand new each day. When I think about what the gospel is to me, in the minds of some, it may seem simplistic, even childish. Yet, in the mind of Barth, quite possibly the greatest theological mind of the twentieth century, it was the most profound theological thought he had ever encountered. I pray it will remain the most profound theological thought that will cross the horizon of my own mind.

Simple or profound, whatever the case may be, the truth of it is the real essence of the gospel, and it is what the gospel means to me: Jesus loves me. Today think about the simple and complex beauty of the gospel message—Jesus loves *you*. –Karch

Morning: Gen 34; Mark 5 — *Evening:* Job 1; Rom 5

WORTHY OF HIS CALLING

*"for at one time you were darkness, but now you are
light in the Lord. Walk as children of light."*
EPHESIANS 5:8

In the book, *Karla Faye Tucker Set Free: Life and Faith on Death Row*, author Linda Strom records that one month before her execution, on February 3, 1998, Karla Faye Tucker included these words in a letter to a friend on death row: "Girl, the world is watching to see if we are for real and if the God we profess is making a difference in our lives." Thirty-one days later, she went home to be with the Lord. In the face of death, Karla was not concerned about herself. She was concerned with how her actions reflected Christ. Even in death, Karla wanted the world to know that her God was real, and *He* had made a difference in her life.

Upon reading Karla's words, I had to stop for a moment to consider how profound they were and how they apply to all of us. As Christians, especially incarcerated Christians, so many others are watching to see if we are authentic and to see if God has truly transformed our lives. The minute we take a wrong step or say the wrong thing, they will point their finger and scream, "I thought you were a Christian!" That is why, as Karla understood, it is so important for us to live our lives worthy of the calling of Jesus Christ. Our lives and sometimes our deaths, as Karla showed us, must reflect who Christ is and what He has done for us.

Have you been walking worthy of His calling? If not, determine today that you will let your conduct show the world around you that your God is real and that He has made a difference in your life. –Solley

Morning: Gen 35, 36; Mark 6 — *Evening:* Job 2; Rom 6

TRUST HIM

*"Into your hand I commit my spirit; you have
redeemed me, O LORD, faithful God."*
PSALM 31:5

T rust is a big issue for many people, especially for those in prison. As a result of going through the rigors of the legal system and ending up on the losing side, we often become bitter. We balk at putting our trust in other people. We build impenetrable walls and let this egocentric attitude affect all our thoughts, words, and actions.

However, when the impenetrable fortress is destroyed by the unstoppable force of God's Holy Spirit, we start to realize that those walls were not hurting anybody but ourselves. Then we understand that we can't even trust ourselves to look out for our own best interests. However, there is One who always has our best interest in mind, upon whom we can cast all our worries and depend upon completely: the One who not only gives life, but gives it abundantly.

Jesus Christ has paid the price for your life. You have been bought by His precious blood. He has ransomed you from death's doorstep. He has reconciled you to your refuge, your rock of strength, your impenetrable fortress. He not only deserves your complete trust, He commands it.

Placing your trust in man, including yourself, will only lead to disappointment, but surrendering your life completely and entrusting your every day to God's loving care will allow Him to guide you through a place full of dangerous situations. So how do you get through this palace of pitfalls, this mansion of mirages, this house of horrors? Trust Him. –Blevins

Morning: Gen 37; Mark 7 — *Evening:* Job 3; Rom 7

OUT OF THE DEPTHS

"Out of the depths I cry to you, O LORD! O Lord, hear my voice!"
PSALM 130:1–2A

We easily develop tendencies when we read Scripture, such as to pass over the nuance of what certain words are attempting to convey. The opening verse of this psalm can easily be one of those cases. What are the *depths*? The context of the depths then is much more than a simple reference to being spatially caught in some deep place. To the Hebrew mind, the depths were a graphic depiction of drowning in deep waters, of being pulled down and swallowed up into the deepest and darkest of waters. They represent the horrors of a drowning person being completely overwhelmed in a way that is utterly inescapable. In the context of this type of predicament, the psalmist cries out to the Lord.

Prison itself can be overwhelming. Even to someone who has spent years here, the potential of being pulled down and swallowed up by despair looms just beneath the surface of the monotony of the everyday routine. This is particularly the case for those confined to segregation. Those who have experienced prison in that capacity understand what it means to cry out of depths on a level most people never will. It was out of those depths that I cried to Him, and the Lord was faithful and heard my voice.

No matter what situations we find ourselves in, how overwhelming or inescapable they seem, or how deep we find ourselves in messes, it is out of those depths we are still able to cry to the Lord; and He will be faithful to hear our voice. While there may not be an immediate change in the situation or circumstances, we can be sure that even in the depths, the Lord sustains us. At present, if you find yourself in the depths, cry out to the Lord, and He will hear your voice. –Karch

Morning: Gen 38; Mark 8 — *Evening:* Job 4; Rom 8

I'VE HAD ENOUGH

*"And he prayed that he might die, and said, 'It is enough! Now,
LORD, take my life for I am no better than my fathers!'"*
1 KINGS 19:4B

T he life of a prisoner can be very difficult and depressing.
Sometimes you just want to give up and beg God to take your
life. However, this feeling is not unique to prisoners: it is also known
to God's people. Elijah, one of the greatest prophets in the Bible, felt
the same way. Shortly after his victory over Baal's four hundred false
prophets on Mount Carmel, Elijah's life was threatened by Queen
Jezebel. Upon learning of Jezebel's threats, Elijah fled into the wilderness and eventually came to rest under a broom tree. Sitting there
alone and feeling like all hope was lost, Elijah came to the end of his
rope. He had enough! Elijah believed there was no reason to go on
any longer. In his depression, he begged God to take his life.

Yet, if you read the rest of the chapter you will see that God meets
Elijah right where he is and comforts him. God reveals to Elijah that,
unknown to him, He was working behind the scenes and His ultimate
plan was being accomplished. Elijah was ready to give up because he
viewed things from his perspective, rather than from God's perspective. We do the same. We become so focused on the seeming hopelessness of our lives that we want to give up. We forget that God has a plan
and a purpose for our lives, and He works behind the scenes to carry it
out regardless of where we are.

If you feel like you have had enough and there is just no use going
on, think about this one thing: whose perspective are you viewing your
situation from—yours or God's? –Solley

Morning: Gen 39; Mark 9 — *Evening:* Job 5; Rom 9

PROTECTIVE CUSTODY

*"The LORD redeems the life of his servants; none of
those who take refuge in him will be condemned."*
PSALM 34:22

I n most prisons, protective custody is taboo. Only those who need to
be protected and who cannot survive on their own in the general
population find themselves in protective custody. While the stigma at-
tached to it may not be quite as heavy as it once was, most people who
have been doing time for a while will still have some sense of its gravity.
In light of the Scripture today, this stigma can finally be overcome.

David was a warrior, fearing nothing and no one but the Lord. Yet,
in the face of insurmountable situations and powerful enemies, he
was forced to fully *trust* in the Lord alone. He clearly understood how
foolish it was to rely on his own strength or on anything other than the
Lord in such circumstances. Because of this, he was not afraid to catch
out and seek his protective custody in the arms of the Lord. So it is with
all of us who have had our lives redeemed by the Lord.

We are all under the protection of something, be it false bravado,
the institution, or any number of fickle and unreliable things. Those
of us who have sought refuge in the Lord can be confident that nothing can harm us or stand against us in a profitable way, especially when
we are under the protective custody of the great God Almighty, the
Creator and Master of the universe. May each day find us comfortable
and confident in His protective custody. –Karch

Morning: Gen 40; Mark 10 — *Evening:* Job 6; Rom 10

BE STRONG AND COURAGEOUS

". . . Be strong and courageous. Do not be frightened, and do not be dismayed, for the LORD your God is with you wherever you go."
JOSHUA 1:9

After the death of Moses, Joshua was given the overwhelming task of leading the children of Israel across the Jordan river into the Promised Land—a land not only filled with milk and honey, but also with Canaanites, Hittites, Hivites, Perizzites, Girgashites, Amorites, and Jebusites. All of whom would have to be driven off the land God promised His people. Knowing that Joshua would face times of uncertainty and fear during the years ahead, God commanded Joshua to be strong and courageous, not to fear or be dismayed because He would be with him every step of the way.

Like Joshua, there will be times when God will give us tasks that seem overwhelming to us—tasks that will lead to situations and circumstances that cause uncertainty and fear. However, as children of God, we can be assured that when we walk in the paths the Lord has set before us, we will not walk alone or in our strength. God will be with us wherever we go, and He will give the strength we need to accomplish what He has called us to do.

When you are faced with tasks that seem overwhelming, be strong and courageous, and do not fear, for the Lord your God is with you. He will go before you, just as He went before the children of Israel, to prepare the way. –Solley

Morning: Gen 41; Mark 11 — *Evening:* Job 7; Rom 11

THE COMPANY WE KEEP

"Do not be deceived: 'Bad company ruins good morals.'"
1 CORINTHIANS 15:33

I can remember a time at the beginning of my incarceration when I would sit around thinking of how life went completely wrong. I would reminisce about the causes of my current predicament, not wanting to believe that it was my fault. These periods of reflection always led back to certain memories in my past and, undoubtedly, to certain individuals I kicked it with. It is hard not to get upset at myself for hanging out with the wrong crowd. I used to think, "How could I ever have let myself get involved with those people?"

Ultimately, I realize my faulty decision-making was the reason I now find myself behind bars. Not once did anyone twist my arm or hold a gun to my head to force me to do what I did. However, I also understand that my choices were influenced by the company I kept. The words of the apostle Paul have a resounding message to the remorseful child of God who finds himself facing the consequences of a lifetime of poor decisions and bad company.

There are lessons to be learned from our past mistakes, and the wisest of us will learn from them quickly. Nowhere in the Scriptures will you find God letting people off the hook for the sinful choices they've made, even if they were guided by the people around them— just ask Adam. Therefore, you are still responsible for your actions, but knowing that your actions and behaviors are influenced by those around you, the choice should be clear. If you're wondering why you cannot stop making poor decisions, and you are constantly struggling to walk in the new life found in Christ, perhaps you may want to take a look at the company you keep. –Blevins

Morning: Gen 42; Mark 12 — *Evening:* Job 8; Rom 12

LONG ARM OF THE LAW

"They show that the work of the law is written on their
hearts, while their conscience also bears witness, and their
conflicting thoughts accuse or even excuse them."
ROMANS 2:15

T hroughout history Christians have developed terms to describe the innate phenomena of a law written on our hearts. John Calvin called it the *sensus divinitatis,* an inherent sense of God that renders us morally accountable to Him. The German idealist, Immanuel Kant, said he could never get beyond what he defined as a *moral law* within his own heart. C.S. Lewis articulated one of the most powerful arguments for the existence of God from this sense of a moral law. John Edward Carnell defined the phenomena as the "judicial sentiment" from which we each know some moral context of what is right and wrong. The point is Scripture tells us it is there. We all experience it.

There are times when, as Christians, we can easily become discouraged as we witness the moral depravity around us. In these times we may feel it is so much easier to live that way, as opposed to striving to live to honor God. Remember though, the long arm of the law written on each heart stands as its own witness to conscience and thought. It may be easy to evade it for a moment, but the condemnation of our hearts cannot be escaped. Each human being understands in an instinctive way that we are morally accountable to God. Because of this, it is altogether better to have the comfort of God's Spirit testifying to the law on our hearts that we are in right standing with Him.

So be of good courage. As Christians we know, "There is now no condemnation for those who are in Christ Jesus. For the law of the Spirit of life has set [us] free in Christ Jesus from the law of sin and death" (Romans 8:1–2). –Karch

Morning: Gen 43; Mark 13 — *Evening:* Job 9; Rom 13

FELLOWSHIP WITH ONE ANOTHER

*"And let us consider how to stir up one another to love
and good works, not neglecting to meet together, as is the
habit of some, but encouraging one another, . . ."*
HEBREWS 10:24–25

At times we are so busy with our personal lives that we neglect coming together for worship with other believers. When I do this, I feel a void within me, like some vital part of my Christian life has withered away. During these times, I often get overwhelmed with the basic mundane circumstances that come from being incarcerated—drawing my strength from self, instead of from God and from my fellow brothers.

On a larger scale, the same applies to the entire body of Christ. When we, as Christians, neglect worshipping together, the entire body suffers. We become self-focused, rather than Christ-focused. We become introverted rather than extroverted. Our main agenda becomes surviving in this chaotic world we live in, rather than participating in the Great Commission. When this occurs, it is easy to let circumstances destroy what little fellowship we do have.

For the unity of the body of Christ, the band of believers that we are, fellowship with one another is of great importance. Worshipping together as a church draws each and every one of us closer to God and closer to each other in unity. Through worship, we not only strengthen ourselves, but the body of Christ as a whole. That is why the writer of Hebrews gave us a dire warning not to forsake our own assembly with one another. When we do so, it is to our detriment.

There is great wisdom in James' words to the first-century church. So, let's heed them by joining together in worship of our God. –Solley

Morning: Gen 44; Mark 14 — *Evening:* Job 10; Rom 14

ADJUSTING TO THE LIGHT

*"If we say that we have fellowship with him while we walk
in the darkness, we lie and do not practice the truth."*
1 JOHN 1:6

Have you ever gone outside on a really bright day after being inside for a long period of time? Or perhaps you've left a dark movie theater only to find yourself blinded by the brilliance of the afternoon sun? Going from one extreme condition to another can often be painful. Having to squint or shield our eyes as they adjust to the brightness of our surroundings can sometimes be an uncomfortable reminder of how diametrically opposed the light and the dark really are to one another.

The apostle John is driving that same point home here as he compares God to light. The contrast to everything light stands for is darkness and represents sin, evil, and wickedness. John says liars are those who claim to walk in the light but continue living in darkness. The two lifestyles are so distinctly separate that a person cannot do one while doing the other. Notice that John does not pretend one could claim to be sinless. His concern is against someone who willfully continues to practice a lifestyle from which Christ has set him free—a person who still clings joyfully to the lightless ways of his past.

Fellowship with God is a wonderful thing to claim, but it is only evidenced by the way we live our lives. Our pasts have been drenched in darkness; now it's time to get adjusted to the light. –Blevins

Morning: Gen 45, Mark 15 — *Evening:* Job 11; Rom 15

HOW FAR?

*"as far as the east is from the west, so far does
he remove our transgressions from us."*
PSALM 103:12

No matter how much we change, some people will always hold our pasts against us. They have kept account of our wrongs and will never let us forget what we have done. Often, they will use our pasts as a weapon against us: refusing to forgive us, condemning us for things we have truly repented. That is a reality of life we must accept. We can do nothing about it, and only frustrate ourselves in our attempts to change their minds and opinions or to convince them to forgive us.

However, we can have peace by resting in the assurance that God has forgiven us for our pasts and removed our transgressions far from us. In other words, our transgressions are no more. God has not simply wiped the slate of our pasts clean; He has shattered the slate to pieces and cast it away as far as the east is from the west! When God looks upon us, He does not do so with condemnation, but with love. He does not see the wrong we have done; He does not see men and women dirty and stained by the sins of their pasts. God sees His children, those He loves, washed and cleansed from all sin by the blood of Jesus Christ (Eph 1:7).

If others have been holding you in bondage because of your past, let it go. Find your peace by forgiving those who refuse to forgive you and your assurance in the truth of the gospel: Christ died so that you may be forgiven. His blood has covered all of your transgressions, and God has cast your sins as far as the east is from the west. That is the gospel—that is the good news. –Solley

Morning: Gen 46; Mark 16 — *Evening:* Job 12; Rom 16

VALENTINE

"Greater love has no one than this, that someone
lay down his life for his friends."
JOHN 15:13

Valentine's Day is associated with love, hearts, flowers, candies, and other things of that nature. Christians, however, are generally oblivious to the roots of Valentine's Day. History attests to two Christians by the name of Valentine who were martyred in the third century under the Emperor Claudius. Some say these are merely separate accounts of the same Valentine. Either way, this early Christian was martyred for his faith.

Valentine, like a number of early Christians, endured the ultimate sacrifice. As a bishop, Valentine may not have wanted to betray his congregation. Or, as one legend has it, he performed marriages forbidden by the Roman government at the time and refused to betray those whom he had married. Whatever led to his martyrdom, he remained firm to the end. He did not betray those whom he would call his friends. Yet, above all of those things, he refused to betray his Lord. He stayed true to his confession of Jesus as his Lord. This is the ultimate display of love and devotion to Jesus. A display of love and devotion that was often played out in the early years of Christianity and, on many levels, is continually played out today in countries where Christians are still persecuted and martyred.

As Valentine's Day is celebrated, let's remember how Valentine's love and devotion for his Lord eventually led him to lay down his life. Most of us will never be asked to physically lay down our lives as Valentine did. Nevertheless, daily dying to self by putting aside our own wants and needs displays a love and devotion for Jesus that extends itself throughout our Christian walk and reflects the great love He has given to us. We may never be a Valentine, but in a daily dying to self, there is no greater love than this. –Karch

Morning: Gen 47; Luke 1:1–38 — *Evening:* Job 13; 1 Cor 1

TOUGH LOVE

"Nathan said to David, 'You are that man!'"
2 SAMUEL 12:7A

Nathan, the prophet, was a trusted adviser to the king of Israel—David. Not only did he declare God's Word to the people of Israel, he was also part of David's royal inner circle. As a trusted counselor and devoted friend, Nathan was not afraid to speak the truth, regardless of the situation.

When David trespassed against God's eternal commands by committing adultery with Bathsheba and murdering her husband, Uriah, he was on a downward slope and falling fast. However, Nathan, being a faithful friend, confronted David with his treachery and helped put David back on the right track. He gave David the truth, however painful, without regard for the consequences should David decide to respond angrily.

Have you ever witnessed a friend do something harmful to others or himself? Did you have the courage to call him on it? We all have opportunities to help others when they're down and out, but how many of us can say we have rebuked a friend when they were in the wrong? Standing up against a friend can be extremely difficult, but it's something we must be willing to do if we truly care.

Being a true friend does not mean you have to smile and nod your head in the face of another's sin. Being a true friend means taking a stand against another's harmful behavior and helping them get back on the right track. –Blevins

Morning: Gen 48; Luke 1:39–80 — *Evening:* Job 14; 1 Cor 2

THE MAN JESUS

"Jesus wept."
JOHN 11:35

For some reason, one thing I love most about the story of Lazarus is that it clearly portrays Jesus' humanity. Nothing penetrates me as deeply as the words: "Jesus wept." My eyes seem to lock onto these two words, and they echo over and over in my mind, *Jesus wept . . . Jesus wept.* These words bring comfort and peace to my soul and make me understand that, like us, Jesus felt deep emotional pain, sadness, and loss. The death of His friend Lazarus and the pain Mary and Martha were experiencing at the loss of their brother hurt Jesus. It hurt Him so much that He wept—just like we do during our times of pain and sorrow.

It is so easy to focus on Jesus' Godhead that we forget about His humanity. Jesus did not walk this earth sheltered and immune from the realities of life. He was not exempt from the pain and heartaches we feel. He was a man of sorrow and acquainted with grief (Is 53:3). Jesus experienced everything that we have, including the pains of life. He understands what it means to hurt. He understands what it means to grieve. He understands what it means to be rejected. He even understands what it means to be betrayed. Like us, Jesus has experienced it all. And because He is one of us and He understands, we can turn to Him for comfort during our times of sorrow and grief.

When you are going through difficulties in life, when it feels like you have no one who understands, let Jesus' humanity assure you that He understands your pain, anguish, and grief. Because He does, He will share in yours. –Solley

Morning: Gen 49; Luke 2 — *Evening:* Job 15; 1 Cor 3

NIGHT

". . . the hour has come for you to wake from sleep. For
salvation is nearer to us now than when we first believed.
The night is far gone; the day is at hand. So then let us cast
off the works of darkness and put on the armor of light."
ROMANS 13:11–12

As Paul begins to sum up his letter to the Romans, he admonishes them in several different ways. This particular section deals with an awareness of the implications of the believers' salvation. Paul encourages them to shake off sleep because night is gone and the day of salvation has arrived. Believers are to know the *time*.

Time has the ability to dominate the person in prison. His existence is defined by the time he has, the time he has served already, or the time he has left to do. Prison time is generally viewed as a period of darkness. Those of us inside prison who are Christians allow this to encroach upon us, and we have a tendency to view salvation as either a one-time event when we confess Jesus or an event that is to take place in the future. Paul expresses that our salvation is nearer to us now than it was when we first believed. So, there is a "both/and" connotation to what salvation involves. Even in the midst of the night, the *day is at hand*.

As we begin to realize and understand the full reality of our salvation in Jesus Christ, we are to step away from those things that belong to the night—even those attitudes that come with doing time—and live like the day is indeed at hand. We walk as His soldiers bearing the armor of light which outshines the darkest nights. –Karch

Morning: Gen 50; Luke 3 — *Evening:* Job 16, 17; 1 Cor 4

HE SUSTAINS US

"The steps of a man are established by the LORD, when he delights in his way; though he fall, he shall not be cast headlong, for the LORD upholds his hand."
PSALM 37:23–24

S top what you are doing and take one long look around you: the concrete, bare walls, steel bars, razor wire. Prison life is a harsh and somber reality. It is where many of us have hit the bottom of the bottom. The odds are that prison is a place you never intended to be, and it is evident from where you are that somewhere along the road in life you have fallen—you have strayed far from the paths that you once desired your life to take. I know I have.

Reality has shown us time and time again that life is not perfect. It is full of ups and downs, highs and lows, twists and turns, heartaches and heartbreaks. Christians are not perfect either. We are finite human beings who have human frailties and weaknesses. Consequently, at some point, no matter how hard we try not to, we will fail. We will fall. It is inevitable. However, the psalmist assures us that when we make the Lord our guide and allow Him to establish our steps, though we fall, we will not be cast headlong. The Lord will uphold our hand; He will sustain us.

It is imperative that today you determine to allow the Lord to guide your steps. That way, when life hits you with one of its unexpected punches and knocks your feet right out from under you, though you may fail and fall, you will not be cast headlong, for the Lord will uphold you. –Solley

Morning: Exod 1; Luke 4 — *Evening:* Job 18; 1 Cor 5

PRIZE OF WAR

*"But I will give you your life as a prize of war
in all places to which you may go."*
JEREMIAH 45:5B

I heard an old ex-convict preacher once talk about miracles. He cried out half a dozen times, "I should have been dead!" How many of us can relate to that statement and attest to the grace and mercy of a forgiving God who has seemingly preserved us against death time and time again? I am constantly aware of the miracle of my life and the many times I should have been dead. However, more miraculous still is the *new* life we have been given in Christ.

Augustine once said he did not believe in miracles until he witnessed the miracle of change in his own heart. In much the same way, many of us can say the same thing. Not only should we be dead, but we should have certainly remained dead in our sins, deserving nothing more. Thankfully, because of Christ our new lives have been given to us as a prize of war, a prize won on the cross at Calvary and given to us wherever we go—even inside prison.

We should be dead, nevertheless we live. Let us use the life we have been given to serve wholeheartedly the One who won our lives for us. And wherever we go, let us display our lives—our prizes of war—to a watching world. –Karch

Morning: Exod 2; Luke 5 — *Evening*: Job 19; 1 Cor 6

ARE YOU TOUGH ENOUGH?

*"Fight the good fight of the faith. Take hold of the eternal
life to which you were called and about which you made the
good confession in the presence of many witnesses."*
1 TIMOTHY 6:12

One of the hardest things I ever had to do was walk away. I had no doubt in my mind that I was right and the officer was wrong. Deep down in my soul I could feel the urge to respond, but I knew this was a lose-lose situation. So, I kept my mouth shut and walked away.

In prison, it is easy to fall into the mind-set that we must look "tough" all the time. We can't let anyone get over on us, or before you know it, everyone will try to test us. There are many ways people will attempt to look tough. Some will fight to let people know how tough they are, while others will just bark really loud and try to sell their toughness without having to fight. However, physical toughness is not what Paul had in mind when he advised Timothy to fight the good fight of faith. The good fight of faith for Paul was placing his unwavering trust and commitment in the sovereign God of the universe. Despite whatever or whomever came against Paul, his faith could not be shaken because he clung tightly to the promise of eternal life to which he was called.

It is easy to put on a show and act tough, but underneath it all, you're just allowing others to determine your actions. The real test of toughness comes from not responding the way other people expect you to. Try swallowing your pride, and then you will see how tough you really are. The next time you are provoked to respond and everyone is watching, expecting you to "go off," try calmly walking away—try fighting the good fight of faith. –Blevins

Morning: Exod 3; Luke 6 — *Evening:* Job 20; 1 Cor 7

STAMPED

*"In him you also, when you heard the word of truth,
the gospel of your salvation, and believed in him,
were sealed with the promised Holy Spirit,"*
EPHESIANS 1:13

Prison is full of men and women who run around displaying their stamp of approval of one gang or another. They fly their artwork proudly, arrogantly daring anyone to speak against it. They proclaim their undying loyalty to those who do likewise. Some are even willing to die for their gang. These people have found a false sense of belonging in something that holds no eternal value. I should know; I was one of them. Like many, I was sealed with a stamp that eventually faded literally and metaphorically. The ink faded on my skin, and the loyalty to something that could never be loyal to me faded in my heart.

Unlike gangs, or prison "families," whose members come and go and whose stamps fade over time, when we put our faith and trust in Jesus Christ, we become part of an eternal family established by the blood of the cross. Our founder, in His love for us, gave His life so that we might live. He has sealed us with the only seal that holds eternal value, a seal that will never lose its luster and never fade. The seal of the Holy Spirit guarantees us that we belong to Christ and are eternally His. Christ has given us the ultimate stamp of approval.

As you walk the halls of your prison today and interact with those who carry temporal stamps of approval, just remember one thing: a man can fly all the artwork he wants, but he is never truly stamped until he is stamped with the seal that is eternal—the seal of the Holy Spirit. –Solley

Morning: Exod 4; Luke 7 — *Evening:* Job 21; 1 Cor 8

PLANTED IN FAITHFULNESS

"I will rejoice in doing them good, and I will plant them in this land in faithfulness, with all my heart and all my soul."
JEREMIAH 32:41

The promise of God through the prophet Jeremiah to bring Israel out of the Babylonian captivity and back to their land is presented here with a depth unique to all of Scripture. The Lord says He will faithfully plant them in the land with all of His heart and all of His soul. This is a powerful and rich assertion.

Most of us tend to see our time in prison as a time of captivity. Maybe it is. However, there are two ways of looking at it. On the one hand, we can see our time as being exiled from our homes and families, knowing that the Lord promises us a joyous return. Or, on the other hand, we can see it as the return itself. Many of us were held captive to one thing or another while on the outside, be it addictions, co-dependency, or any number of vices. Our coming to prison to be freed from those things is, in its own way, liberating. When we begin to look at it in this light, we are in a much better position to serve the Lord and to rejoice in what He has done for us in and through this liberating return.

In terms of perspective, try and think of prison time not as captivity, but as liberation. View it as being faithfully planted by the Lord in this place, in this time, so we may honor and glorify Him in the freedom from the things that once bound us. At the same time, we can be certain that He has faithfully planted us where we are with all of His heart and all of His soul. –Karch

Morning: Exod 5; Luke 8 — *Evening:* Job 22; 1 Cor 9

REMOVE AND RENEW

"Create in me a clean heart, O God, and
renew a steadfast spirit within me."
PSALM 51:10

King David had it all: money, power, and fame. All these things are what the world tells us will make us happy, but David still wanted more. He let himself fall into the snare of an unsatisfying life. He took something that was not his, another man's wife, and did it by any means necessary. In the process, David sinned against God, who had established him as the king, and thereby created a rift in their relationship. Giving into his fleshly desires had tremendous consequences in David's life. As David learned, God does not tolerate or make allowances for sin in our life no matter who we are or how pious we may think ourselves.

Have you ever felt that if you could make just a little more money, if you could just find the next pretty girl, or if one more hit could finally take all the cares away, then everything in your life would be better? Today's secular-driven society repeatedly advertises worldly things promising a happier life. Our human lives are constantly spent searching for that "something" to fill the void in our hearts, but as David discovered, that void is only filled by God. And, also like David, once we discover that we have tried to supplant God with material possessions or sinful relationships, we must humble ourselves and cry out to the Almighty Father.

Read David's stories in 2 Samuel 11 and 12, then read Psalm 51 and ask yourself, "Have I put something in between my relationship with the Lord?" If so, isn't it time to remove and renew? –Blevins

Morning: Exod 6; Luke 9 — *Evening:* Job 23; 1 Cor 10

THE MEANEST MAN IN TEXAS

"And the Lord appointed a great fish to swallow up Jonah."
JONAH 1:17A

The story is often told about Clyde Thompson, the meanest man in Texas. Clyde was incarcerated for the murder of several hunters who trespassed on his property. Shortly after his incarceration, he quickly established a reputation for being one of the most dangerous men to ever walk the halls of a Texas prison. Within a few short years, he had not only killed several prisoners, but had attacked numerous guards as well. No matter where they housed Clyde Thompson, he always found a way to escape from his cell and strike with violence at the least provocation. Eventually, prison administrators were forced to place Clyde in the old morgue underneath the prison and weld the door shut behind him. The only connection between Clyde and humanity was a small slot his food was passed through to him.

One day, disobeying all the rules, a guard slipped a small Bible down the food slot to Clyde. He was never the same again. Soon, Clyde was released from his living tomb and began spreading the gospel of Jesus Christ to his fellow prisoners. No one could believe this was the same man who, only a short time ago, would kill you for simply looking at him too long.

The story of Clyde Thompson makes me realize that sometimes God will put us in a place where we will have no choice but to listen to Him. For Clyde, it was an old morgue with the door welded shut; for Jonah, it was the belly of a whale; for you and me—it may be right where we are. The very prison we find ourselves in could be the appointed place God has determined to be used to get our attention. The question is: Are we listening? –Solley

Morning: Exod 7; Luke 10 — *Evening:* Job 24; 1 Cor 11

RESPECT

"Be imitators of me, as I am of Christ."
1 CORINTHIANS 11:1

I n every penal institution I have ever been in, there is always a degree in which people demand *respect*. How that demand is played out varies from place to place, and the word itself means different things to different people. These various meanings, and the various degrees in which they are demanded, serve to create a dynamic for trouble. After some inevitable altercation, combatants emerge with the excuse that one or both had been disrespected. Regardless of how much the degrees of demand vary, and no matter how many different meanings the word accumulates, inside prison respect always connotes some form of self-love. The total opposite of what real respect is.

Immanuel Kant developed a philosophically decisive definition of the word respect. He sees respect directed toward something (or someone) that thwarts our self-love. It cannot be compulsory by either inclination or fear. Concerning persons, we respect those who exercise their duty in a way that deserves respect, whether we are inclined to give it or not. Those who we respect we seek to emulate—we have a desire to be like them. This is what Paul is getting at as he encourages the Corinthians to be imitators of him as he imitates Christ. There is no other person who has ever lived who exercised his duty in a way that even his enemies respected Him. Paul understood this; and as he respected Christ, he sought to emulate Him.

The Corinthians knew what kind of life Paul lived. In him they had a visible representation of Christ. Inasmuch as we do not have Paul with us, there is somebody we can look to that is seeking to imitate Christ. We can look at their lives and imitate them as they seek to imitate Christ. Look for that person who deserves that type of respect and imitate him. –Karch

Morning: Exod 8; Luke 11 — *Evening*: Job 25, 26; 1 Cor 12

QUARTER

"You adulterous people! Do you not know that friendship with the world is enmity with God? Therefore whoever wishes to be a friend of the world makes himself an enemy of God."
JAMES 4:4

I remember a time in high school, studying the Middle Ages, when I became fascinated with knights. Their tales of courage, honor, dedication, and loyalty always amazed me. One of the most interesting facts I discovered was that often times when two kings were at war and their knights were battling each other, there was an unwritten rule of engagement: if a knight were to submit and surrender his arms, he would be given quarter. It didn't matter how savagely the knight fought or how dangerous he might be in the future; his life would be spared. Most of the time, he would be ransomed back to the king he fought for and sent away in disgrace.

I find James' statement true that being friends with the world puts us at odds with God. In fact, it makes us His enemies. What a scary thought, to be at odds with the Creator of the universe. However, that's the most amazing thing about His grace in that while we were still sinners, He offers us quarter through His Son, Jesus Christ. He doesn't destroy us or lock us in some dark dungeon, even though we certainly deserve it. He showers us with His mercy and grace. And the best part is, He doesn't ransom us back to our old master; He allows us to fight for the winning side.

Have you bent your knee and surrendered your life to the Most High God? Are you tired of fighting a losing battle? Accept the quarter He's offering you today and declare your own sworn loyalty to the King of kings (1 Tim 6:15). –Blevins

Morning: Exod 9; Luke 12 — *Evening:* Job 27; 1 Cor 13

A HELPING HAND

*"But Moses' hands grew weary, so they took a stone and put it
under him, and he sat on it, while Aaron and Hur held up his
hands, one on one side, and the other on the other side . . ."*
EXODUS 17:12

S hortly after their exodus from Egypt, the Israelites faced Amalek
in battle. While the Israelites fought below, Moses watched from
the top of a nearby hill with the staff of the Lord raised in his hands.
As long as Moses held the Lord's staff up, Israel prevailed in battle.
However, when his arms got weak and he lowered the staff, Amalek
prevailed. Seeing that Moses was growing weary, Aaron and Hur took
a stone, placed it under him, and held up his hands. The Israelites
prevailed in battle because Aaron and Hur were willing to stand with
Moses, and Moses was willing to accept the help of those God had
placed in his life.

God has not designed us to walk through life or to fight our battles
alone. Not only does God go before us as He did Moses, He has given
us "Aarons" and "Hurs" to stand with us to help hold up our hands
when we grow weary, people who are willing to come alongside us and
help us through the battles we face. However, like Moses, we must be
willing to accept the help of the people God has placed in our lives.
There will also be times when we will have to be the Aaron or Hur to
someone else, times when we will be required to come alongside another brother or sister and help hold up their hands when they grow
weary.

God never intended the Christian walk to be a solo experience. He
has placed fellow believers in our lives for a reason. Let us never fail to
accept their help or to offer ours. –Solley

Morning: Exod 10; Luke 13 — *Evening:* Job 28; 1 Cor 14

PLEDGE OF ALLEGIANCE

*"And I tell you, everyone who acknowledges me before men, the
Son of Man will acknowledge before the angels of God,"*
LUKE 12:8

In reading this particular discourse of Jesus, it is easy to sterilize what is being said. For those of us who have run afoul of the law at any time in our lives, the idea of confession creates an almost knee-jerk reaction, as if confession were a bad thing. Luke's gospel account was originally penned in Greek and the word translated as *confess* loses something in translation. The word literally carries the idea of pledging allegiance.

In this light, to confess Jesus before men carries with it much more weight than merely telling people we believe in Jesus. As much as the name of Christ is bandied about these days, we can see why the demands here are much greater than a mere vocal assertion. There is a demand for an avowal of commitment—an announcement or pledge of loyalty and dedication that leads to action for our entire lives. The wonderful thing about this is, we see Jesus offering this same allegiance toward us. He committed His life as an act of loyalty and dedication to us, and His pledge of allegiance was signed in His own blood for us.

Take a minute to think about what this allegiance cost Jesus, as well as the benefits we receive from it. As we do so, think about what it means to confess Jesus before men today—to pledge your allegiance to Him. –Karch

Morning: Exod 11, 12:1–21; Luke 14 — *Evening:* Job 29; 1 Cor 15

YOU SAID WHAT!

*"Let no corrupting talk come out of your mouths, but
only as such as is good for building up, as fits the
occasion, that it may give grace to those who hear."*
EPHESIANS 4:29

I offended someone the other day by saying something I thought
to be very minor. At the time I said it, I was not even aware of the
impact my words had on him until he approached me a few days later
and expressed his feelings. Naturally, I wanted to get defensive and say
he was nit-picking by bringing up something so minor, but I listened to
him. After thinking about it, I was able to see where he was offended.
And the truth was, he was right; I did say something that was not very
becoming of who I am in Christ.

As Christians, we are a light unto the world, and at all times are
to let our light shine in front of others (Matt 5:16). This includes our
speech. It is easy to get caught up in the penitentiary mentality and
let our mouths run-off without giving thought to how our words may
impact those around us—even when we are not aware they are listening. However, Paul exhorts us to let no corrupt talk come out of our
mouths, but only such that is good for building others up so that it may
give grace to those who hear it. If our speech is not building others
up and imparting grace to those who hear it, then we need to rethink
what we have to say before we say it.

None of us are perfect. However, we live in an environment where
others are constantly watching and listening. Let not only our actions,
but also our speech, show them that we are for real about the God we
profess. –Solley

Morning: Exod 12:22–51; Luke 15 — *Evening*: Job 30; 1 Cor 16

THE KING OF HEARTS

"Search me, O God, and know my heart!
Try me and know my thoughts!"
PSALM 139:23

T hough David was a king, he was not born into the monarchy, so his ascendency to the throne was in many ways a unique experience that afforded him a rare vantage point of what it meant to be a king. As a boy he was anointed by Samuel to lead the people of Israel, but it was a long and difficult thirty years later when he finally ascended to the throne in Jerusalem. David understood what it meant to be low and high, and what it meant to be ruled and to rule.

As David understood this, he knew it was one thing to have a person's allegiance—even their loyalty—but it was something altogether different to have their heart. There is a famous discourse recorded between Napoleon and Count Montholon that took place after Napoleon's exile to the rock of St. Helena. Napoleon also knew what it meant to rule and he was now experiencing what it meant to be ruled. He knew what it was like to be high; but as a vanquished exile, he experienced what it was like to be low. Their discourse concerned the person of Jesus Christ. Napoleon marveled at how the King Jesus had a worldwide empire built on people's hearts. No other monarch in history could ever attest to having the hearts of his subjects. Both David and Napoleon clearly understood this.

Today we do not understand monarchies the way civilizations did in the past. However, we do know where our hearts are. As you think about the King of your heart, see yourself connected to a vast empire ruled by a King who knows each of us intimately. Seek to give more of your heart to Him each day until he has it all. –Karch

Morning: Exod 13; Luke 16 — *Evening:* Job 31; 2 Cor 1

STICKS AND STONES

"There is therefore now no condemnation for
those who are in Christ Jesus."
ROMANS 8:1

Y ou hear it all the time: "You're not a Christian, you're a fake! God will never forgive you for what you've done. The only place you belong is in hell." Simple words strung together and hatefully thrown are often the most hurtful weapons and cut us the deepest. Yet, there are times when it's our conscience, not other people, who launch the harshest assaults at us. How many times have you thought, "I don't understand how God could forgive me," or "I've done things that can't be forgiven."

Well, I've got some good news. It's probably news you've already heard, but just haven't found a way to believe. There is now *no* condemnation for those who are in Christ Jesus. That doesn't mean some condemnation; but absolutely none—zero. However, if you've constructed your house out of glass instead of the solid Truth of God's Word, it will never withstand the onslaught when the world, or your own conscience, launches hate-filled attacks at you. On the other hand, if Christ is your Chief Cornerstone, then sticks and stones, or anything else thrown at you, are all harmless.

Submit to God's Word in your life. In other words, don't just read it to read it—apply it and believe in the promises He's given you. Understand also, that no matter what the world says or what your own conscience may try to tell you, you who are in Christ are saved from God's wrath. No stick, stone, or hurtful word can change that. –Blevins

Morning: Exod 14; Luke 17 — *Evening:* Job 32; 2 Cor 2

THROUGH THE VALLEY

*"Even though I walk through the valley of the shadow
of death, I will fear no evil, for you are with me;
your rod and your staff, they comfort me."*
PSALM 23:4

Psalm 23 is one of the most recognized passages in the Bible. Historians believe King David wrote this psalm during his flight from King Saul, who sought his life. What is unique about this psalm is that David was not looking for a way out of his predicament. Rather, he was trusting God to see him through it. The depth and strength of David's trust in God permeates this entire passage. In the face of imminent death, David feared no evil because he knew that though he must walk through the valley of death, he did not walk alone—God walked with him.

Many times we cry out to God to deliver us from some "valley of death" we are facing. Whether it is our incarceration, a sickness, a broken relationship that brings pain into our lives, or simply a fearful and unpleasant situation we encounter, we want God to miraculously intervene—to simply take that which is troubling us away. So we cry out to God, begging and pleading with Him to deliver us. Many times God does deliver us. But then there are those times when He does not deliver us, times like David experienced, when we must walk through the dark valleys of life. Yet, as David clearly understood, when God does not deliver us from these pits of darkness, He is there to walk us through them, comforting and strengthening us along the way.

There is great comfort in knowing that though the valley seems deep and wide, God will see us through it. So, when you find yourself walking through life's deep, dark valleys, don't just look for a way out. Instead, look for God's strength to see you through. –Solley

Morning: Exod 15; Luke 18 — *Evening:* Job 33; 2 Cor 3

AGAIN AND AGAIN

"Again the word of the LORD came to me:"
EZEKIEL 16:1

Some days I get sidetracked. There were times early in my walk with Christ when I would get sidetracked for a few days at a time. This is pretty much a universal experience for all believers. By being sidetracked, I mean we get caught up in the everyday machinations of life. We spend considerable amounts of time thinking about when the next letter or visit is coming—or if they will come at all. For Ezekiel there were a lot of things going on that would allow for him to become sidetracked. His nation had been destroyed. His people had been taken into captivity, split up, and enslaved. Worries could easily have encroached upon his relationship with the Lord. However, Ezekiel reminds us how the Lord mitigates those things that distract us by continuing to speak to us in His Word.

We can take comfort in knowing the Lord will not allow us to become too sidetracked before He begins to get our attention. While it is important that we remain sensitive to how He does this, the most important thing is He continues to do it again and again.

Our Lord has given us personal letters in His Word. He stands ready to visit us in the Scriptures and speak to us. Next time you notice yourself getting sidetracked by all of the distracting things that come with life, go to Him so you, too, can say, "Again the word of the LORD came to me." –Karch

Morning: Exod 16; Luke 19 — *Evening:* Job 34; 2 Cor 4

A FATHER'S EMBRACE

*"And he arose and came to his father. But while he was still
a long way off, his father saw him and felt compassion,
and ran and embraced him and kissed him."*
LUKE 15:20

R aising children is a difficult job any way you cut it. Providing for our children's physical, emotional, and spiritual needs is a daunting task, one which most of us learn to do as we go. Sometimes we get it right and other times we fall flat on our faces. Nevertheless, the best fathers are the ones who never give up, the ones who stay the course even when it looks like all their efforts have been in vain. These are the fathers all children secretly wish they had.

The parable of the prodigal son was used by Jesus to teach spiritual truths concerning forgiveness and salvation. We often focus on the change in disposition of the wayward son and his disgruntled brother, but what about the attitude of the father? After the independent young man decided he would rather take his chances in the world than be under the care and protection of his father, his daddy was still there for him, to welcome him back.

While we may not be typical fathers to our children, we can still be there for them in other ways, loving and caring for them. Through the appropriate channels of communication, whether it's a letter, phone call, or a visit, we need to let them know that regardless which direction they choose to take in life, we will always be here to welcome them back into our arms with a father's embrace. –Blevins

Morning: Exod 17; Luke 20 — *Evening:* Job 35; 2 Cor 5

PEACEMAKERS

"Blessed are the peacemakers, for they shall be called sons of God."
MATTHEW 5:9

I walked into my cell after a long, tiring day only to find myself confronted with a mess: my cellmate's clothes scattered all over the floor; his dirty, smelly boots sitting right beneath the spot where I lay my head, and there appeared to be dried toothpaste stuck to the side of the sink. The grit beneath my feet told me that my cellmate, once again, tracked in half of the dirt from the rec yard. And, of course, he was passed out in his bunk with his mouth hanging half-opened, snoring—with the light on.

Let's face it: living in a 5' x 9' concrete box with another man is not always easy. Cellmates often get on your nerves, frustrate you, and make you ready to fight, much like I was that night. However, I thank God that, over time, He has taught me a different way of life. Instead of the old hardhead I used to be, I am now a peacemaker—even when I do not want to be, and even when it is not easy. The easiest thing for me to have done that night would have been to reach up and snatch my cellmate right out of his bunk and teach him some long overdue manners. Yet, that would not have been very becoming of a *son of God*.

If your cellmate has you past the breaking point and you are ready to explode, just remember one thing: "Blessed are the peacemakers, for they shall be called sons of God." No, being the peacemaker is not always easy, but it is what we are called by our Heavenly Father to be. And with God's help, all things are possible. –Solley

Morning: Exod 18; Luke 21 — *Evening:* Job 36; 2 Cor 6

ALCHEMY

*"But he knows the way that I take; when he has
tried me, I shall come out as gold."*
JOB 23:10

People throughout the Middle Ages searched for a chemical formula that would cause a material change in the elemental makeup of base materials. Particularly, people sought a method to change things like lead into gold. The professionals of this enterprise were sanctioned and employed by kings to use whatever means necessary to find such a formula. These self-styled professionals were called alchemists.

The name has its roots in an ancient Greek word meaning "to pour." For us, God—the King Himself—becomes the ultimate alchemist. He knows the formula for taking the base and worthless things we are, and by pouring His Spirit into our lives, He effects a substantial material change within us so that we will emerge from this transformation process as *gold*.

Wherever you are today, realize God knows that place; He knows the way you take. In pouring His Spirit into your life, He has already begun the process of conforming you into the image of Christ. As this is the case, know that when the very complex and sometimes painful process of transformation is complete, you will most assuredly come forth as gold. For evidence of this process, take a look at what the Lord has brought you from even now, and you might sense a hint of gold already. –Karch

Morning: Exod 19; Luke 22 — *Evening:* Job 37; 2 Cor 7

NIGHTLIGHTS

"The LORD is my light and my salvation; whom shall I fear?"
PSALM 27:1A

When I was a young boy, maybe five or six years old, I was terrified of the dark. I couldn't sleep in a room by myself unless I had a nightlight on. If I didn't have one, I thought something horrible would creep in the darkness and would "get me." But when there was a nightlight on, I had this innate sense of security because there was light around.

King David, the author of Psalm 27, likewise had a sense of security. However, it wasn't in a cheap, plastic nightlight. David's security came only from the Lord. When surrounded by enemies and faced with imminent death, he didn't trust in his own ability or in any created thing. David placed his complete and absolute trust in the Lord God Almighty, and by waiting on Him, David found courage.

I eventually outgrew my fear of the dark and my dependence on nightlights. But looking back, I just exchanged one fear for another. If it wasn't the dark, I feared rejection by others, failure in my marriage, or going to prison. At some point in my life, I can distinctly remember facing each of these things. I can also remember always placing my trust in the wrong things, whether myself or secular solutions. Now, I have matured in my faith and my understanding of God's love for me. God is my strength, my stronghold, my deliverer. I now place my trust in Him alone. Ask yourself, what, or who, do I put my trust in; and "Am I still turning on nightlights?" –Blevins

Morning: Exod 20; Luke 23 — *Evening:* Job 38; 2 Cor 8

IT IS WELL

"Be merciful to me, O God . . . for in you my soul takes refuge; in the shadow of your wings I will take refuge, till the storms of destruction pass by."
PSALM 57:1

In the late 1800s, a fire destroyed everything Horatio G. Spafford owned. While he was struggling to recoup his losses, his young son took fever and died. As he began to slowly emerge from his grief, his family planned a voyage to England. However, Horatio was forced to stay back in order to attend an unexpected court hearing and planned to take another ocean steamer to meet his wife and three daughters in England. His life was shattered once again when he received an emergency Teletype from his wife informing him that their ship sank at sea; she was the only member of their family to survive. While Horatio was standing on the deck of his ship looking out toward the sea where his three daughters drowned, wrestling with the emotions raging inside of him, God gave him the words to the hymn, "It Is Well with My Soul."

Horatio Spafford experienced tragedy of such magnitude that is unknown to most of us. Yet, even in the midst of his loss, he understood that his refuge was found in the shadow of God's wings. Instead of allowing the pain and anguish to overwhelm him, Horatio turned to God, knowing that ultimately, no matter the circumstances, all would be well. In his own words, he proclaimed, "Whatever my lot, Thou has taught me to say: It is well; it is well with my soul."

Even in the midst of our struggle and heartaches, when life seems to overwhelm us, we can take refuge in the shadow of God's wings. We can also say, "It is well with my soul." –Solley

Morning: Exod 21; Luke 24 — *Evening*: Job 39; 2 Cor 9

TURN ASIDE

"And Moses said, 'I will turn aside to see this
great sight, why the bush is not burned.'"
EXODUS 3:3

Moses was minding his own business, tending his father-in-law's flocks when he came upon a burning bush. Seeing this, he turned aside to see what it was all about. This is often how the Lord comes to us. He solicits our attention in order to speak to us in His Word. We will be minding our own business, maybe tending to our routine devotional pattern for the day, when we see something that catches our attention.

However our burning bush experiences come to us and catch our attention, what is key is the turning aside to see the sight. In this portion of Scripture we see that when God *saw* Moses turn aside, it was then He began to speak. When we read the Word of God and something catches our attention, it is important to turn aside so that we may see why the Scriptures say this, or why it says things in a certain way.

We may not see many bushes burning in prison; but we do know that God Himself is a consuming fire, and He has revealed Himself to us in His Word. Even in prison, we have both His Word and the time to read it. What's more, there are plenty of things in His Word capable of getting our attention. Once the Lord has our attention, may we always be ready to turn aside. In doing so, we can be sure that the Lord sees us and be confident He will speak to us. –Karch

Morning: Exod 22; John 1 — *Evening:* Job 40; 2 Cor 10

FINDING FAVOR

*"But the LORD was with Joseph and showed him steadfast love
and gave him favor in the sight of the keeper of the prison."*
GENESIS 39:21

S old into slavery by his brothers and unjustly accused of rape by
his master's wife, Joseph was familiar with the short end of the
stick. To most people, Joseph's life was a series of bad breaks and difficult dilemmas they would not wish on their worst enemy. Ultimately,
the story of Joseph didn't end in prison. In fact, it was there that God
turned Joseph's fateful circumstances upside down.

Being incarcerated is probably one of the worst things a person
can ever experience. Whether you're new to the system or you've been
down for some time, it never gets easy. So many things happen on a
day-to-day basis that you might find yourself asking, "God, are you really there?" Joseph realized God had a plan and purpose for his life.
Even though there were times when it didn't always appear that way,
God was with Joseph.

If you've ever struggled with finding a purpose amidst your own
fateful circumstances, know that indeed there is one. Joseph's foray
into Egyptian servitude led him, by the hand of God, to find favor in
Pharaoh's eyes and eventually, to be in a position to save his family
from famine. Paul likewise confirms this in the New Testament: "And
we know that for those who love God all things work together for good,
for those who are called according to his purpose" (Rom 8:28). The
common denominator between Joseph's story and Paul's indicative
statement is God-centeredness. Keep God first in your life and favor
will find you. –Blevins

Morning: Exod 23; John 2 — *Evening:* Job 41; 2 Cor 11

THE POWER OF PRAYER

*"Rejoice always, pray without ceasing, give thanks in all
circumstances; for this is the will of God in Christ Jesus for you."*
1 THESSALONIANS 5:16–18

I was six years old when my mother became a Christian. Growing up,
I watched her life change as her faith and trust in God strengthened. Many times, I witnessed her down on her knees praying for her
children. Even as I grew into an adult and strayed far away from God,
I always knew my mother never ceased praying for me. She never gave
up, and she never stopped praying, although it took many years and
much heartache before her prayers were answered.

I learned a valuable lesson from my mother: there is power in
prayer. Prayer is how we draw close to the heart of God and safely lay
all of our cares and concerns at His feet. When we pray for those we
care about, we show God we trust Him with those we love the most.
However, as my mother experienced, there will be times when it feels
like the prayers are not being answered. Yet, just as my mother learned,
sometimes prayers are answered long before we have any reason to believe that they are. Today, this is why I pray for my daughter and for
those dear to me, just as my mother prayed for me.

What about you? Are there loved ones in your life you would like
to see saved? What about your children or your spouse? If so, begin
the task of praying for them without ceasing. In doing so, you place
those you love the most in the hands of the One who loves them even
more. –Solley

Morning: Exod 24; John 3 — *Evening:* Job 42; 2 Cor 12

JUST US

*"so that he might be just and the justifier of
the one who has faith in Jesus."*
ROMANS 3:26B

T he experience of justice has not been a pleasant one for most people inside prison. In fact, the old play on the word justice— *just us*—implies that it is really about those with the power to distribute injustice at will, and with impunity.

To think of this from a Biblical perspective, we can see how God, in His position of power and authority, could not help but righteously condemn sinful humanity as guilty. To justify man and maintain His own righteousness and justice, He had to send His only son, Jesus, to receive the penalty for the sins of mankind. Since no human sought God, nor was anyone righteous according to the law, it is as though God the Father told the Son, "It's just us." If things were to be made right, and through Jesus the world was to be reconciled by God, it had to be that way. Within the eternal counsel of the Godhead it was, "just us."

Our justification comes to us as a gift because of what Jesus accomplished for us through His righteousness. Jesus bore our guilt for us and took the punishment that was rightfully ours. Out of this, God's righteousness has been revealed so that "He might be just and the justifier of the one who has faith in Jesus." To understand the justice of God through what Jesus has accomplished for us helps us to understand justice in a whole new way. It makes the experience of justice pleasant. –Karch

Morning: Exod 25; John 4 — *Evening:* Prov 1; 2 Cor 13

ALWAYS

"And behold, I am with you always, to the end of the age."
MATTHEW 28:20B

J esus sent His disciples into a volatile environment knowing they were going to face humiliation, persecution, and loneliness. He understood what was coming far better than they did, yet He did not hesitate to give them such a dangerous task. He did not quail at sending them on such a lonely road. Have you ever asked yourself, "How could Jesus knowingly give His friends and followers such excruciatingly difficult commands to obey?"

The answer lies in the last words of the resurrected Lord in Matthew's gospel account. After commissioning His disciples to go out into the world and make disciples, Jesus comforts them by promising to be with them always, until the end of eternity. What a relief, I bet, that was! Here was their Lord, fresh from the grave, whose very presence before them was a testament to His power to fulfill His promises. Now they unequivocally knew that when He said He was going to ride it out with them, He meant business.

Being a disciple behind bars puts a new dynamic on the Great Commission. Sure, Paul preached the gospel both in chains and out, but He was the gold standard of the missionary. Most of us have never considered making disciples for Jesus while doing time. However, as Christians, we are commanded to do so regardless of our location. Evangelizing in prison isn't an easy task. Whether we do it directly by preaching the truth or indirectly by living a godly lifestyle, one thing we can be sure of is that Jesus' promise is still in effect today. He is with us, always. –Blevins

Morning: Exod 26; John 5 — *Evening:* Prov 2; Gal 1

TEMPTED

*"God is faithful, and he will not let you to be tempted beyond
your ability, but with the temptation he will also provide
the way of escape, that you may be able to endure it."*
1 CORINTHIANS 10:13

Every morning as we sip our first shot of coffee on the edge of
our bunks, listening to the slamming of steel doors and endless
chatter, we are greeted with something we never really think about: a
day full of trials and temptations. Will we look at that dirty magazine
our cellie left lying on the table in plain sight? Will we lie to the officer
about where we are going just so we can get off the line or out of the
cell? Will we buy that stolen hamburger out of the chow hall? Will we
respond to the constant disrespect around us in the violent way we
used to? Or will we send angry letters home, wondering why we have
not heard from anyone?

We are bombarded with temptations all day long that will test our
Christian character and our commitment to Christ. No one is exempt.
Yet, Scripture is plain: God will not allow us to be tempted beyond
what we can handle, and when we are tempted, God *will* provide the
way of escape. Yet, we have to stand strong and temporarily endure the
lures of temptation while we seek Christ's help to overcome them, because in Christ's suffering, He is able to help us when we are tempted
(Heb 1:18).

When you are tempted to step out of your Christian character today, look for the way of escape God has provided. You just may be surprised how easily you will find it. –Solley

Morning: Exod 27; John 6 — *Evening*: Prov 3; Gal 2

PATRICK

*"For this perhaps is why he was parted from you for a while, that
you might have him back forever, no longer as a bondservant
but more than a bondservant, as a beloved brother . . ."*
PHILEMON 15–16A

I n Paul's letter to Philemon, the bondservant Onesimus was sent
back to his owner. Yet, Philemon was to receive Onesimus as more
than a bondservant—he was now a brother. Today, as people wear
green and associate St. Patrick's Day with shamrocks and everything
Irish, there is a much richer story behind Patrick. Like Onesimus,
Patrick was a slave who had escaped his captivity. He had been a slave
in Ireland for six years when he finally escaped and returned to his
home in Britain.

Those of us who have spent time in prison can relate to the desire
Onesimus and Patrick had to be free from their captivity. The funny
thing about both of them is that they returned to where they had experienced bondage in order to represent the transforming power of
the gospel of Jesus Christ. Consequently, once Patrick returned to the
land of his captivity, the lasting influence of his preaching changed
Ireland forever.

We often see former convicts coming back inside to do ministry, but
what about those of us who are transformed by the gospel and don't
leave? The same desire should manifest itself in us, the desire to see others come to know the Lord. Even as an old man, Patrick never forgot his
former captivity as a slave, just as those of us who remain, can't forget
ours. Yet, knowing Christ lends to us a testimony that we are now more
than convicts, just as Onesimus and Patrick were more than bondser-
vants. We are co-heirs and fellow laborers with Christ. –Karch

Morning: Exod 28; John 7 — *Evening:* Prov 4; Gal 3

WITH ARMS WIDE OPEN

"Beloved, let us love one another, for love is from God, and whoever loves has been born of God and knows God."
1 JOHN 4:7

When people like us come to Christ, we bring with us a lot of excess baggage. Because of the lifestyles we have lived as hardened prisoners, criminals, and gang members, it is difficult for us not to allow our past behaviors to seep into our Christian walk and affect our relationships with other believers. We cannot simply divorce ourselves overnight from the negative behavior patterns and ideologies we lived with for so long. They are ingrained in us, and often, they unknowingly stand between us and our brothers or sisters in Christ.

However, as Christians, we gravely err when we allow our pasts to dictate how we interact with our joint heirs in Christ. The truth is, no matter how we try to overcome these issues alone, we will only fail. There is only one thing that can transcend the boundaries we have erected within and among ourselves. Only the love of God resounding in our hearts can break down the barriers of racism, prejudices, hate, and anger that many of us have allowed to separate us from other believers. When we immerse ourselves in the love of God, we cannot help but allow that love to flow out from us and embrace others with a genuine love, free from all of the excess baggage we have carried for so long. It is only then that we can approach each other with arms wide open.

As the apostle John so eloquently stated, "Beloved, let us love one another, for love is from God, and whoever loves has been born of God and knows God." So, let us continuously allow the love of God to search our hearts and destroy the barriers that prevent us from loving one another. –Solley

Morning: Exod 29; John 8 — *Evening:* Prov 5; Gal 4

GLYCERIN

"Tell the righteous that it shall be well with them,
for they shall eat the fruit of their deeds."
ISAIAH 3:10

I n the middle of Isaiah pronouncing judgment on Judah and Jerusalem, he offers this comfort to those who have been living well and who have sought to honor and follow the Lord. In the midst of the woes and judgment against the wicked, oppressors, and those who bring evil upon themselves is the promise to the faithful that they will be well and eat the fruit of their good deeds.

Glycerin comes from a Greek word that means "sweet." Today it is representative of a substance used to sweeten various foods and drinks. Something about the sweet taste appeals to our palate and we enjoy it. In this sense, the fruit we reap as faithful servants will have the same sweet taste. Yet, it transcends mere taste-buds and encompasses all of life. We will enjoy an overall sweetness of life as a reward for our righteous deeds as servants of the Lord. Even in the middle of chaos and confusion, our focus should be on faithfully serving the Lord with the understanding that the fruit of our labor will be sweet.

Being in prison implies judgment. This is oftentimes disheartening for those of us who seek to overcome our pasts in order to now honor and follow the Lord. Faced with this, as you consider how Isaiah slips in this encouragement in the midst of judgment, let it be an encouragement to you to press on and know that we will taste the sweetness of our labor when we are afforded the opportunity to eat the fruit of those deeds performed in His service. –Karch

Morning: Exod 30; John 9 — *Evening:* Prov 6; Gal 5

WHATCHA GONNA DO?

*"Submit yourselves therefore to God. Resist the
devil, and he will flee from you. "*
JAMES 4:7

W hen I first hit the county jail, I quickly learned there were three
television shows you didn't mess with: *The Young and The Restless,
Jerry Springer,* and *COPS.* These were jailhouse staples no matter what
section of the jail where I lived. For the life of me, I could never figure
out why guys locked up had a fascination with a show about getting
arrested. Then it dawned on me: it was the resistance, the potential
for one of the criminals to overcome the authorities. These men were
literally rooting for the "bad boys" as the theme song went.

The human condition has been ravaged by sin. One manifestation
of that is our unwillingness to submit to authority. Whether we're right
or wrong, our initial inclination usually is one of rebellion. Let's be
honest, no one naturally wants to be subjected to rules. But is that how
God intended us to be? Did he create Adam and Eve to be the ultimate
authority, ungoverned and without restrictions? I think Eve would be
the first one to tell you, "No."

In contemplation of what a Christian lifestyle looks like, we need to
consider that sometimes our first impulse isn't necessarily the correct
one. James lists several imperatives that, at first glance, probably seem
strange, especially for those of us who still root for the bad guys when
watching *COPS.* However, the defining mark of a Christian is humility,
capped by our submission to God. Resistance is reserved for the evil
one. So, "bad boys, bad boys, whatcha gonna do?" –Blevins

Morning: Exod 31; John 10 — *Evening:* Prov 7; Gal 6

THE REAL DEAL

"You will recognize them by their fruits . . ."
MATTHEW 7:16

I watched two guards escort past me one of the meanest looking dudes I had ever seen in my life. His face was covered in scars, all scrunched up, and hard as granite. When they placed him in the empty cell next to me, I let him get settled in then called him to the bars, "Hey, bro, I'm Solley, you need anything, let me know." In one of the softest and kindest voices I had ever heard, he answered, "I'm Hector, and I am good right now. God bless you, bro." I stood there stunned. God bless me? Get the heck out of here! I hated phony Christians. I had been around them all my life, and the last thing I needed was one living next to me 24 hours a day, 7 days a week, 365 days a year.

I soon discovered that Hector was far from phony. He was the real deal, a light shining in the midst of one of the darkest places I had ever been: administrative segregation—a prison inside a prison. As I grew close to him, I learned Hector was confined to administrative segregation as one of the original founders of a violent Texas prison gang. When he gave his life to Christ, he struggled and fought his own internal battles, but never turned back. The Christ-like fruit Hector bore told everyone that he was for real. Hector would become my spiritual father until his death three years later.

As Christians in a dark world, a place where Christianity has often been used for ulterior motives, the fruit we bear must tell those around us we are the real deal. Our lives must always represent the God we serve because, whether we like it or not, we will be recognized by the fruit our lives bear. –Solley

Morning: Exod 32; John 11 — *Evening:* Prov 8; Eph 1

LIVING TO TEACH

"May my teaching drop as the rain, my speech distill as the dew, like gentle rain upon the tender grass, and like showers upon the herb."
DEUTERONOMY 32:2

In the closing chapters of Deuteronomy, Moses stands before Israel and reminds them of how far the Lord has brought them. He encourages them to press forward into the land the Lord promised them and admonishes them to adhere to all the Lord instructed them to do. This encompasses all Moses taught them from the time he led them out of Egypt.

As Moses prefaces one of his final discourses, he prays that his teaching will be nourishment for the people; that it would nourish them as the rain nourishes the grass and herbs. We should have the same attitude toward how we present the Lord's instructions to those around us. Within the confines of prison, the largest way we display the way of the Lord is through how we live our lives. As people see who we are now in contrast to who we used to be, they are reminded of how the Lord changes people's lives. As they see us press forward in faith toward where the Lord is leading us, they too will be encouraged to do the same. When they see us refuse to compromise the instructions the Lord has given us in His Word, they cannot help but recognize the legitimacy of the Lord's work in our lives.

As we live out our faith in this way, people around us are nourished as the rain nourishes the grass and the herbs. Live your life in such a manner where others are taught the way of Christ. –Karch

Morning: Exod 33; John 12 — *Evening:* Prov 9; Eph 2

GIVING BACK

*"The point is this: whoever sows sparingly will also reap sparingly,
and whoever sows bountifully will also reap bountifully."*
2 CORINTHIANS 9:6

G iving from our own resources isn't an easy thing to do. What little financial support we receive from our family or friends is important to us (and them). While the state provides our most basic necessities, it is a blessing to be able to afford deodorant, coffee, and a soup or two. Yet, have you ever considered blessing someone else?

What an amazing opportunity we have. All around us are people who are going through tough times, and while we all know the guys who do not hesitate to ask for a handout, there are just as many who will not. For whatever reason, they will get by on the bare minimum and never say a word. Wouldn't it be a wonderful display of compassion and love to sacrifice some of your own blessings for someone who doesn't receive much from anyone? Think about what it would mean to you if someone, for no apparent reason, supplied a few basic comforts for you during a difficult time. How grateful would you be? Would you be interested in knowing why they did it?

Opportunities such as these are perfect times to share the gospel. When the Lord opens your heart to give a material blessing, He may be opening their heart to receive a spiritual one. Providing temporal needs to those less fortunate is also a great way to live out your faith. Remember the second commandment where Jesus stressed, "You shall love your neighbor as yourself" (Lev 19:18, Matt 19:19). What greater display of love than sharing the gospel with someone, and what better use of your own resources than facilitating that? –Blevins

Morning: Exod 34; John 13 — *Evening:* Prov 10; Eph 3

WISE COUNSEL

*"Oil and perfume make the heart glad, and the sweetness
of a friend comes from his earnest counsel."*
PROVERBS 27:9

There have been times when God placed people in my life to give me wise counsel and I refused to listen. One instance in particular stands out. It was March 24, 2006, and my father pulled into my driveway. As soon as my wife saw who it was, she begged me to tell him to leave. She knew the lifestyle my father was living and feared he would lead me astray, and she would lose me. Inside, I knew that she was right. However, for many reasons, I did not listen. That was the biggest mistake of my life. The next day, my father and I were arrested for bank robbery. Had I listened to my wife that day, life would be a lot different for me, my wife, and our daughter.

God will put people in your life who truly love you, care about you, and want what is best for you. However, you will not always want to listen to their wise counsel because it is not what you want to hear, or you think their advice is ill-founded or given with ulterior motives. Yet, it is only a true friend or loved one who will give you wise counsel even when they know you do not want to hear it.

Who has God placed in your life to give you wise counsel when your feet begin to slip off the straight and narrow path? Are you listening, or are you being hardheaded like I was? If so, the cost may just be a little more than you are willing to pay. Think about that. –Solley

Morning: Exod 35; John 14 — *Evening:* Prov 11; Eph 4

HAMMER OF GOD

"Behold, I make of you a threshing sledge, new, sharp, and having teeth; you shall thresh the mountains and crush them, and you shall make the hills like chaff; you shall winnow them, and the wind shall carry them away, and the tempest shall scatter them. And you shall rejoice in the LORD; in the Holy One of Israel you shall glory."
ISAIAH 41:15–16

Isaiah makes the statement in today's Scripture concerning Jacob, also known as Israel, the "offspring of Abraham" (v. 8, 14). Just prior to this he calls "Jacob" a *worm*. I recall reading where Martin Luther said that when he came before the Lord he felt like a worm. The same type of experience is common to Christians, particularly Christians who are all too aware of the decadence of their pasts. There is an overwhelming sense of inadequacy for serving the Lord at times because of these feelings. So how do worms do anything worthwhile for Christ?

In light of the Scripture today, we see how God says, "I will *make* of you . . ." God Himself makes us instruments of righteousness who are set apart to do and act according to His will and purpose. In this instance, He makes us threshing sledges—hammers of God—to thresh out the mountains into dust that the wind blows away. These mountains can be any number of things in our immediate environments which hinder the dissemination of the gospel. The Lord shapes us into His hammers to obliterate these things.

Even in the days when we may feel like worms, we can know that we are being forged as the hammers of God. In our growth as believers, we must always ask what the mountains may be that we are being shaped to thresh, all the while thanking the Lord for shaping us to be useful for the purposes of His kingdom. –Karch

Morning: Exod 36; John 15 — *Evening:* Prov 12; Eph 5

YOU GONNA REPRESENT THAT?

*"For I am not ashamed of the gospel, for it is the
power of God for salvation to everyone who believes,
to the Jew first and also to the Greek."*
ROMANS 1:16

From street gangs to prison gangs, ideologies to religions, and convict codes to honor among thieves, most of us have represented many different things in our lives. We have held fast to what we believed. And for many of us, the scars on our bodies attest to the fact that we will represent what we believe in, no matter the cost. We were the first to get out there and the last to lay it down when the gas hit. In prison, we know what it means to represent *that*!

Why then are we so feeble in representing the God we serve? God has reached down into our lives, rescued us from many toils and snares, and even delivered many of us from death. Yet, we self-consciously hide our Bibles when walking to the church house, or hesitate and look around when another brother asks us to pray with him in the dayroom or the chow hall. We have a King who died for us, who gave His life so that we might live, and we hesitate to stand up for Him. Yet, we had no problem representing the things that held us in bondage. Shame on us! Like the apostle Paul, we should not hesitate to stand up and boldly proclaim that we are not ashamed of the gospel of Jesus Christ, because we know what He has done for us and what He will do for others.

Let us never be ashamed to represent to the fullest that which we profess—our Lord and Savior, Jesus Christ. As you go about your day today, ask yourself this one question: You gonna represent that? –Solley

Morning: Exod 37; John 16 — *Evening:* Prov 13; Eph 6

BAD TO THE BONE

*"The fool says in his heart, 'There is no God.' They are corrupt,
they do abominable deeds, there is none who does good."*
PSALM 14:1

In the opening line of this psalm, David recognizes the depravity of man. When Paul begins his section on man's depravity in his letter to the Romans, he opens the section quoting this same verse. Both David and Paul understand the wickedness that rested within their own hearts and knew that the same wickedness runs through every single human heart.

A strong sense of this depravity drove Augustine's theology in the fourth century. Centuries later it was picked up by men like Luther and Calvin, and served to shape reformation theology. In recent years the journalist, Malcolm Muggeridge, claimed that the doctrine of man's depravity was one Christian doctrine that was empirically verifiable. Although people readily acknowledge the depravity of men's hearts, they mistakenly try to mask the guilt produced by its corruption. Through various means we attempt to bury our "abominable deeds." This practice tends to be much more pronounced within the walls of prison. Our exclusion from society fosters a sense of shame that exacerbates the realization of the evil within our own hearts. We are, in a very real way, bad to the bone. Nevertheless, in knowing the Lord, we know the rectification for our depravity.

From David to Muggeridge, inasmuch as depravity was a reality to them, they also recognized the towering nature of the grace of God that redeems us from our depravity. The psalm closes with an admonition to rejoice because of God's grace toward us. As we recognize where the Lord has brought us from, we too should rejoice in the fact that our corruption has been overcome. Knowing this to be true, there is no way man can ever say, "There is no God." –Karch

Morning: Exod 38; John 17 — *Evening*: Prov 14; Phil 1

HOPEFUL GRIEVING

*"But we do not want you to be uninformed,
brothers, about those who are asleep, that you may
not grieve as others do who have no hope."*
1 THESSALONIANS 4:13

Losing a loved one is a difficult experience, especially for those incarcerated. One reason for this hardship is the great divide between ourselves and those we care about. In addition, the limited information we receive, coupled with the lack of control we now face, make coping with death overwhelming. The regret of not being there, alone, is enough to cripple the toughest of us.

However, our grief doesn't have to be permanent; nor does our sense of loss need to dominate our emotional response to the passing of our Christian friends and family. Paul doesn't encourage the Thessalonians not to grieve, but to do so with hope. People who think this world is all there is, or that death is the last straw, undoubtedly have a hard time reconciling death. Those of us who are in Christ Jesus, however, need not look so despondent. We know there is something greater on the horizon.

When you experience the loss of a loved one and the tears begin to fall, don't let every tear be one of sorrow; cry a few tears of joy, too. The same God who resurrected Jesus from the tomb will one day lift all His children. At the sound of a trumpet call, those who have fallen first, then those who are still alive will be caught up together in the clouds (1 Thess 4:16–17). What a glorious day that will be! –Blevins

Morning: Exod 39; John 18 — *Evening:* Prov 15; Phil 2

CROSS EXAMINATION

"Let us test and examine our ways, and return to the LORD!"
LAMENTATIONS 3:40

Our lives can be compared to the steering system on an automobile. If the steering is just a little bit out of line, the vehicle will drift to one side or another. As a result, the misalignment in the steering actually pulls the vehicle to the left or to the right. The farther you drive the vehicle without correction, the farther it will drift. In the same way, sin serves as the misalignment that causes us to drift off course. Many times our misalignment is through those apparently inconsequential sins like laziness or indifference to the things of God. No matter the sin, the longer we travel in it, the further we drift from our relationship with the Lord. Realizing the potential for our lives to drift, it is necessary to consider the importance of self-examination.

Most of us, however, never really think about self-examination as we grow in our relationship to the Lord. Yet, Jeremiah exhorts us to *test and examine our ways* so we will be able to have the necessary checks and balances for any misalignment in our lives. As Christians, we examine ourselves primarily in light of the cross. We examine ourselves by asking how our lives express gratitude for what Jesus has done for us, and how our lives imitate His self-sacrifice.

Let us take Jeremiah's exhortation to heart and take time each day to test and examine ourselves through the lens of the cross of Jesus Christ. As we take seriously self-examination, the Word of God speaks to our hearts and shows us the areas where we are drifting. When we understand where we are drifting, we are in a better position to repent and return to the Lord. –Karch

Morning: Exod 40; John 19 — *Evening:* Prov 16; Phil 3

HATERS

"If the world hates you, know that it has hated me before it hated you. If you were of the world, the world would love you . . ."
JOHN 15:18–19A

When I first chose to make Christ the Lord of my life, I had to make a lot of changes. One of those changes was to disassociate myself from some of the people I ran with for years, not simply the individuals, but the destructive ideology they had. Someone I was once very close to, who had stood side by side with me through some very dangerous and trying times during my incarceration, could not accept some of the changes in my belief system. One day, during a heated conversation, he muttered these words: "I hate you, man. You make me sick." It stunned me to hear my friend and one time "brother" say this to me.

I now understand that when we choose to follow Christ, especially in a prison setting, the world will hate us because being a Christian challenges the norms of our environment. We are prisoners; we are supposed to be hardened criminals, gang-bangers, and racists—tough guys and gals—not peaceful followers of Christ who express a genuine love and concern for all men. And when our lives challenge the belief system of others, they will hate and despise us—just as they hated and despised Christ. We cannot expect anything different, nor can we apologize for who we are in Christ.

Do not be surprised when those around you hate you for your decision to follow Christ. Simply love them anyway and continue to be a shining light in the midst of this dark world. Who knows? Maybe your love in response to their hate will drive the hater out of them. –Solley

Morning: Lev 1; John 20 — *Evening:* Prov 17; Phil 4

FREEDOM

*"Now the Lord is the Spirit, and where the
Spirit of the Lord is, there is freedom."*
2 CORINTHIANS 3:17

Paul always addresses the pressing needs of those to whom he is writing. An example of this is his first letter to the Corinthian church where he speaks of a person who is imprisoned to a certain sin (1 Cor 5). Likewise, in his second letter to the Corinthian church, Paul addresses the same situation, except he calls for forgiveness and restoration for the one who *had been* in bondage to sin (2 Cor 2:1–11). Paul then proceeds to map out how this forgiveness and restoration works with a primary emphasis on the ministry of reconciliation and the freedom that comes with it (2 Cor 5).

The concept of freedom is a powerful idiom inside prison. I recall a conversation with a brother who talked about preaching inside prison being powerful when it is conducted through a "hermeneutic of freedom." There is much to be said about his insight. Those of us inside prison understand the importance of freedom. We also realize a sense of freedom that comes with a call to surrender to Jesus. From this realization, we proceed with the ministry of reconciliation to disseminate the freedom Jesus has won for us. For this same reason, Paul was able to encourage believers to understand fully how it is we have been entrusted with in the ministry of reconciliation, because *where the Spirit of the Lord is, there is freedom.*

As you reflect on the freedom you have been given in Christ, look for those around you who desperately need that same freedom. Utilize the ministry of reconciliation that has been entrusted to you as a believer in Jesus by speaking in the idiom of freedom to those in bondage around you. As you do so, you convey the richness of forgiveness and restoration that is available in Christ. –Karch

Morning: Lev 2, 3; John 21 — *Evening:* Prov 18; Col 1

TRUE FREEDOM

"So Jesus said to the Jews who had believed him, 'If you abide in my word, you are truly my disciples, and you will know the truth, and the truth will set you free.'"
JOHN 8:31–32

Freedom, as any prisoner can attest, is a word that is never far from one's mind. It doesn't matter if you've done six months or twenty years, if you have six months left or they told you you're never getting out, the thought of freedom has a resounding effect on a prisoner. There is another sense of the word, however, that carries much greater significance and has eternal ramifications. Speaking to those who already believed in Him, Jesus declared a new kind of freedom: freedom from the bondage of sin. And, much like the Jews with Him then, it's a freedom that many people today don't quite understand.

Our condition as fallen human beings has left us in a state of slavery. We are bound by the effects of sin; it's our master, and without God's grace we will never be truly free. While many will agree with that assessment, they think that a simple mental acknowledgement of Jesus as their Savior will unlock those chains. To the consternation of the Jews back then, and for many now, Jesus put conditions on true discipleship. He says the only way to know the truth that will free you from sin's yoke is to abide in His word.

Nominal Christianity is a blemish on the face of the Church today, and many people are falling victim to the lie of "easy believism." In this, there is no real abiding, and thus, no true freedom. Jesus said, "If you love me, you will keep my commandments" (John 14:15). The key to true freedom is not found in mere mental assent, but in faith evidenced by obedience to our Lord and Savior. –Blevins

Morning: Lev 4; Ps 1, 2 — *Evening:* Prov 19; Col 2

LOVE ONE ANOTHER

"There is no fear in love, but perfect love casts out fear."
1 JOHN 4:18A

In a prison environment absent of genuine love, one of the greatest things we can do for those around us is to love them as Christ loves us. However, this is very difficult for prisoners to do. Because we are afraid of what others will think about us, we would much rather fade the whole dayroom than show or tell another inmate that we love them. Yet, as the apostle John informs us, "perfect love casts out fear" (1 John 4:18). By loving others, we exhibit Christ's love for them and break down the tough-guy barriers we have built between one another.

The Bible teaches us to feed our enemies if they are hungry (Rom 12:20), to pray for one another (James 5:16), and to encourage one another (1 Thess 5:11). These are all simple commandments we can follow out of love. If I see my brother hungry and I am able, I can feed him. If I see him in need of prayer, I can pray for him. If I see him down and out and in need of encouragement, I can come alongside him, encourage him, and lift him up. It is not often through some great act that we show our love to those around us. As Christians, we show daily the love we profess for another through the little things we do. Much more than lip service, it's genuine.

It has been said that people will not care how much you know until they know how much you care. Show those around you today that you care by loving them as Christ has loved you. In Christ's own words, "By this, all people will know you are my disciples" (John 13:35). –Solley

Morning: Lev 5; Ps 3, 4 — *Evening:* Prov 20; Col 3

SALT

"Salt is good, but if salt has lost its taste, how shall its saltiness
be restored? It is no use either for the soil or for the manure pile.
It is thrown away. He who has ears to hear, let him hear."
LUKE 14:34–35

In Luke's gospel Jesus' comments about salt are written after a discourse on discipleship. These passages pertaining to salt are broadly interpreted as referring to the preservative aspects of salt in the first century. Salt was used to preserve meats and other materials. However, salt has a corrosive aspect as well, also referred to in Scripture (Deut 29:23, Judg 9:45). When nations were conquered, their fields were often times sown with salt to keep crops from ever growing there again.

On naval ships, sailors have to constantly wash the decks of the ship with fresh water to keep sea salt from literally eating the ship out from under them. Similarly, if we take Jesus' meaning to be in reference to the corrosive nature of salt, the passage takes on a whole new meaning. Christians are to be the salt of the earth and we are being sown into the field of the earth so that sin will no longer grow. As the gospel spreads throughout the earth, the salt metaphor serves to illustrate how the power of the gospel eats away at the pervasiveness of sin throughout the world.

What do the fields in which we find ourselves laboring look like? How pervasive is sin around us? Is the saltiness of our lives serving to eat away at and erode the sinfulness of the culture we live in? As you consider these things, begin to think of yourself as the salt of the earth that keeps sin from spreading further. –Karch

Morning: Lev 6; Ps 5, 6 — *Evening:* Prov 21; Col 4

THE JOY OF YOUR SALVATION

*"Your words were found, and I ate them, and your words
became to me a joy and the delight of my heart, for I am
called by your name, O LORD, God of hosts."*
JEREMIAH 15:16

In Old Testament times, God communicated with and revealed Himself to His people through prophets. Prophets such as Jeremiah were literally the mouth pieces of God—He spoke to His people directly through them. This forced the prophets to know God's Word intimately. Consequently, it became part of who they were. To Jeremiah, God's Word became a joy and the delight of his heart because He knew he belonged to God and was called by His name.

As Christians, we are called by God's name. We are His. As His people, God communicates with and reveals Himself to us today. He does this through the Holy Bible. The Bible is God's spoken word in written form. The more we consume God's Word, the more and more it becomes part of who we are. As we meditate on what God has to say to us and allow it to permeate every area of our lives, God's Word will become a joy to us and the delight of our hearts. We will hunger for God's Word and feel spiritually parched without it.

We are fortunate to have God's Word at our fingertips. Many Christians across the world today do not. Let us never take this blessing God has given us lightly. Meditate on God's Word daily, and let it become a joy to you and a delight to your heart. –Solley

Morning: Lev 7; Ps 7, 8 — *Evening:* Prov 22; 1 Thess 1

LIGHT IT UP

*"The light shines in the darkness, and the
darkness has not overcome it."*
JOHN 1:5

T here are few places on earth darker than the penitentiary. Yet, at that same time, there are not many places that stay as well lit as a prison. The lights around and inside a prison are always on so that some level of visibility is maintained. Nevertheless, while prisons are physically well lit, they are psychologically and spiritually very dark. Prisons have a type of darkness much worse than any physical darkness. A particular darkness unique to prison cripples men and women mentally. It destroys their health, hope, and dreams and often leads to despair.

Thankfully, no prison possesses the security to prevent the presence of Christ. The opening chapter of John's gospel account is a penetrating attestation to Jesus as the light of the world. The light of Christ in John's mind seems to be directed specifically at the kind of darkness so prevalent inside prisons. And no matter how deep and thick that darkness may be, it does not and cannot overcome the light of Jesus Christ. The interesting thing is how Jesus shines His light in places like prison. He changes people inside prisons and uses them to radiate His light.

Anybody who has walked the halls of prison for any amount of time knows all too well the type of darkness that destroys people's lives. Yet, we also catch glimpses of the light of Jesus in those who believe in Him. A simple glimpse of the light of Jesus in others helps us to understand that His light is the only light that serves to encroach upon the darkness. As you follow Jesus, shine His light in the middle of the darkness around you—the darkness cannot overcome it. Be the spark that lights things up. –Karch

Morning: Lev 8; Ps 9 — *Evening:* Prov 23; 1 Thess 2

PRICELESS

*"Again, the kingdom of heaven is like a merchant in
search of fine pearls, who, on finding one pearl of great
value, went and sold all that he had and bought it."*
MATTHEW 13:45–46

I remember a few years ago a MasterCard commercial listed items of value and their prices. It progressively presented thematic purchases and then concluded with some intangible whose value was listed as priceless. The tagline went something like, "There are some things in life money can buy; for everything else, there's MasterCard."

Life does have copious amounts of stuff to offer, so many things we can eagerly spend our entire lives pursuing. But could there be something else out there we haven't yet experienced, something that may even be beyond our ability to imagine? In prison, some tend to live from commissary day to commissary day, measuring their worth by the size of their lockers. Others count their wealth by the number of letters they receive. They place all their stock in human relationships.

However, the most valuable thing anyone could ever possess is probably the one most of us take for granted. The gift of salvation trumps any possession or credit card promise. It overrides anything you can put on a commissary list or receive from the mail room. It's the reason why the poor widow could put her two small copper coins in the offering box (Mark 12:41–44). It's why men leave all they've ever known to take the gospel to countries where people who own Bibles are killed every day. Think about the gift you've been given, and then think about what it's truly worth. –Blevins

Morning: Lev 9; Ps 10 — *Evening:* Prov 24; 1 Thess 3

HE LOVES US

"Who shall separate us from the love of Christ? Shall tribulation, or distress, or persecution, or famine, or nakedness, or danger, or sword?"
ROMANS 8:35

In our Christian walk, there will be times when we feel as if God has abandoned us, as if He has removed us from His love. It will seem like our heartfelt prayers and our cries of anguish fall on deaf ears, and for some reason, God has turned His face from us. In our anguish, we will feel like Jesus did on the cross when He cried out, "My God, my God, why have you forsaken me?" (Mt 27:47).

Yet, we are not forsaken. God's love is always there. However, there are times when we become so caught up in our distress, our anger, our pain, our sorrow that we cannot feel God's love or see evidence of it in our lives. So, we question it. Yet Paul, who had experienced distress and persecution like none of us ever have or ever will, knew without a doubt that nothing—no tribulation, distress, persecution, nakedness, danger, or sword—could separate him from the love of God. He did not let his feelings or circumstances undermine the *fact* that God loved Him. Paul knew his Lord and Savior loved him. And because Christ's love sustained him, he was more than a conqueror in all the trials and tribulations he faced (v. 37).

We must understand that God loves us, too. And as rough as our lives may seem at times when we feel unloved and alone, God's love is right there to sustain us. As Paul did, let us take comfort in knowing nothing can separate us from the love of our God. –Solley

Morning: Lev 10; Ps 11, 12 — *Evening*: Prov 25; 1 Thess 4

WALKING TALL

"Blessed be the God and Father of our Lord Jesus Christ! According to his great mercy, he has caused us to be born again to a living hope through the resurrection of Jesus Christ from the dead,"

1 PETER 1:3

On April 8, 1945, Dietrich Bonhoeffer preached from this text to a small group of prisoners at Flossenberg, Germany. Seconds after the service concluded Bonhoeffer was taken away to be hanged. In his book, *Bonhoeffer: Pastor, Martyr, Prophet, Spy*, biographer Eric Metaxas captures the final moments of Bonhoeffer's life as well as his final words to his fellow prisoners: "This is the end, but for me it is the beginning of life." The New Testament book, 1 Peter, is considered a classic exposition of the riches Christians have in the midst of suffering for righteousness sake. It is little surprise, then, that Bonhoeffer would choose this text to minister to those around him who were suffering for what was right.

Those who are familiar with the life of Bonhoeffer are still struck with the calm reserve with which he handled his imminent death. He did not panic; he calmly walked tall to the gallows. One of the medical doctors commented that he had never witnessed a man die with such dignity. As we think about how Bonhoeffer both lived and died, it compels us to strive to live the same way. We are moved to understand the great mercy of God, to understand what the living hope is that He has caused us to be born into on the same level as Bonhoeffer did.

As our understanding of God's great mercy and our understanding of the hope He has caused us to be born into begins to increase, we, too, can live our lives in a way that commands the attention of others. Our living hope is borne out through the resurrection of Jesus Christ. Like Bonhoeffer, we, too, can walk tall throughout life with our eyes on the beginning of life. –Karch

Morning: Lev 11, 12; Ps 13, 14 — *Evening:* Prov 26; 1 Thess 5

FIRE TESTED

*"so that the tested genuineness of your faith—more precious than
gold that perishes though it is tested by fire—may be found to result
in praise and glory and honor at the revelation of Jesus Christ."*
1 PETER 1:7

Gold is one of the world's most precious metals. Being found in
such small amounts across the earth's surface, it is a highly limited resource. However, gold is used for all manner of things. From
electrical plating to art decorations to jewelry, its uses trace back to
some of the earliest civilizations in history. Even the Bible records the
use of gold by the early Egyptians and Israelites.

Modern day refinement of gold is an elaborate process which involves the use of cyanide and many other chemicals. However, the way
in which ancient cultures went about purifying their precious yellow
metal was quite simple. They just heated it up. The hotter the gold
became, the more impurities rose to the surface and were removed.
So the best gold is that with the least amount of impurities: the gold
that's been refined by fire.

Peter makes an apt analogy comparing the Christian's faith to the
testing of gold by fire. As Christians, we certainly experience trials and
tribulations, especially in prison. Consequently, those troubles refine
our faith. Just as the ancient cultures purified gold with fire, God uses
those difficult times to draw out the impurities within us. It is God's
way of shaping and molding us into the pure vessels He wants us to be.
So the next time the heat gets turned up on you and times get rough,
remember the master craftsman is refining you by fire. –Blevins

Morning: Lev 13; Ps 15, 16 — *Evening:* Prov 27; 2 Thess 1

PATIENTLY WAITING

*"I waited patiently for the LORD; he
inclined to me and heard my cry."*
PSALM 40:1

I t is easy to get in a rush and want everything right here and right
now. If we are honest with ourselves, we'll admit that impatience
is what landed most of us in prison. While others were toiling away
working nine to five, we were out hustling and bustling, trying to get
ours when we wanted it, the way we wanted it—no matter the cost.
And many times, we carry over that old pattern of behavior into our
Christian lives. We pray and ask God to move in a circumstance or situation, and when He does not answer in our time frame, we become
frustrated and discouraged, and often try to take matters into our own
hands—simply because we lack patience.

In our Christian walk, there will be times when we pray and pray,
fall on our knees, and beg God for something in our lives; and it seems
as if we are talking to the ceiling, that God is not listening. It is during
these times we must exercise the gift of patience—bearing up without
complaint—knowing that God *does* hear us and in His time, will answer. This quality of restraint, standing firm in the midst of the storms,
is what separates the immature believer from the mature one. When
we display patience in our lives, we will eventually be able to declare as
the psalmist did, "I waited patiently for the LORD; he inclined to me
and heard my cry."

When you find yourself wanting to revert back to the old mentality
of getting it right here, right now, remember that God does not operate on your timing. To make it as simple as it can be: when waiting on
the Lord—be patient. He hears you. –Solley

Morning: Lev 14; Ps 17 — *Evening*: Prov 28; 2 Thess 2

REMEMBER CHRIST JESUS

"Remember not the former things, nor consider the things of old."
ISAIAH 43:18

Years ago, there was a storm of controversy surrounding the conversion of David Berkowitz, "The Son of Sam." People had a hard time accepting the fact that Jesus Christ could save a serial killer. One Christian apologist defended Berkowitz's salvation by commenting that for him to know the love of Christ, and still have to live with the horrors of his past crimes, was a type of hell in and of itself. Many of us can attest that there is some truth to that statement. It is often difficult knowing and understanding the love of Christ while, at the same time, having prison remind us daily of the guilt and shame of our pasts.

The Israelites also had a great deal to be guilty and ashamed about because they had turned on the Lord and on one another. They committed crimes against their God and against each another. Throughout Isaiah 43, the Lord affirms again and again His declaration to forgive them, redeem them, and restore them. In the middle of this, He demands they not be weighed down with the guilt and shame of the past—He tells them to forget it. Our salvation has been accomplished in the person and work of Jesus Christ, and those old things have passed away. We are not to look to the old things any more, but rather, look to what Jesus has done for us and how He has opened an avenue for a new way of life.

What *former things* of your past are still burdening you? How many times do you find yourself feeling guilty or ashamed over what your life used to be? Remember Christ Jesus. Leave those things behind and look to Him who has redeemed you. Our hope is in the new thing He is doing in our lives, not in our pasts. –Karch

Morning: Lev 15; Ps 18 — *Evening:* Prov 29; 2 Thess 3

HEARTSICK

"The heart is deceitful above all things, and
desperately sick; who can understand it?"
JEREMIAH 17:9

H ave you ever wondered why you find yourself repeatedly in the
same type of bonehead situations? I remember, when I was
growing up, trouble always seemed to find me. Whether it was busting
out a neighbor's window or getting into fights at school, my backside
became intimately familiar with tree switches and brown leather belts.
Even as I got older, and supposedly wiser, I kept finding myself doing
really dumb things—from trying to drive home loaded on Xanax and
Budweiser to carrying guns around with a really short temper. Over
and over again I'd say to myself: "Well, I won't do that again." But,
nevertheless, I'd be back in trouble before too long.

On a personal level, I can honestly say that none of the lessons
learned kept me from doing something just as stupid the next time.
And on a larger scale, history has proven that the whole of humankind
experiences a similar stubbornness. However, the seventh century B.C.
prophet, Jeremiah, astutely diagnoses this painstaking condition—
heartsickness. The state of fallen humanity's heart is one of wickedness, deceit, and rebellion. Sure, we might've done some really nice
things in our lifetime, but ultimately, left to our own devices, we will
do some really wrong things. The enduring effects of the fall on our
hearts are like a debilitating disease. The good news is, we have the
best doctor.

God has promised to create within us a clean heart (Ps 51:10; Ezek
36:26). So, just as Jeremiah prayed for the Lord to heal him of this
inner infirmity, we too may call upon the Lord to cure our heartsickness. –Blevins

Morning: Lev 16; Ps 19 — *Evening:* Prov 30; 1 Tim 1

JUST A LITTLE BIT

*"And the Lord's servant must not be
quarrelsome but kind to everyone, . . ."*
2 TIMOTHY 2:24

I had a very bad day, and my night seemed no better. No matter how hard I tried, I could not take my mind off of all of the problems in my life. For hours I lay in my bunk tossing and turning, trying to slow down my mind. Just as I was about to give up on sleep, I heard the officer on duty slowly making his way down the run conducting a security check. Several cells down, he stopped to talk to someone else who was still awake. In the quiet of the night, I heard him tell someone in broken English, "I know it's hard, but don't give up. Stay strong." As the officer walked by my cell several moments later, I pulled the covers over my head and repeated his words over and over in my mind: *I know it's hard, but don't give up. Stay strong.* Peace washed over me, and I quickly drifted off to sleep.

Though the officer never knew I heard his words that night, he taught me a valuable lesson: a little bit of kindness goes a long way. Whether it is a kind word or kind act, we never truly know the impact our kindness has on those around us. It is no wonder Paul instructs us to be kind to one another. It is our kindness to others in a world full of unkind acts that can make the difference in someone's life. Maybe, like the officer's kind words that quiet night, our kindness will give someone the strength to make it just one more day.

I encourage you to make an attempt to go out of your way today to show kindness to at least one person you do not know. Remember, it only takes just a little bit. –Solley

Morning: Lev 17; Ps 20, 21 — *Evening:* Prov 31; 1 Tim 2

ACCEPTANCE

*"The saying is trustworthy and deserving of full
acceptance, that Christ Jesus came into the world to
save sinners, of whom I am the foremost."*
1 TIMOTHY 1:15

Most people in prison have had some form of experience with
drugs and alcohol. As a result, most prisoners have heard of
the Serenity Prayer—a centuries old prayer attributed to St. Francis of
Assisi. The prayer's first petition asks the Lord to help us to accept the
things we cannot change. For Christians, one thing which must be accepted is that we are sinners and there is nothing we can do to change
this truth. Until we accept the fact we are sinners, we can never come
to the point of accepting that Christ came to save us in the midst of
our helplessness.

Far too often we display the tendency to take our focus off what
Jesus has accomplished for us. We easily come to a place in our spiritual development where we become self-righteous, as opposed to simply accepting the righteousness of Jesus being attributed to us. We are
quick to point out the faults of others and are unable to recognize or
accept the work Christ may be doing in their lives. The more rampant
this becomes, the more damaging it is to us and those around us because it becomes more difficult for us to merely accept grace. Paul
understood he was a sinner when Jesus saved him, and as an old man
who was mature in the faith, admits he was the chief of sinners.

The key to knowing and serving Jesus Christ is accepting that He
saved you apart from anything you did or could do for yourself. So,
simply accept the one thing you cannot change and completely trust
Jesus to do what he says he will do—He is trustworthy and deserving of
full acceptance. –Karch

Morning: Lev 18; Ps 22 — *Evening:* Eccl 1; 1 Tim 3

DIVERT THEIR GAZE

*"For what we proclaim is not ourselves, but Jesus Christ as
Lord, with ourselves as your servants for Jesus' sake."*
2 CORINTHIANS 4:5

Witnessing for Christ is a remarkable thing. It's such an empowering feeling to testify to the glory of God and what He's done in our life. The blessings of living a Spirit-filled life are manifested in numerous ways, and sharing those experiences is a natural occurrence. However, when we tell others about the amazing grace we have encountered, whether it is physical healing, financial blessings, or just carrying us through the dark times of being incarcerated, it is easy for people to misappropriate their awe. When others hear about our breakthroughs, there is a tendency to focus on the recipient of the blessing and not the giver of the blessing.

When he traveled on his missionary journeys, proclaiming the gospel, Paul always redirected the attention away from himself and back to Jesus. He knew the people hearing the gospel message would easily attribute the good things he was doing to a mere man, when instead their focus should be placed firmly on the Lord.

Likewise, when you are sharing your personal testimony it should always point back to the Redeemer. Telling others about the wonderful changes taking place in your life should never be about yourself. Give credit where credit is due, and constantly divert their gaze to the source of the light within you. –Blevins

Morning: Lev 19; Ps 23, 24 — *Evening:* Eccl 2; 1 Tim 4

DOING GOOD

*"And let us not grow weary of doing good, for in due
season we will reap, if we do not give up."*
GALATIANS 6:9

Have you ever asked yourself why you even try to do good? I
know I have. Some days I wake up in prison, take one long look
around me, and ask myself, "What's the use? Why do I try so hard
to do the right things, be a better person, and help others along the
way?" At times, it just seems like no matter how much good I do, it
is all to no avail. Then I read verses like Galatians 6:9 and see things
in a whole new light. What if the farmer, after all of his toiling and
planting, looked across his bare field and seeing no crop to reap said,
"That's it, I quit. What's the use?" He would never enjoy the benefits
of the harvest season when he could reap what he had so strenuously
sown.

Sometimes, doing good is not easy. It is hard, and it is tiring. There
will be times when we want to give up, especially, when it feels like all
we are doing is to no avail; and we cannot see any fruit for our labor.
Yet, the apostle Paul tells us that if we do not grow weary in doing
good, if we do not give up, just like the farmer who patiently awaits
harvest time, we will reap the reward in due season—when the crop
is at its fullest and brings maximum gain. That is God's promise to us.

When you grow weary of doing good, and you eventually will,
you can lean on the promises of God found in Scripture to give you
the strength you need to keep moving forward and to keep pressing
on. –Solley

Morning: Lev 20; Ps 25 — *Evening:* Eccl 3; 1 Tim 5

STRAIGHT-LACED

*"For we do not have a high priest who is unable to
sympathize with our weaknesses, but one who in every
respect has been tempted as we are, yet without sin."*
HEBREWS 4:15

Have you ever experienced times when you are really going through it? Does it ever seem as if everything is coming at you all at once, and you just want to explode? In the midst of these times we can easily slip into the mindset that this is somehow unique to us—that nobody else knows what it is we are experiencing. And when it comes right down to it, nobody really knows what it's like because each person and each situation is unique. The more credence we give to this mindset, the more prone we are to give in and fall into sin.

The author of Hebrews makes it clear that we are not alone in our struggles. They are not foreign to God. Jesus was tempted in every way that we are; He can relate to our situations, circumstances, and temptations. Yet, inasmuch as He experienced these things, He did so without sin. He stayed straight-laced and focused in the thick of it. As we understand what Jesus accomplished, it ought to bring us comfort. Looking to Him will generate confidence and strength so we, too, may endure in the midst of the trying times that are bound to come.

Maybe you have recently come through a time of intense temptation and trial. Maybe you are going through one right now. If so, look to Jesus, realizing that He knows and can relate to what it is you are experiencing in a way that no mere human can. From Him, we can all gain our confidence, strength, and endurance even in the middle of the worst of times. –Karch

Morning: Lev 21; Ps 26, 27 — *Evening:* Eccl 4; 1 Tim 6

FAITHFULNESS

"Let not steadfast love and faithfulness forsake you; bind them around your neck; write them on the tablet of your heart."
PROVERBS 3:3

As a child growing up, it was common knowledge among my six siblings and me that our father was unfaithful to our mother. Often times, Dad's girlfriend lived as close as the "girl next door." Dad did not even attempt to hide his unfaithfulness from Mom. To be fair, Mom was not a saint either. When Dad found himself doing a long prison sentence, Mom found her a boyfriend. She eventually divorced my father to marry him. Though my parents were together for many years, their relationship was never built on faithfulness and consequently, did not last.

Faithfulness is an endearing quality and one of the most important aspects in any relationship. Without faithfulness there is no trust, and without trust, there can be no real relationship. This was the case with my parents. Though they were married, they lacked a relationship based on mutual love and trust. What my parents' unfaithfulness essentially did was demonstrate a lack of value for their relationship. That is why being a faithful person matters. It says that we value those we are in relationship with, whether they be a spouse, friend, fellow-believer, or most importantly, God.

As Christians, we are called to be relational people. Because of this, it is important that we be faithful men and women others can depend on and trust. Our actions should show that we value our relationship with God and the personal relationships He has given us. Like the proverb instructs: we must bind faithfulness around our necks and write it on our hearts. –Solley

Morning: Lev 22; Ps 28, 29 — *Evening:* Eccl 5; 2 Tim 1

WHERE'S YOUR HEART?

"For where your treasure is, there will your heart be also."
LUKE 12:34

I remember a conversation I had one day with a guy who was the top ranking official of the prison gang I had been involved with for almost a decade. In the midst of the conversation, he asked me a rhetorical question. As rhetorical questions are wont to do, it caused me to think. The initial hesitation in my heart, however, struck like lightening and showed me very clearly that the gang I had dedicated myself to for years was no longer my treasure. My heart was no longer in it. As I thought about what that meant, it made me question where my heart was. Only a few short months later I came to know Christ, and shortly thereafter, I left the gang. That conversation taught me a lesson though. I learned that simply because we claim to represent something, it doesn't necessarily mean our heart is in it.

So, today I often ask myself similar rhetorical questions relating to my ties with Jesus Christ. What am I not willing to give up for Him? Is there anything I am unwilling to do for Him? What do I treasure most right now? How these types of questions register in my heart and mind, tell me where my heart is. They serve as a gauge for what it is I treasure most in life and help me keep my focus on the hope I have in Christ.

Where is your focus? What treasures do you seek? Where's your heart? Ask yourself these same types of questions. And, as the answers emerge, pray that the Lord will deepen your commitment to Him. Ask Him to strengthen your ties to Him so that He becomes to you the supreme treasure that He truly is. –Karch

Morning: Lev 23; Ps 30 — *Evening:* Eccl 6; 2 Tim 2

FROM PURPOSELESS TO PURPOSEFUL

*"[God] saved us and called us to a holy calling, not because
of our works but because of his own purpose and grace,
which he gave us in Christ Jesus before the ages began,"*
2 TIMOTHY 1:9

When we were dead in our trespasses did we serve a purpose?
Did we fulfill any intentional design or achieve some objective?
Sure we did, if you consider demonstrating to the world the inherent
wretchedness of mankind. The sinfulness we displayed was evidence of
fallen humanity and the awful state of those who are separated from
God.

But now we've been redeemed, washed, and cleansed by the blood
of the Lamb. Our purpose is now a righteous purpose found only in
Christ. We have been called to a higher purpose, one which involves
service and humility. We have been graciously granted a new life based
on nothing we've done, but according to His mercy. We are to live out
our new life at His behest. Sharing the gospel with others, studying
God's Word, applying it to our lives, and teaching it to our friends and
family are all ways of fulfilling our new purpose.

Don't ever think that just because you're locked up you've lost
your purpose or have nothing to live for. God's Holy Spirit is working
in you, and you can be confident that what He begins He will see to
completion. Your responsibility is to take the holy calling He's called
you to and serve Him with your whole heart, mind, and strength.
That means getting actively involved in what God is doing around
you. So, pray for opportunities where you can pursue God's calling
on your life and best serve Him. You might be surprised where He
leads you. –Blevins

Morning: Lev 24; Ps 31 — *Evening:* Eccl 7; 2 Tim 3

DEFENDING THE FAITH, GENTLY

*". . . always being prepared to make a defense to
anyone who asks you for a reason for the hope that is
in you; yet do it with gentleness and respect,"*

1 PETER 3:15

As ironic as it may seem, one of the first fights I saw in prison was between a Catholic and a Jehovah's Witness. What started as a simple debate about the doctrines of their faiths turned into a heated argument and concluded with blows being exchanged. Of course, being the heathen I was at the time, I enjoyed every minute of it. When all was said and done, I popped off sarcastically, "Now that is what I call defending the faith!"

I look back on that incident with a different perspective. I now understand how detrimental to the faith the actions of those two individuals were, especially in a prison context, where everyone is watching those who profess to be believers. Like these two individuals discovered, as believers in Christ, we will encounter those who do not share our beliefs, who question the reason for our faith, and who often do so aggressively. However, if we respond in like-manner, our defense of our faith simply becomes a defense of our pride. We become more focused on proving we are right than proclaiming the gospel in a manner worthy of Jesus Christ. This is the reason Peter warns believers to always be ready to give a defense for the hope that is in us, but to do so with gentleness and respect. When we do so, those who slander or revile us for our good behavior will be put to shame (v. 16).

When confronted with someone who asks you to give reason for the hope that is in you, defend the faith; but defend it in gentleness and respect worthy of the One who has placed the hope in you. –Solley

Morning: Lev 25; Ps 32 — *Evening:* Eccl 8; 2 Tim 4

FINISH THE GAME

*"I have fought the good fight, I have finished
the race, I have kept the faith."*
2 TIMOTHY 4:7

I n the second *Young Guns* movie, Billy the Kid rescues a couple of the Lincoln County Regulators from a lynch mob. After the rescue, the outlaws are contemplating what to do next and Billy the Kid tells a story about three men playing a game. In the story, a fourth man runs up and says the world is coming to an end. One of the players scrambles to go be with his family, the second runs off to party, and the third man says he shall stay to finish the game. The moral of the story is that against all odds, and in the midst of impending disaster, players find many things that take priority over the game.

Paul writes his final letter understanding he is about to die. Nevertheless, his focus does not waver, for there is no greater priority for him than the outcome of his devotion to Christ. The essence of his statement to Timothy is that he has finished the game. Against all odds, in the face of opposition by the Roman Empire and his own people, and in the midst of his own impending death, Paul fights the good fight to the very end, finishes the race, and keeps the faith—he finishes the game.

Too often, prison can be overwhelming. The odds feel like they are stacked against us. We seem to face insurmountable opposition and there are times when disaster looms around every corner. Yet in Christ, we find the strength to finish the game. For that reason—even in the midst of all you face—keep fighting the good fight. Stay adamant in your faith, and stay focused so you finish the game. –Karch

Morning: Lev 26; Ps 33 — *Evening:* Eccl 9; Titus 1

MEANINGLESS TO MEANINGFUL

"I said in my heart, 'Come now, I will test you with pleasure;
enjoy yourself.' But behold, this also was vanity. "
ECCLESIASTES 2:1

From the moment we are born, we are constantly learning to seek things that please us the most. As babies, we scream and cry to get what we want. As kids, we learn to ask for things we want, as well as to pout when we do not receive them. As adults, we work to have what we want in life, and even learn to make sacrifices to acquire the things we value most. Throughout our early years, and even into adulthood, we are conditioned to believe that the greatest things in life are self-centered, materialistic achievements. But is that really all that life's about?

Solomon expresses in Ecclesiastes that the meaning of life is not found in the material things of this world. He purposely seeks out pleasure and wisdom to discover the exact meaning of his earthly existence. Solomon had it all—wealth, women, and wisdom; and he could tell you none of it brought him lasting satisfaction. So what conclusion does he come to? Solomon tells us that meaning is found in fearing God and obeying His commandments.

Our life, as Christians, should not be about how much money we can accumulate, what position we can hold, or even how much knowledge we can obtain. These are all self-gratifying investments the world tells us will make us happy, but ultimately leave us empty. We should be focused and dedicated to the service of others by living in reverence and respect to God and His eternal decrees. –Blevins

Morning: Lev 27; Ps 34 — *Evening:* Eccl 10; Titus 2

SELF-CONTROL

"A man without self-control is like a city
broken into and left without walls."
PROVERBS 25:28

W hen King Solomon reigned, most cities were built with high, thick, defensive walls which protected them from invaders. When times of trouble came, the city's doors were tightly barricaded, and the city's inhabitants inside were safe. To conquer a city, the enemy would first have to overcome its walls. Without high walls of protection, cities were left defenseless and were quickly overcome by invading armies. Her defensive walls were a city's most important military asset.

Likewise, self-control is one of our most important spiritual assets, especially in prison. Prison is a place where, at all costs, we must learn to exercise self-control. When we do not, we leave ourselves wide open to attacks from the enemy. At the right opportunity, when our defenses are down, the enemy will strike; and once again, we will pay the price for our lack of self-control. It is no wonder Solomon compared a man without self-control to a city broken into and left without walls; without self-control, a man is defenseless. He allows the enemy free passage into his life to pillage and rob at will. By default, he allows his enemy to control him. That is why we so often give in to temptations and commit sins we know we should not, sins that leave us asking ourselves, "Why did I do that again?"

Have you been allowing the enemy to ransack you like a city without walls because of your lack of self-control? If so, ask God to help you in this area of your life. Ask Him to help you build your self-control because it is the essential defensive barrier in your life. –Solley

Morning: Num 1; Ps 35 — *Evening:* Eccl 11; Titus 3

O BROTHER!

"If anyone does not obey what we say in this letter, take note of that person, and have nothing to do with him, that he may be ashamed. Do not regard him as an enemy, but warn him as a brother."
2 THESSALONIANS 3:14–15

O ften times we find ourselves in situations where a brother or sister does something that has the potential to bring shame to the name of Christ and His church. This is particularly the case among Christians inside prison because there are few secrets here. For those of us who truly desire to serve the Lord in a real way, these become difficult situations. Generally, our reactions fall on the side of one extreme or another. Either we ignore these instances as though they did not happen at all, or we levy heavy judgment and condemnation against the offending brother or sister.

Among his final thoughts in the small letter to the believers in Thessalonica, Paul instructs Christians on how to handle the brother or sister who creates bad situations by their negative actions. Paul explains that if anyone "who bears the name of brother" does not follow the guide for conduct we have in the Scriptures, we are to have nothing to do with that person (1 Cor 5:11). The specific reason is so the person might become aware of his or her error and be ashamed. The emphasis is not to ignore or condemn, but to call it what it is so the brother or sister will do better next time. Thus, we do not *regard him as an enemy, but warn him as a brother.*

So, the next time a Christian you know blows it or is not living according to the way Scripture instructs us, we can't be quick to disregard them as a non-Christian. We are instructed to warn him *as a brother* and hope he does better in the future (Gal 6:1). –Karch

Morning: Num 2; Ps 36 — *Evening:* Eccl 12; Phlm 1

EYES WIDE SHUT

"For the word of the cross is folly to those who are perishing,
but to us who are being saved it is the power of God."
1 CORINTHIANS 1:18

H ow many times have you heard somebody talking bad about Christians? It's a frequent occurrence in prison. Stand in one place too long and you'll hear someone verbally assault the name of Jesus, the Bible, or something else regarding our faith. Many look down their noses at Christians because they think we're weak and are trying to hide behind the Bible, or they think the Word of God is nonsense. It's not hard to get the sense that quite a few inmates have a low tolerance for the gospel of Jesus Christ.

Yet, we who are being saved cling to it like it's a matter of life or death. We have seen the fruit of God's grace in our own lives, and now we can't live without it. It's not a deceptive tool to fool everyone or a shield to keep others from hurting us. It's life-giving water, sustaining us and cleansing us, leading us toward our eternal inheritance.

What should our attitude be toward those who casually or maliciously criticize the gospel? The Word of God tells us not to be surprised. There are some who will find it foolish. And what do most people do with something they find foolish? They often ridicule it, mock it, or treat it with contempt. Therefore, our response should be one of patience and humility. We must realize that the foolishness of God is wiser than men, and God will choose the foolish and the weak things to shame the wise and the strong. Rejoice that the cross of Jesus Christ is the power of God to us who are being saved. If you find yourself surrounded by those who find it foolish, pray for their eyes to be opened. –Blevins

Morning: Num 3; Ps 37 — *Evening:* Song of Sol 1; Heb 1

DEAR GOD

"For you are my lamp, O LORD, and my God lightens my darkness."
2 SAMUEL 22:29

Depression can be overwhelming. It can slowly seep into your life and incapacitate you; it can leave you feeling as if life is not worth living, that there is no hope for a better tomorrow. I should know. There were times in my life when I sank so deep into a world full of dark depression that I did not even have the strength or desire to get out of bed in the morning. I would lie there all day, with my head under the covers, lost in a world of sadness. There was no one who understood what it felt like or how dark my world had become. I couldn't even pray.

However, I learned a trick that, no matter how depressed I was, God always seemed to lift the sadness inside of me. I started writing letters to God. Because I had no one to talk to about how I was feeling, I would get a piece of paper, sit by myself, and tell God how I felt and why. It was always difficult to begin writing. I never knew exactly where to start, but once I began, all of the feelings poured out of me onto paper. As I wrote and wrote, it felt like someone turned a flashlight on and shined it into my heart, lightening the darkness inside of me. I felt hope because I knew someone was there, someone cared—God did.

If depression is overwhelming you, remember, God is just a letter or a prayer away. God will lighten the darkness in your life called depression and turn your sorrow into a song of deliverance, just as He did for King David when he experienced difficulties in his life. –Solley

Morning: Num 4; Ps 38 — *Evening:* Song of Sol 2; Heb 2

DEAD MAN WALKING

"We know that our old self was crucified with him in order that the body of sin might be brought to nothing, so that we would no longer be enslaved to sin. For one who has died has been set free from sin."
ROMANS 6:6–7

R omans 6 is Paul's great theological exposé of what it means to be a dead man. Paul uses striking images to convey the idea that we are dead men. We were baptized into Christ's death, buried with Him in that baptism, and are united with Him in His death. Through this, we also share in His resurrection and walk in a new life. The initiation of these things comes through the crucifixion of our old self. From this we understand Christians are in effect, dead men walking.

Over the years, Hollywood has depicted death row scenes where prisoners are escorted to the execution chamber accompanied by the haunting call, "Dead man walking!" While this may not be a spoken reality, it is most certainly a troubling reality in the silent recesses of the hearts and minds of men and women serving time on death row. Even so, as haunting as it is, there is a distinct irony behind it which points to freedom—an ultimate release toward a final liberation from the harsh confines of prison. In much the same way, realizing it or not, men and women walk through the world within the harsh confines of sin. The Christian, however, has already been crucified—executed— and has been liberated from the chains of sin.

For the believer in Jesus Christ, the call "Dead man walking!" no longer carries a haunting aspect; it is a clarion call of freedom from sin, where Christ has set us free from our captivity to sin. –Karch

Morning: Num 5; Ps 39 — *Evening:* Song of Sol 3; Heb 3

THE POWER OF FORGIVENESS

"Be kind to one another, tenderhearted, forgiving
one another, as God in Christ forgave you."
EPHESIANS 4:32

Julie Aftab was working to help support her family in a small office in Pakistan when a Muslim man walked in and noticed a small, silver cross hanging from her neck. The man asked her if she was a Christian, to which Julie quietly responded, "Yes." The man repeated this question three times. Each time, Julie unashamedly admitted she was a follower of Christ. What happened next would change Julie's life forever.

The man left and came back with an accomplice and a bottle of battery acid. He threw the battery acid at Julie, instantly melting the right side of her face and leaving deep burns on her arms and chest. When she tried to flee, they grabbed her, held her down, and poured battery acid down her throat, destroying her esophagus. When the men informed the authorities that Julie insulted Islam, no hospital would admit her. Finally, one doctor reluctantly agreed to treat her. Julie was sixteen.

After ten years and thirty-one surgeries, Julie has forgiven the men who did this to her and shares with others that her experience brought her closer to Christ. In forgiving, she has freed herself from all the anger and emotional pain she once felt. Julie's story is tragic, but it is a beautiful story of the power of forgiveness.

What about you? Have you been hurt by others in the past? Do you live with mental, emotional, and physical scars others have caused? If so, God is calling you to forgive those who have hurt you. He is calling you to let go and give to Him all of the anger and pain that you feel. –Solley

Morning: Num 6; Ps 40, 41 — *Evening:* Song of Sol 4; Heb 4

REVOLUTIONARY

*"He has delivered us from the domain of darkness and
transferred us to the kingdom of his beloved Son, in
whom we have redemption, the forgiveness of sins."*
COLOSSIANS 1:13–14

Virtually everyone in prison has engaged in some form of rebellion. To one degree or another, each of us has rebelled against the law. Inasmuch as our rebellious activities were against the laws of a particular state or nation, most of us never considered our activities as actually being *revolutionary*. For the most part, we were merely functioning according to the principles of the kingdom we belonged to: the kingdom of darkness.

While the state may have viewed our activities as rebellion against the law, we were actually operating within the framework of the kingdom of this world as rebels against the kingdom of God. The real revolutionary activity was performed by Him who snatched us out of the dominion of the kingdom of darkness and placed us within a new kingdom.

God has undermined the principles of the kingdom of darkness and, as a true revolutionary, set up another kingdom. Paul uses a play on words in order to capture what has actually taken place in redemption and the forgiveness of sin. Deliverance and redemption carry related meanings. Through God's revolutionary activity, we have been delivered; and in that deliverance we have redemption.

Think about the extremes Jesus went to in order to accomplish our deliverance and redemption. There is no greater revolution throughout history. Thank Him for what He has done, and understand you are part of a revolution that has established a kingdom that can never be overthrown. –Karch

Morning: Num 7; Ps 42, 43 — *Evening:* Song of Sol 5; Heb 5

COMPASSION

"When he saw the crowds, he had compassion for them, because they were harassed and helpless, like sheep without a shepherd."
MATTHEW 9:36

Music composer Eric Genuis walked with his son and eight year old autistic daughter through a hospital where he went to perform. As they rounded a corridor, he noticed a woman sitting outside of a hospital room alone—face buried in her hands as she cried deep, heart-wrenching sobs. He pulled his children close and whispered, "Be quiet." Unable to comprehend what her father said, Eric's autistic daughter stopped directly in front of the crying woman. After staring at her for a few seconds, she placed her forehead against the woman's head. Suddenly, she began sobbing as deeply and mournfully as the woman. As this total stranger wrapped Eric's daughter up in her arms and cried, he asked himself, "Why did I ever think it was okay to pass by someone suffering so much without doing anything to help?"

How often do we, as incarcerated Christians, simply walk by those we know are hurting without giving them a second thought? We see them every day: the guy on the line who seems lost in a world all of his own, the man called down to the chaplain's office and given the terrible news about a loved one's death, the one who has not seen his children in years and lives with so many deep regrets. How about the one whose wife or girlfriend moved on with her life and left him far behind?

If we are to be imitators of Christ, we can all take lessons from Eric's little girl. Let us not simply pass by the helpless and hurting, but rather, let us reach out to them with Christ's love and compassion. –Solley

Morning: Num 8; Ps 44 — *Evening:* Song of Sol 6; Heb 6

EXCEPT FOR THESE CHAINS

*"And Paul said, 'Whether short or long, I would to God
that not only you but also all who hear me this day might
become such as I am—except for these chains.'"*
ACTS 26:29

When I was baptized, I was in administrative segregation on a high security unit. It was right at one year after my conversion when my name came up on the list of those who had requested baptism. As I stripped down to my boxers and stuck my hands out of the slot to be handcuffed, the two floor officers were being relieved for their break. My door rolled and I stepped onto the run. Almost all of my tattoos were visible to the officers and all four of them took a long look at me when, one of them said, "That ain't washin' off." And they all began to laugh. I nodded and grinned as I walked by.

After being baptized, I came back onto the wing, still dripping wet. The two relief officers looked up at me from the bottom of the stairs and they began to laugh again. One said, "I told you it wouldn't wash off." As this was going on, a Scripture thundered in my mind as the cold steel of the handcuffs rested on my wrists: *I would that they were as I am—except for these chains.* I knew a freedom they could not fathom.

We have a freedom we should desire to share with everybody. With the exception of our chains, our bars, or fences, we should want the world to have the freedom we have been given in Christ. Far too often we let our chains, bars, or fences dampen our understanding of our freedom, and the need of others to have it. Let us thank the Lord for our freedom and desire others to have what we have, except for our chains. –Karch

Morning: Num 9; Ps 45 — *Evening:* Song of Sol 7; Heb 7

A NAME LIKE NO OTHER

*"And there is salvation in no one else, for there is no other name
under heaven given among men by which we must be saved."*
Acts 4:12

H is name was Jesus and He walked the earth almost two thousand
years ago. Since that time, men and women have been calling
on His name for the salvation of their souls. The gospel accounts of
His life and ministry indeed depict a special individual, but He was
much more than meets the eye. He was God incarnate, the Divine in
human flesh, and He had a mission. Jesus' work on the cross intricately
links His precious name with our gift of salvation. The sacrifice of the
only perfect One paid sin's penalty for the many, who could never
have found redemption any other way.

While the world will tell you that all religions are just different
paths up the same mountain, don't be fooled. Christianity stands
alone as the only path to God, as its many exclusivity claims purport.
You either take them as truth or you deny them. You cannot take the
middle ground—it just doesn't exist.

Jesus made this abundantly clear when He stated, "I am the way,
and the truth, and the life. No one comes to the Father except through
me" (John 14:6). Our salvation is entirely a gift from God and cannot
be earned or bartered. God's justice demanded satisfaction and there
was only one way that could happen: "For our sake He made Him to be
sin who knew no sin, so that in Him we might become the righteousness of God" (2 Cor 5:21), and "you shall call His name Jesus, for He
will save His people from their sins" (Matt 1:21). Thank you, Lord
God, for that sweet, sweet name—a name like no other. –Blevins

Morning: Num 10; Ps 46, 47 — *Evening:* Song of Sol 8; Heb 8

YOUR FIRST LOVE

*"But this I have against you, that you have
abandoned the love you had at first."*
REVELATION 2:4

When we first come to Christ, everything seems new. We are eager to tell everyone about our salvation and to spread the gospel message. We are in love with what Christ has done for us and the hope that we now have in Him. Yet, as time goes by, we still maintain our faith; we still believe and are thankful for what Christ has done for us, but the newness fades. The Christian life ceases to be one of joy and becomes one of routine. Our enthusiasm diminishes and our message grows silent. We essentially abandon the love for Christ we first had.

In Revelation 2, John is instructed to warn the church of Ephesus against this very thing. Even though the church had endured patiently and not grown weary, they had abandoned the works that they did at first; they abandoned their first love. They were warned that if they did not return to their first love, repent and return to the works they did at first (v. 5), their lampstand would be removed from its place (v. 6). At first glance, it appeared as though the church of Ephesus was on solid ground. They toiled, endured patiently, did not bear with those who were evil, tested those who called themselves apostles and bore up for Christ's name sake. Yet, they missed it. They lost the love they once had for Christ—and for that, they risked losing it all.

Are we like the church at Ephesus? Have we abandoned the love we had for Christ? If so, we risk losing it all. Today, let us determine that we will repent and return to our first love—the *original* love we had for Christ. –Solley

Morning: Num 11; Ps 48 — *Evening:* Isa 1; Heb 9

FINE IN THE FIRE

"Behold, I have refined you, but not as silver; I have tried you in the furnace of affliction."
ISAIAH 48:10

The band Ten Years sings a song titled "Fix Me" that says, "I'm fine in the fire and I feed on the friction, I'm right where I should be, don't try and fix me." After hearing the song, I remember thinking about biblical personalities like Job, Joseph, and Isaiah. Most Bibles add a footnote to our text in reference to the word "tried." An alternate translation could just as well read, "I have *chosen* you in the furnace of affliction." Whether tried or chosen, there is no escaping the reality that there are times when we will find ourselves in the furnace of affliction. It is in the times of trial where God tries us or chooses us.

In light of God choosing us in the trying times, we cannot consider the fires of affliction to always be a bad thing. As challenging and painful as those times are, they are a necessary condition of our relationship to the Lord. Prison can easily be seen as a furnace of affliction. While it may never be the place where we desire to be, we can know it is a place where the Lord tries us or chooses us. It is the place where he refines us for His service.

As you consider your time of trial as the place where God chooses you, do you realize you are right where you should be during the refining process? Have you come to a point of full submission to Christ in the midst of the refining fires? If not, realize you are where you are for a reason, and feed on the friction so you can say with confidence that you are fine in the fire. –Karch

Morning: Num 12, 13; Ps 49 — *Evening:* Isa 2; Heb 10

YOU BETTER RECOGNIZE

"Yours, O LORD, is the greatness and the power and the glory and the victory and the majesty, for all that is in the heavens and in the earth is yours. Yours is the kingdom, O LORD, and You are exalted as head above all."

1 CHRONICLES 29:11

Have you ever been so caught up in your own accomplishments that you neglect to give credit where credit is due? Isn't it easy sometimes to think that any success we may have in life is a direct result of our own power? It's kind of like a Pro Bowl-caliber running back that rushes for over 100 yards and two touchdowns on his way to winning the Super Bowl but never thinks to mention his offensive line.

King David didn't have a problem giving credit to the one who was responsible for his success and good fortune. He went from tending sheep to ruling a nation, but he was intimately aware by whose hand his ascension came. He constantly gave praises to the Lord, offering psalms of thanksgiving and recounting his many blessings. Even when David went through a tough time after his sin with Bathsheba and the death of their son, he understood the importance of worshiping God for who He is.

Like David, we too can learn to praise God in all things. That may sound funny considering our current situation; but if our trust is in Him, then we can be confident everything is under His control. Remember, He is not just head over some things but all things. He is God over the free man as well as the incarcerated man. So with that thought in mind, why don't we give the Lord our recognition and praise? –Blevins

Morning: Num 14; Ps 50 — *Evening:* Isa 3, 4; Heb 11

MESS TO MESSAGE

*". . . 'Go home to your friends and tell them how much the
Lord has done for you, and how he has had mercy on you.'"*
MARK 5:19

I n Mark 5 we are told the story of the demon possessed man from
the country of the Gerasenes. This man was insane. He lived naked
among the tombs of the dead, and every time others tried to control
him by binding him with shackles and chains, he wrenched the chains
apart and broke the shackles. All day and night, he roamed through
mountains crying out and beating himself with rocks. Simply put, his
life was a mess.

Then he met Jesus, and his life was instantly transformed. Jesus
cast out the legion of demons living inside of him, restored him to his
right mind, and clothed him. As Jesus was leaving, the man begged
to go with Him. However, Jesus had other plans. Jesus told him, "Go
home to your friends and tell them how much the Lord has done for
you . . ." What Jesus did in those simple words was turn the mess that
had been this man's life into a message!

Our being confined within prison walls demonstrates that we have
made a mess out of our lives. However, when we met Jesus, our lives
were transformed. We have been restored to a right relationship with
God and set in our right minds. Moreover, like the demon-possessed
man from the country of the Gerasenes, we now have a story to tell—a
story of how Christ has taken the mess of our lives and turned it into a
message about His love, mercy, and grace. This is a message we are duty
bound, as Christians, to share with others. Today, fulfill that duty. Share
with someone how Christ has turned your mess into a message. –Solley

Morning: Num 15; Ps 51 — *Evening:* Isa 5; Heb 12

INTO STRANGENESS

*"Not many days later, the younger son gathered all he
had and took a journey into a far country, and there
he squandered his property in reckless living."*
LUKE 15:13

Most people of the Western world have heard of the biblical parable of the prodigal son. No matter their religious background, this story is deeply ingrained into Western culture. While most people may not know the story's origin, they can recount how the young son demanded his half of the inheritance from the father, only to waste it on the fast life.

An interesting aspect of the prodigal son's story is how the concept of "far country," as we have it in English, was captured when the Scriptures were translated into German. The idea in German can be loosely described as "strangeness." The young son did not only go away from his father and home, he went into a place that was altogether strange to him. Those of us in prison have also ended up in a place of strangeness through our own riotous living. No matter how long we have been locked up, there is something about prison that is foreign— something we cannot get used to. Something about prison speaks to our very being and calls us back home.

In the parable, the son finally comes to his senses and returns to his father. The thrust of the strangeness of prison, likewise, bids us to return to our Heavenly Father. No matter how long we have to serve inside of prison, we turn to Him knowing He calls us out of this strangeness and back home. He stands ready to receive us. Even if it means our return to Him beyond these walls will only be in eternity, He stands to welcome us home. –Karch

Morning: Num 16; Ps 52, 53, 54 — *Evening:* Isa 6; Heb 13

OUR FIRST REACTION

"The Lord is at hand; do not be anxious about anything,
but in everything by prayer and supplication with
thanksgiving let your requests be made known to God."
PHILIPPIANS 4:5B–6

O ften, while doing time, unfortunate circumstances and situations beyond our control enter our lives. We will receive bad news from home. Our wives and children will struggle mentally, emotionally, and financially with us being gone. Appeals will be shot down. Parole will be denied. In some cases, wives will leave us and loved ones will pass away. Our first reaction is usually one of anxiety or fear. We become anxious and stressed over things we really cannot fix, but we try to anyway. And when we fail, we usually become angry and frustrated.

Yet, as Christians, we sell ourselves short by trying to carry all of our burdens and fix all of our problems alone. We rob ourselves of God's peace when we fail to turn to Him during times of stress and anxiety. When faced with things beyond our control, prayer should not be our last resort; it should be our first reaction. As Paul instructs, we should "not be anxious about anything, but in everything, by prayer and supplication with thanksgiving let [our] requests be made known to God." It is then that "the peace of God, which surpasses all understanding, will guard [our] hearts and [our] minds in Christ Jesus" (v. 7). What Paul is saying is don't be anxious about it, pray about it.

When unfortunate situations and circumstances enter our lives that are beyond our control, let us not be anxious about it—let us pray about it. Let us turn to our Father in heaven who will give us His peace that passes all understanding, in the midst of our storms. –Solley

Morning: Num 17, 18; Ps 55 — *Evening:* Isa 7; Jas 1

CHURCHMEN

*"But if we walk in the light, as he is in the light,
we have fellowship with one another, and the blood
of Jesus his Son cleanses us from all sin."*

1 JOHN 1:7

The responsibility to maintain fellowship with the wider body of Christ should always be viewed as an honor and privilege—regardless of an individual's particular situation or calling. Fellowship should never be viewed as a burden or work. Of course, there are a variety of callings on the lives of individuals, even inside prison. Not everybody will view this topic through the same lens. Whatever a person's calling or title, we should have a deep passion for the church of Jesus Christ and the fellowship of believers. If I were to be pigeonholed into accepting one title over another, I would want to be identified as a "churchman." It is one of those old titles which have largely fallen out of use today much like "statesman" has in the political world.

I am convinced, for the life of the Christian inside prison to be sustained with any real vitality, the role of fellowship should be one of priority. John understood the importance of fellowship, and he equates it with walking in the light. Thus, all believers should enjoy a community of believers. We should be eager to participate in worship and fellowship with other believers. We are built up together to be better equipped to serve Christ.

Look for the believers around you and extend the hand of fellowship to them. Even if you are in administrative segregation, you can still shout down the run at those around you. Encourage them to be churchmen. Build one another up as representatives of Christ who serve the community of believers, and the wider population, through reflecting the tight-knit bonds Jesus shared with His disciples. –Karch

Morning: Num 19; Ps 56, 57 — *Evening:* Isa 8, 9:1–7; Jas 2

ASKING FOR DIRECTIONS

*"Jesus said to him, 'I am the way, and the truth, and the
life. No one comes to the Father except through me.'"*
JOHN 14:6

D riving around or wandering in circles looking for your destination is frustrating even for the most tranquil of people. Having to stop and ask for directions is embarrassing—especially for men. We absolutely hate asking anyone to help us find our way, and it is made even worse when we are given bad directions.

Receiving bad directions happens more and more frequently today. Society is flooded with false religions claiming to lead us to some secret knowledge or some "deep" mystical enlightenment, but in reality, these voices only serve to keep us lost. Jesus makes a remarkable claim in John 14:6. He asserts that He is the only way to God, a one-way-in type of entrance which excludes all other routes. Jesus' words to His disciples at the Last Supper make it clear that in order to find our way to the truth and receive everlasting life, we must follow Him. All of the other mystic religions that teach their followers they can arrive at the same place through many ways are just false directions designed to keep you wandering in circles. It's the equivalent of asking for directions from someone who never wants to see you reach your destination.

Remember, "the gate is wide and the way is broad that leads to destruction, and there are many who enter through it." But "the gate is small and the way is narrow that leads to life and there are few who find it" (Matt 7:13, 14). –Blevins

Morning: Num 20; Ps 58, 59 — *Evening:* Isa 9:7–21, 10:1–4; Jas 3

WHY WAIT?

"The harvest is plentiful, but the laborers are few."
LUKE 10:2

H ow many times have we had grand visions about what the Lord is going to do with our lives once we get out of prison? We have our whole futures planned out. For many of us who are Christians, we are going to be great missionaries, prison ministers, powerful evangelists, pastors, teachers, counselors, youth ministers, and the list goes on and on. We are going to use the amazing stories of our lives to touch the world and transform many lives for Christ. We are going to be mighty witnesses of the power of the gospel! These visions and plans are very pious and noble, yet, why must we wait?

All you have to do is take a good look around to see that we live in an environment ripe for harvest. We are surrounded by shattered dreams, broken lives, pain, sorrow, guilt, regret, misery, and hate—all of the things that make the soil of one's heart ripe for the message of the gospel. Yet, our grand plans of doing great things when we are released prevent us from seeing the fertile fields we are standing in right now. We often neglect the harvest for vision of future wonder. When we do so, we do a grave injustice to those hurting here and now. The words of Christ silently echo to us down through time, "The harvest is plentiful, but the laborers are few."

When you walk out of your cell today, stop and look around you. You are in the midst of a bumper crop! The harvest is plentiful. So, why wait? Set aside those grand visions for now and reap the harvest God has set before you. –Solley

Morning: Num 21; Ps 60, 61 — *Evening:* Isa 10:5–34; Jas 4

DARKNESS

"It was now about the sixth hour, and there was darkness over the whole land until the ninth hour,"
LUKE 23:44

We seldom associate the presence of God with anything dark or fearful. In fact, we often question where God is in the dark and fearful times. At Sinai, Israelites were afraid of the darkness, yet God was where the thick darkness was. And, as Moses drew near to the darkness where God was, the people kept their distance. Like the Israelites, it is ingrained in us to flee, or stand aloof from, those things that seem dark and fearful to us. We have developed ideas that shape our conceptions about God because of our inclinations to flee from what appears to be dark and fearful—ideas which say God could never be in the darkness. As a result of such ideas, God seems far away in those dark times when we experience fear, pain, or suffering.

Elie Wiesel recounts his experiences in Nazi concentration camps in his little book, *Night*. At one point, he tells a story of seeing a little boy hanged for stealing bread. Wiesel recalls, as all the prisoners in the camp were forced to watch the execution, a man behind him continued to cry softly, "Where is God? Where is God in this?" Wiesel writes that an inner voice struck him deep within his soul as he heard the words, "Right there on the gallows." In the midst of the most horrible darkness of the twentieth century, God was in the midst of it. Wiesel's story helps us to understand that even we can never discount God's presence.

Prison time is often dark and we can easily ask, "Where is God?" Yet, may we always remember that in one of the darkest times of history, it was God in the flesh who hung in the midst of the darkness. May we always seek God's presence, even in the midst of the darkness. –Karch

Morning: Num 22; Ps 62, 63 — *Evening:* Isa 11, 12; Jas 5

IT'S NOT THE END OF THE ROAD

"And this is the promise that he made to us—eternal life."
1 JOHN 2:25

I can't tell you how many times I've looked around the dayroom and seen that look. You know: the one that lets you know a guy's time is really getting to him. The look that says depression is right around the corner. The look that confirms the hopelessness they are feeling inside. I can't speak for everyone, but I can definitely remember a time when I was starting the front end of a life sentence and thinking my life was over. Thoughts of despair kept swimming through my consciousness, reminding me that there was nothing to look forward to, no hope.

Oh, what horrible lies we believe when our attention is set on this world and not on the eternal life we have in Christ. True, we may have squandered opportunities for living a happy life outside of prison, but you know what? It's only temporary. Our real solace and peace comes from the ever-living Word of God and all that He has promised to His children. We began living eternally the moment we accepted and received Him. No life sentence, or any prison term for that matter, can derail the glorious plans of God Almighty.

The next time you are tempted to believe your life is over, or incited to believe prison is the final chapter in your existence, remember, "you have been born again, not of perishable seed but of imperishable, through the living and abiding Word of God" (1 Pet 1:23). So, do not fret, this is not the end of the road. –Blevins

Morning: Num 23; Ps 64, 65 — *Evening:* Isa 13; 1 Pet 1

QUIT RESISTING

"You stiff-necked people, . . . you always resist the Holy Spirit."
ACTS 7:51

Q uit resisting! The last time I heard those words, I was face down in the middle of someone's front yard, getting the stuffing kicked out of me. One cop had his knee on the back of my neck pressing my face into the mud and grass while another cop had my right arm twisted so far behind my back that I could feel the muscle tearing. Then there were two more—one kicking me in the ribs while the other attempted to do what appeared to be the figure-four on my legs. All of them were yelling, "Quit resisting!" I learned very quickly that there are consequences to resisting.

In Acts 7, Stephen referred to the Jews as a stiff-necked people, uncircumcised in heart and ears, and charged them with always resisting the Holy Spirit (v. 47.). In a practical sense, we are often like those Jews. As Christians we are often led by the Holy Spirit to do certain things, yet we constantly disobey. We resist the Holy Spirit's guidance in our lives, and when we do so, we become stiff-necked and hard-hearted. Just like I learned the day I was getting my ribs kicked in by the police: there are consequences to resisting—and the more you resist, the greater the consequence. Likewise, the more we resist the Holy Spirit, the more our hearts become calloused to His conviction. Before we know it, we have strayed so far away from the Christian path that we often cannot find our way back.

Where is the Holy Spirit leading you today? Are there things in your life He is telling you to get rid of, someone you need to pray for, people you need to forgive? If so, quit resisting. –Solley

Morning: Num 24; Ps 66, 67 — *Evening:* Isa 14; 1 Pet 2

CAN THEY SMELL IT?

"For we are the aroma of Christ to God among those are
being saved and among those who are perishing, to one
a fragrance from death to death, to the other a fragrance
from life to life. Who is sufficient for these things?"
2 CORINTHIANS 2:15–16

Nothing smells very good in a South Texas prison during summer's one-hundred degree heat. So, one afternoon the unexpected smell of pizza inside the dayroom got everyone's attention long before anyone saw the sergeant walk by with two large boxes of fresh pizza. The sudden change from the ordinary smells of the prison dayroom to the pleasing aroma of pizza was a sharp contrast inescapable to anyone's senses.

Of course, there are many smells associated with prison, few of which are pleasing aromas. When something does smell good, it tends to catch our attention in a way that those in the world miss. Similarly, as believers our lives should arrest the senses of others in the same way. Others ought to sense in us what Christ has accomplished for us. Those who do not know Christ ought to be made aware of their own need of salvation, while those who are believers should be encouraged and strengthened by what they see in us. Paul's allusion here is the lives of Christians exude an aroma that points others to the victory we have in Christ.

Far too often we settle for merely blending in with prison life. Yet, we should stand out in the way the smell of that fresh pizza did—one that grabs everyone's attention. We represent a marked difference between what is ordinary and normal inside places like this. Can others sense Christ Jesus in you? Can they smell Him? –Karch

Morning: Num 25; Ps 68 — *Evening:* Isa 15; 1 Pet 3

SPIRITUAL TUTOR

*"But the Helper, the Holy Spirit, whom the Father will
send in my name, he will teach you all things and bring
to your remembrance all that I have said to you."*
JOHN 14:26

In grade school, I remember having to learn something new each year. Whether it was math, science, or English, every year I was introduced to new concepts and had to be taught what I didn't know. The classes I thrived in and enjoyed the most were the ones with the best teachers—those who cared about their students and invested time and effort into making sure no one in class was left behind. Sometimes they stayed late after class if anyone had questions, or they scheduled times when they could individually tutor students. Those were the teachers I remember the best, because they cared.

There's a similar principle behind the activity of the Holy Spirit in a believer's life. Jesus promised His disciples a Helper, one who would teach them all things. This wasn't some casual, temporary instructor who would teach them and then move on, but a permanent, life-long tutor. The Spirit of Truth, who was poured out on the day of Pentecost and dwells in all believers, is our spiritual tutor. He convicts us of sin, righteousness, and judgment as well as comforts us and provides us strength (John 14:16–17, 2 Cor 1:3–7, Eph 3:16). He goes above and beyond in a way no earthly teacher ever could.

Just as we needed good teachers in grade school, as Christians, we need the tutelage of the Holy Spirit. He is the teacher of all teachers. So, today, look to Him for instruction and comfort and allow Him to lead and guide you in all things. –Blevins

Morning: Num 26; Ps 69 — *Evening:* Isa 16; 1 Pet 4

IF YOU LOSE IT ALL

"It is he who remembered us in our low estate,
for his steadfast love endures forever;"
PSALM 136:23

A short time ago, I was going through a period in my life where I thought I was losing everything that meant the most to me. My mother-in-law passed away, my marriage was in shambles, I had not seen my daughter in a year, and my father was diagnosed with terminal cancer. As I struggled with the idea of losing those who meant the world to me, I could not help but ask God, "Why?" Yet in the midst of my loneliness and confusion, I was honestly able to tell God that I knew He loved me, and if I lost it all, I would still serve Him.

At times, it is easy to believe we are traveling life all alone and to feel like we have lost everything. Our friends have abandoned us; wives or girlfriends have left us. Our children have not written or visited us, and loved ones have passed away. We feel such an overwhelming sense of loss that it constantly weighs upon our minds. Yet we are not alone. God is with us. Even while we were dead in our trespasses and sins—in our lowest estate—God remembered us and demonstrated His own love toward us by sending Christ as a propitiation for our sins. How much more now, as His adopted children, can we have assurance that God remembers us, is with us, and will never leave us nor forsake us. Though we may feel alone, like we have lost it all, we have one thing we can count on—God's enduring love.

When life gets overwhelming and you feel like you have lost everything that means the most to you, know that God has not forgotten you. His love for you endures forever. Even if you lose it all, His love remains. –Solley

Morning: Num 27; Ps 70, 71 — *Evening:* Isa 17, 18; 1 Pet 5

THE CHOSEN

"even as he chose us in him before the foundation of the world, that we should be holy and blameless before him."
EPHESIANS 1:4

T he first chapter of Ephesians is a towering attestation to the sufficiency of Jesus Christ. In the first few verses, Paul lays out how it is in, by, and through Christ that we have been chosen, redeemed, made holy, and blessed. It is all about Him. Paul has the tendency to always bring the focus back to Jesus. He seldom gets away from the centrality of what has been accomplished for us by the person and work of Jesus.

Due to the close proximity of the Christian community inside prison, the interaction between believers on the inside often turns toward theological discussion. Questions emerge concerning various doctrines, the proper Christian ethic, and the end times. Relating to each of those topics are questions surrounding the concepts of predestination and election. Keeping Paul's focus in mind, we realize that the Father predestined and elected Jesus—He is the chosen One. Only in Him can we become part of that elect—we, too, become the chosen.

As we find ourselves thinking about these things, we should maintain Paul's same focus. Particularly, when we are discussing them with other believers, it is important not to lose the focus Paul had. In the midst of our thinking and talking about what it is we believe, we need to always keep Jesus at the center of our focus. In doing so, we are much better equipped to understand and rejoice in the fact that He is the chosen One, and that we too are chosen in Him. –Karch

Morning: Num 28; Ps 72 — *Evening:* Isa 19, 20; 2 Pet 1

HOMECOMING

*"In my Father's house are many rooms. If it were not so, would
I have told you that I go to prepare a place for you? And if
I go and prepare a place for you, I will come again and will
take you to myself, that where I am you may be also."*
JOHN 14:2–3

T here is always a certain joy felt when a loved one who has been
gone for a long time returns home. There are usually hugs and
smiles, maybe even a few tears. Soldiers returning home from war experience it, college kids coming home after a long semester away experience it, and of course, men in the penitentiary longingly anticipate
what it is going to be like when they return home after a lengthy stint
in prison.

Yet, have you ever wondered what that day is going to be like when
Christ returns to take us to our eternal home in heaven? He has promised to prepare a place for us in the Father's house. One day He will
return to take us with Him to that very location, so that where He is,
we may be, also. What an incredible homecoming it will be when God
finally brings all His children home.

Though the journeys we each have taken in life have led us in all
different directions, as believers in Christ, our final destination is the
same. We will return to the heavenly home Christ has gone to prepare
for us. Our heavenly homecoming will be a glorious occasion for rejoicing. As the song says, I can only imagine! –Blevins

Morning: Num 29; Ps 73 — *Evening:* Isa 21; 2 Pet 2

GOING AND GOING AND GOING

"Train up a child in the way he should go; even
when he is old he will not depart from it."
PROVERBS 22:6

Most of us were raised in dysfunctional homes where the only training we received was in dysfunction. As we grew older and went out into the world on our own, we carried our dysfunctional behavior, which we learned from our dysfunctional families, with us. In turn, our dysfunctional lives are a dysfunctional example to our children who, without some type of intervention, will grow up to be dysfunctional adults. Statics say that seventy percent of our dysfunctional children will follow in our dysfunctional footsteps through prison doors. It is a dysfunctional cycle that keeps going and going and going.

Unless we want to see our children living right where we are, we must do something about it today. We are the only ones who can put a stop to the cycle of dysfunction that has plagued our families generation after generation. The old proverb is correct: "Train up a child in the way he should go; even when he is old he will not depart from it." On the other side of the coin, when we do not train them up right, they take the wrong way and will not depart from *that* path.

Even though we are incarcerated, we are the greatest influence in our children's lives. As men and women who have been transformed by Christ, we must pass a new legacy on to our children. Namely, we must break that cycle of dysfunction that has held our families bound for so long. We must do all that we can to set our children's feet on the right path by showing them that in Christ, there is new life—a better life. It is only being in Christ that will keep them out of prison. –Solley

Morning: Num 30; Ps 74 — *Evening*: Isa 22; 2 Pet 3

ORGANIZED CRIME

"but God shows his love for us in that while we
were still sinners, Christ died for us."
ROMANS 5:8

Throughout the letter to the Romans, Paul navigates the details of his carefully crafted arguments pertaining to man's inherent sinfulness, the justice of God's law, and man's debt to God for having violated that law. So, by the fifth chapter we begin to get an understanding of our position. As sinful human beings, we owe a debt to God we simply cannot pay. For satisfaction of His justice to be made, something must be done that we could never do.

It is not justice for an innocent person to pay for the criminal violations of the guilty, and in a very real way, it is criminal for the innocent to suffer the punishment due to the guilty. Those of us inside prison have a heightened sense of awareness of the innocent suffering for the guilty in that, to one degree or another, we have seen it happen or have had it happen to us. The innocent guy gets caught up and fades the heat for the guilty one. Nevertheless, this is the heartbeat of the gospel and is exactly what made the cross a scandal to those who first heard it. While we were still sinners (guilty), Jesus (the innocent) suffered our punishment for us. In our minds it is almost criminal.

Thinking about what Jesus has done for us, how He willingly submitted to the will of the Father in order to be the perfect satisfaction for His justice, we can see there is a direct organization to it all. Theologians deem it as the covenant of redemption that took place within the Godhead itself. As sinners who have been redeemed from our guilt through the innocent sacrifice of another, it can be seen as a final vindication of the ultimate organized crime. –Karch

Morning: Num 31; Ps 75, 76 — *Evening:* Isa 23; 1 John 1

STAR GAZING

*"He determines the number of the stars; he
gives to all of them their names."*
PSALM 147:4

Have you ever looked skyward on a clear night and wondered about the infinite number of tiny shining lights off in the distance? You were probably able to make out a few constellations, the Big and Little Dipper or Orion's Belt. If you had a telescope, you could probably pick out a few more. Perhaps you picked up a *Popular Science* magazine and read about the billions of distant stars all across the universe. Even with all their expensive equipment, astronomers are still discovering more stars.

Sometimes it's hard to reason our way back from the created universe to the all-powerful Creator. We overlook the connection or we may have other things in our life distracting us from realizing the truth. Yet, according to Norman Geisler, the Principle of Causality states that everything that comes to be is caused by something else. We can trace everything around us back through a series of interrelated causes, but much like Aristotle found out, there has to be a First Cause or a Prime Mover. Something or someone had to set it all into motion. Think about it for a second. If there was a big bang there had to be a big banger. Nature attests to the awesome and incredibly powerful Creator (Rom 1:20).

The next time you gaze up at the sky on a clear night and catch a glimpse of some of those billions of tiny stars, remember they didn't just happen to be there. They didn't just spontaneously appear: God has hung each one it its place and given them a name according to His perfect will. If God has paid so much attention to the stars, how much more significant is the fact that God desires to have a relationship with you? –Blevins

Morning: Num 32; Ps 77 — *Evening:* Isa 24; 1 John 2

OUR GOD

*"fear not, for I am with you; be not dismayed, for I
am your God; I will strengthen you, I will help you, I
will uphold you with my righteous right hand. "*
Isaiah 41:10

At times, the life of a prisoner can be very difficult and discouraging. The mundane lifestyle drags us down so much that it is easy
to become so focused on our circumstances that we lose sight of how
much God cares for and loves us or how much He sustains us through
our struggles and hardships. We allow discouragement and depression
to set in, and we forget who our God is and who we are in Him.

That is why I love Isaiah 41:10 so much. It reminds me of who God
is and His care and concern for each one of us. Though God is speaking to a specific people in this text, the words reveal to us the heart of
God. He loves and cares for His people and is utterly devoted to them.
He promises that He is with them: He is their God, He will strengthen
them, He will help them, He will uphold them with His right hand.

Like the Israelites in this passage, we are God's children. He loves
us and is devoted to us. He is there with us as we walk down these
desolate halls. He strengthens us when we are weak. He helps us when
it seems like all hope is gone, and He upholds us with His right hand
when we cannot stand. We can take great comfort knowing that God
is *our* God. –Solley

Morning: Num 33; Ps 78: 1–37 — *Evening:* Isa 25; 1 John 3

GROUND ZERO

"And they sang responsively, praising and giving thanks to the Lord,
'For he is good, for his steadfast love endures forever toward Israel.'
And all the people shouted with a great shout when they praised the
LORD, because the foundation of the house of the LORD was laid."
EZRA 3:11

T he Israelites began rebuilding Jerusalem through a special commission from King Artaxerxes. The people had been in captivity
under brutal Babylonian regimes and their homeland had lain in ruins for decades. The temple's destruction was a particularly devastating
aspect of the Babylonian campaigns. Now, however, Israel would see it
rebuilt. Ezra records the people's response as they celebrated the laying of the foundation. The rubble had been cleared, the soil broken
at ground-zero, and praise and thanks were shouted to the Lord as the
foundation was laid.

Those of us in prison understand what it's like to be in captivity.
Some of us even know what it is like being captive under brutal regimes and have watched all that we associate with our home slowly
fade. Nevertheless, as Christians, we have similar reasons to give thanks
and praise to the Lord. In the New Testament, Christ points to Himself
as being a temple which would, upon being destroyed, be raised again
in three days (John 2:19). Through His resurrection, He has become
the chief cornerstone of the temple of His body, the church, which is
made up of believers—living stones (1 Pt 2:5).

Christ is our ground-zero. The foundation of the Lord's house has
been laid in the person and work of Jesus. Our praise and thanks to
the Lord ought to reflect the same response of the people in Ezra's day
for what has been done for us in Christ. Like Ezra, we can proclaim He
is good and that His steadfast love endures forever. –Karch

Morning: Num 34; Ps 78: 38–72 — *Evening:* Isa 26; 1 John 4

THE CONTENT OF OUR CONTENTMENT

*"Keep your life free from love of money, and be content with what
you have, for he has said, "I will never leave you nor forsake you."*
HEBREWS 13:5

Recently, while watching television in the dayroom, I was amazed by some of the commercials. Most were advertisements appealing, in some way or another, to people's sense of unfulfilled dreams. Our culture has adopted a philosophy of life in which "good" is never good enough. We spend most of our lives chasing a better life because we are so dissatisfied with the one we have.

People in the free-world would hardly believe someone incarcerated can live a content life. In fact, most people in prison would never admit their contentment. It is, however, possible. When you stop placing your hope in material things and start placing your hope in the eternal promises of God, earthly things no longer matter so much. It is then, that no matter what situation you find yourself in, you can be content.

The writer of Hebrews understood this as he wrote to Jews who had not quite grasped the wondrous content of those promises. Paul understood this while he wrote in chains waiting to find out the outcome of his imprisonment (Phil 4:11). Christ, Himself, is the *content* of our contentment, and our hope is in Him and Him alone. So, who cares if the grass looks greener on the other side of the fence? Where we are headed, there won't be any fences. All those things the world chases after will have disappeared, and we'll still be standing with Jesus, the content of our contentment. –Blevins

Morning: Num 35; Ps 79 — *Evening:* Isa 27; 1 John 5

THE PRODIGAL

"Bring quickly the best robe, and put it on him, and
put a ring on his hand, and shoes on his feet . . .
let us eat and celebrate. For this my son was dead,
and is alive again; he was lost, and is found."
LUKE 15:22–24

T he story of the prodigal son moves me every time I read it. I believe it is because I see myself in this man who had so much at his
disposal. But, in his ignorance and immaturity, he chose to waste it all
away on things that held no real significance. When all was said and
done, he stood alone in his filth and his shame and said the only thing
he could, "I will return to my father." When his father saw him coming,
he ran to his son, kissed him, and embraced him in all of his filthiness.
As Scripture tells us, in his love, he forgave his son and restored him
completely. He rejoiced because his son had finally returned.

Like the prodigal son, many of us have strayed away and lived lifestyles that were not becoming of who we are as children of God. We
have wasted many years and many resources that our Father has given
us on pleasures in life that hold no real value. We long to return to the
Father and beg His forgiveness. However, how often do we waddle in
the pig pens of life before we finally reach the point where we say, "I'm
going home. I will return to my Father."

If like the prodigal son, you have strayed away, yet your heart longs
to return, know that you have a Father who loves you and awaits your
return—a Father who longs to restore you to your rightful position in
Him. –Solley

Morning: Num 36; Ps 80 — *Evening:* Isa 28; 2 John 1

THE NOTHING

"And lead us not into temptation, but deliver us from evil."
MATTHEW 6:13

I n the 1980s, most American kids had seen or heard of the movie, *The NeverEnding Story*. The protagonist of the movie is a young boy who enters another world through the pages of a book and is faced with the challenge of saving that world from being destroyed by the onslaught of an enemy known only as the "Nothing." The Nothing is portrayed as this substance-less void that swallows up everything. Theologians since the time of Augustine have attempted to define evil in much the same way. By Augustine's standard, evil is substantive only inasmuch as it corrupts that which is inherently good. It is the nothing that has been eating away at God's good creation since Adam's sin in Eden.

This traditional definition of evil is not without its problems. For instance, if evil is nothing, then what are we being delivered from in Christ? What is the point of Jesus instructing us to pray to be delivered from evil? As we think about this, it begins to make sense that we should pray to be delivered from the nothing that eats away at the goodness of the life God has called us to and prepared for us. It is so easy to get caught up in the mundane and mediocre—the nothing—that swallows up the richness of God's designed purpose for us.

The prayer for deliverance from evil is much broader than a prayer to be delivered from individual bad circumstances or situations. While certainly a part of it, there is much more. As you approach each day, pray the Lord's Prayer from Matthew 6. Ask the Lord to deliver you from the nothing that attempts to eat away at the good the Lord has planned for your life. –Karch

Morning: Deut 1; Ps 81, 82 — *Evening*: Isa 29; 3 John 1

PEOPLE OF INTEGRITY

*"Whoever walks in integrity walks securely, but he
who makes his ways crooked will be found out."*
PROVERBS 10:9

O kay, just admit it. We have not always been people of integrity. We have lied, cheated, conned, robbed, abandoned, and betrayed. You name it and we have probably done it at some point in our lives. No matter how much we try to justify our criminal lifestyles, our destructive behaviors, or our demented actions, the reality is that our ways were very, very crooked. We were far from being people of integrity.

Because of our pasts, many label us immoral reprobates, devious miscreants, lost causes, no good, or the proverbial "waste of tax payers' resources." Yet, our pasts, or the labels others put on us, do not have to determine who we are, nor dictate our future. Regardless of the lifestyles we once lived or the character flaws we had, we *can* be people of integrity—people others *can* depend on and trust. As new creations in Christ, we *can* walk through life securely, knowing we are not the people we used to be (2 Cor 5:17). Plus, there is an additional benefit: as people of integrity, we no longer have to look over our shoulders, wondering and waiting for what we have done to find us out or catch up to us.

Though your past may be full of things you are not too proud of, know that you no longer have to walk in the ways of the crooked, nor do you have to conform to the labels others put on you. So, today, choose integrity. Choose to be the person God has called you to be. –Solley

Morning: Deut 2; Ps 83, 84 — *Evening:* Isa 30; Jude

WHAT'S IN A NAME?

"Because he holds fast to me in love, I will deliver him;
I will protect him, because he knows my name."
PSALM 91:14

In Shakespeare's *Romeo and Juliet,* Juliet asks the famous question, "What's in a name? That which we call a rose by any other name would smell as sweet." However, there is something in God's name and something in knowing His name. David writes Psalm 91 conveying what he has heard from the Lord. The Lord will deliver those who cling to Him in love and He will protect those who *know His name.*

We can easily slip into a type of "Christianity of convention." We know all the spiritual platitudes about faith, hope, and love and we have tendencies to make the theological virtues out to be banal. Yet, we forget we are baptized in the name of Jesus Christ (Acts 19:5). There is only one name given under heaven by which we must be saved (Acts 4:12). At the name of Jesus every knee will bow (Rom 14:11; Phil 2:10–11).

Spend time today thinking about the name of Jesus. Think about the truth David conveys to us in Psalm 91. Not only do we have the Lord's protection, we know that all the promises of God are "Yes" in Christ (2 Cor 1:20). The old hymn says, "There is just something about that name," and we would be correct to say there is everything about that name. As we think about the name of Jesus today, know that the creator of the universe responds because we know His name. –Karch

Morning: Deut 3; Ps 85 — *Evening*: Isa 31; Rev 1

LIFE'S ROAD MAP

"Your word is a lamp to my feet and a light to my path."
PSALM 119:105

L ife is rough. We are not born with an instruction manual that teaches us who we are or the purpose for which we were created. We can't open the glove box and find a map to point us in the right direction. We wander down the dark roads of life searching for who we are and where we are going. Often times, we end up following someone who is headed the wrong way, or we listen to others who can only give us wrong directions. Eventually, we lose our way and end up in places like prison.

Yet, despite all the wrong roads in life we have taken, we still have hope. We are not utterly lost! There is something that will light our way and set our feet on the right path. It is called the Bible—the living, breathing Word of God (Heb 4:12). In the Bible, we discover who we are, why we were created, and where we are going. The Bible is not only our road map for life, but it is our instruction manual as well. From Genesis to Revelation, God speaks to us through His Word, and gives us direction and instruction for life. It is no wonder the psalmist declared in praise, "Your word is a lamp unto my feet and a light unto my path."

If you find yourself headed down the wrong, dark roads of life time and again, open God's Word and let it be a lamp unto your feet and a light unto your path. You will never get lost following God's road map. –Solley

Morning: Deut 4; Ps 86, 87 — *Evening:* Isa 32; Rev 2

NO FENCE STRADDLING

*"No one can serve two masters, for either he will hate the
one and love the other, or he will be devoted to the one and
despise the other. You cannot serve God and money."*
MATTHEW 6:24

For most of my life, if you asked if I were a Christian I would have
hastily said, "Yes." That thought used to amuse me because, although I always believed in God, I couldn't tell you a lick about His
son, Jesus. I didn't read my Bible or go to church. My life more closely
resembled what my great-grandfather would've deemed a "heathen"
more than a saved child of God.

Today, I realize my false profession of faith wasn't an exclusive experience. The sights that surround me now don't amuse me anymore.
Instead, they bring me great sorrow. Many people run around wearing the name "Christian" like it is some nominal name tag. Professing
Christ, they sinfully continue in the ways of the world. We've all seen
them: those who claim to be Christian but still represent a color and
lock alphabets when shaking their homeboys' hands or the ones who
profess faith in the risen Lord but walk around with a stack of photo
albums stuffed with pornography.

Jesus explains during His Sermon on the Mount that there is no
middle ground. When it comes to discipleship, it's right or left, hot or
cold, Jesus or the world. True living faith is expressed in our daily lives
in that it's a lifestyle not a label. If we say we're Christian and we aren't
living for God's glory, we're only playing games. Ask yourself, "Have I
truly made Jesus Lord of my life?" If the answer is "No," then you might
want to reevaluate on which side of the fence you really stand. –Blevins

Morning: Deut 5; Ps 88 — *Evening:* Isa 33; Rev 3

SHIFTING SANDS

"And the rain fell, and the floods came, and the winds blew and beat against that house, and it fell, and great was the fall of it."
MATTHEW 7:27

At the close of His Sermon on the Mount, Jesus illustrates the importance of obeying His teachings through the analogy of two builders: one wise and the other foolish (Matt 7:24–29). Those who hear His words and follow them are like a wise man who builds his house upon a rock. When the storms and floods come, his house stands. On the other hand, those who hear His words and do not act on them are like the foolish man who builds his house on sand. When the floods and winds come, his house falls. And great is its fall.

Although this passage points to future judgment, it has an immediate application. Many times, we build our lives on foundations of sand: false religions, ideologies, wealth, pride, the street life, prison codes. Whatever the case may be, we have built our lives upon a foundation that is unstable. If you are incarcerated, it is evident the sand you built your life upon shifted beneath your feet and left you lying flat on your back. However, God is in the reconstruction business. He has provided you with a sure foundation to build your life upon: Jesus Christ (Is 28:16; 1 Pt 2:6).

The foundation your life is built upon will be proven when the floods come and the winds blow. Do not be found wanting! Be like the wise man. Do not just hear Christ's words, act on them. Build your life on the solid rock of Jesus Christ. –Solley

Morning: Deut 6; Ps 89 — *Evening:* Isa 34; Rev 4

TOTAL RECALL

"That which is, already has been; that which is to be, already
has been; and God seeks what has been driven away."
ECCLESIASTES 3:15

I n most instances, prison time seems stagnant. The days neither drag
on nor fly by. We are often frustrated with trying to get through one
day or frustrated because we have accomplished nothing in the time
that has passed. Either way, there is the inevitable sense that life is passing by, and there are so many things we are missing. This experience
brings to mind the old idea that time is the ultimate destroyer. Time
eats away at everything until eventually nothing is left.

In terms of time, prison serves only to emphasize our awareness of
its passing. However, traditional linear concepts of time as past, present, and future cannot bind God. He created time. Inasmuch as we
often misunderstand His creation, we may well be misunderstanding
time as well. There are various theories concerning time, but as believers in God, we are not bound to any one of those existing theories.
Based on the Scripture for today, we see how our ideas of past, present
and future are not as clear as they appear at a glance. The present already has been and the future already has been as well. God has it all
worked out so that there is an immediacy of the future working within
the present. The key is, "God seeks what has been driven away."

Whatever time we feel we are losing while in prison, we can be
comforted in knowing that God has it all worked out already. He knows
what we have missed. The time we have lost, He will ultimately recall
and redeem. –Karch

Morning: Deut 7; Ps 90 — *Evening:* Isa 35; Rev 5

GET OFF THE GAS

*"Do not lie to one another, seeing that you have
put off the old self with its practices"*
Colossians 3:9

I t's a known fact that in prison you can be anybody you want to be. Everybody has heard the countless "drug lord" stories, "big-time pimp" episodes, and "stone-cold gangster" sagas. After hearing these tall tales you begin to think you're living in a *Scarface* movie and not the real world. You rarely hear about the drug, alcohol, or sexual addictions or the less "glamorous" crimes people don't like to talk about.

Likewise, you have probably figured out there aren't many Tony Montanas or Pablo Escobars out there. However, most people are glamorizing their pasts because they are ashamed of what really happened, or they are trying to impress others because they think people won't like who they truly are. But what do you tell people when you've committed your life to serving Christ and the candy-coated paint jobs and six-figure drug deals no longer mean anything to you? First, you should understand there is nothing glorious about why you're incarcerated. It doesn't matter if you were a kingpin or a pinhead; we all messed up and were once labeled sons of disobedience. Second, our lives now should reflect an aversion to those things, not an exaggeration of them. Paul tells us to consider ourselves dead to the evil ways which separated us from God and commands us not to lie to one another.

We don't need to continue feeling guilty for our pasts because we can be confident that we are forgiven. However, we must not be proud of our pasts or embellish our sinful history. Yet, our pasts can be useful. Telling others the struggles we faced and the depths of our depravity is a powerful testimony to God's amazing grace in our lives. All we have to do is be truthful about it, and get off the gas. –Blevins

Morning: Deut 8; Ps 91 — *Evening:* Isa 36; Rev 6

CALLED OUT

"And if it is evil in your eyes to serve the LORD,
choose this day whom you will serve . . . But as for
me and my house, we will serve the LORD."
JOSHUA 24:15

In Joshua 24, what is essentially his farewell address, Joshua stands before the tribes of Israel and reminds them of all the Lord has done for them as a nation from the time of Abraham to their successful conquering of the Promised Land. He reminds the children of Israel of God's faithfulness to them, even in times of disobedience, and warns them of the harsh consequences of following after other gods. Then he calls them all out. He gives them an ultimatum: choose this day whom you will serve. Joshua leaves no room for maneuvering nor does he allow the Israelites to weasel their way out of it. The children of Israel have to make a decision that day.

Like the children of Israel, we are being called out. Each day we are faced with the same ultimatum they were. We must make a conscious decision who we will serve: the gods of our pasts—our sinful lifestyles, addictions, false belief systems that held us in bondage—or the Lord who has rescued us from danger, time and time again, and has sustained us through times of hardship and trouble. Will our daily actions tell the world around us that we serve the Lord, or will they only serve as a testament to the fact that we are still trying to serve the false gods of our pasts?

So what's up? You are being called out. What are you going to do? I hope that, like Joshua, you will be able to say with confidence, "As for me and my house, we will serve the LORD." –Solley

Morning: Deut 9; Ps 92, 93 — *Evening:* Isa 37; Rev 7

JUST BUMPIN'

*"But someone will say, 'You have faith and I have works.' Show
me your faith apart from your works, and I will show you my
faith by my works. You believe that God is one; you do well. Even
the demons believe—and shudder! Do you want to be shown,
you foolish person, that faith apart from works is useless?"*
JAMES 2:18–20

J ames brings his argument to a head here as he deals with the tension of faith and works. He demands tangible evidence that extends beyond mere words. Faith, in James' mind, is something more than assertions. Faith has an active aspect to it that works itself out in a way that can be demonstrated. Real faith can be seen.

Those of us inside prison understand the foolishness of hearing someone say that they have faith without displaying any corresponding evidences that confirm it. Far too often, we see those who have lost sight of the conclusion James is advocating. Without some type of evidence to confirm our faith, we are essentially just bumpin'. We claim we have faith, but there is nothing demonstrating that it is for real. James points out even demons have that type of faith and it is useless.

We can't be just bumpin' when it comes to what we really believe. When witnessing about what Christ has done for us to those around us, we have to realize how suspicious and skeptical most people inside prison are. Therefore, if we do not display the type of evidences James advocates, those we are trying to witness to will see us as just talking. As we live out the tension between faith and works, everyone around us knows we are doing more than talking. When we show our faith by our works, we have a much stronger witness to the power of Christ. –Karch

Morning: Deut 10; Ps 94 — *Evening:* Isa 38; Rev 8

BIRD WATCHING

*"Look at the birds of the air: they neither sow nor reap
nor gather into barns, and yet your heavenly Father
feeds them. Are you not of more value than they?"*
MATTHEW 6:26

I was lying in my bunk the other day reading when a bird landed on the run in front of my cell. Setting my book down, I silently watched as the tiny bird pecked at the bare, concrete floor in search of something to eat. Quietly, I reached into my locker, grabbed a pack of crackers, and threw one on the run. Suddenly, the bird cocked his head, listening, and then flew away. Just as quickly as the bird left, he returned. As I watched God's tiny creation gobble up the cracker, I could not help but think of Christ's words in Matthew 6: "Look at the birds of the air: they neither sow nor reap nor gather into barns, and yet your heavenly Father feeds them. Are you not of more value than they?"

Many times, we forget about this. We forget how valuable we are to our heavenly Father. When we are faced with times of need, we worry and worry, wondering if He is going to provide for us. We often worry so much that we cannot do anything else but worry. We wake up worrying, we go about our day worrying, and when we lie down to go to sleep, we worry some more. Yet, we worry for nothing. God knows the things we need. He will provide for us just as He provided for that tiny bird when I reached up into my locker and threw him a cracker.

Even in prison, you can trust and depend on God to meet all of your needs. He is faithful and will provide for you because you are His. And as His child, you are of great value to Him. –Solley

Morning: Deut 11; Ps 95, 96 — *Evening:* Isa 39; Rev 9

FORGETTING TO REMEMBER

*"Remember not the sins of my youth or my transgressions;
according to your steadfast love remember me, for
the sake of your goodness, O LORD!"*

PSALM 25:7

D avid prayed for the Lord not to remember the sins of his youth nor his transgressions. However, David's youth as a shepherd boy tending his father's sheep seems petty compared to the sins of our youth and the protracted transgressions of our entire lifestyles. How could it not? Being a shepherd boy in the hills of Israel simply does not compare to being a youngster in the typical American city today. There is far too much in the modern age that helps to compound sin and transgression.

Thinking along these lines, nevertheless, actually drives David's point home. No matter what volume of sin or transgression we may have accumulated in our pasts, we have to appeal to the same steadfast love of God. In His love, and for the sake of His goodness, we appeal to the Lord not to remember the sins of our pasts. We are asking Him to forget those sins and through His love, remember us. Because we can be sure God never acts contrary to His steadfast love and goodness, we can ask Him to forget in order to remember.

If God can forget our pasts and through His steadfast love remember us, then surely we can forget those things which brought us to prison. We can put those things behind us and know that because of God's steadfast love shown to us specifically in Christ, He remembers us. –Karch

Morning: Deut 12; Ps 97, 98 — *Evening:* Isa 40; Rev 10

ETERNAL CONSEQUENCES

*"Jesus said to her, 'I am the resurrection and the life. Whoever
believes in me, though he die, yet shall he live, and everyone who
lives and believes in me shall never die. Do you believe this?'"*
JOHN 11:25–26

C onsequences. There are consequences for every decision we
make. The incarcerated realize this fact of life probably more
than most. Doing time has a way of making one think about consequences. However, there are consequences for good decisions as well.
While most of us have spent endless hours contemplating the consequences of our poor decisions, what about contemplating the consequences of our good ones, or more specifically our best one?

When we put our faith in Jesus Christ, we're not trusting in merely
a morality teacher or even some comic book superhero. We're putting
our belief in the Son of the Living God—the One promised to Adam
and Eve long ago, the One who claimed to be the Good Shepherd, the
One who asserted Himself as the only way to God (Matt 16:16; Gen
3:15; John 10:11, 14; 14:6). Jesus Christ is the very content of our faith,
and putting our trust in Him has some serious consequences.

Jesus stated that the one who believes in Him will have everlasting
life. While there is no doubt this earthly life we experience is fading
fast, our hope should never rest here. Although this life is spotted with
the negative effects of our bad decisions—some worse than others—all
who put their faith in Jesus can take comfort in His promise of glorious, eternal consequences. –Blevins

Morning: Deut 13, 14; Ps 99, 100, 101 — *Evening:* Isa 41; Rev 11

THE DISCIPLINE OF PRAYER

"Then Jesus went with them to a place called Gethsemane, and he said to his disciples, "Sit here, while I go over there and pray."
MATTHEW 26:36

For six years, I had a very difficult time praying. My prayers were either full of painful shame I felt for hurting my family by returning to prison, or silent cries for God to forgive me. Because of my lack of a healthy prayer life, I felt far away from God and even further away from the forgiveness He offered. I was spiritually sick. Now, several years later, I am closer to God than I have ever been in my life. Furthermore, I am spiritually healthy and enjoy the forgiveness God has graced to me. Why? I learned how to pray.

Christ demonstrated the importance of the spiritual discipline of prayer. Shortly before His crucifixion, when the weight of the world was literally on His shoulders, He sought time alone with the Father to pray. It was through prayer that Christ communicated and fellowshipped with God, brought His burdens to the Father, and received the power he needed to carry out the tasks set before Him. In addition to Christ demonstrating the importance of prayer, we are commanded throughout the New Testament to pray (Mt 5:24; Rom 12:12; 1 Cor 7:5; Eph 6:18; Phil 4:6).

Prayer is the most important spiritual discipline in our lives. Without prayer, we drift further and further away from proper fellowship with God. If you have found this to be the case and your prayer life lacking, I encourage you to begin praying for fifteen minutes every morning and evening. You will be surprised how much thirty minutes a day communicating with the Father through prayer will transform your life. –Solley

Morning: Deut 15; Ps 102 — *Evening:* Isa 42; Rev 12

COUNTING THE DAYS

"So teach us to number our days that we may get a heart of wisdom."
PSALM 90:12

E veryone knows what it's like to count days. Those of us in prison especially know what it is like to count days. We count days until commissary, days since the last letter, days since the last visit, and days until the next visit. However, our day-counting comes mainly by way of numbering the days, months, or years, until that elusive parole interview or release date. As a result, we become professionals at counting the days.

Psalm 90 is a prayer by Moses contrasting the eternality of God with the finitude and fleeting nature of humanity. Inasmuch as we get caught up in counting the days of things temporally important to us, it is altogether wise to reorient our focus on those things which are eternal. If we have a discharge date from life itself where we appear before an Almighty God for an eternal pardon or condemnation, then our hearts are inclined toward wisdom by taking stock of eternal things here and now. A degree of wisdom is attributed to us when we begin to understand eternal things, and only then, do we gain a more clear perspective in numbering our days.

As our relationships with the Lord grow, let us look to Him for the proper numbering of our days. Ask Him, as Moses did, to teach us to rightly number our days. In doing so, we begin to take on an eternal perspective of all things from which our hearts become wise—even wise unto salvation (2 Tim 3:15). –Karch

Morning: Deut 16; Ps 103 — *Evening:* Isa 43; Rev 13

SICK CALL

"He heals the brokenhearted and binds up their wounds."
PSALM 147:3

B eing sick or injured in prison is horrible, especially when you're left with no choice but to go to medical. Frustration sets in knowing that whatever is wrong with you will more than likely be prescribed two non-aspirin and a blood pressure check. In prison, your left arm could be falling off and the best treatment you're going to receive is an ice-pack and a Band-Aid. Well, maybe it's not that bad—maybe!

Sometimes, though, the most serious injuries aren't physical. The worst types of traumas are the internal ones that affect the heart and mind. Prison has a way of inflicting unspeakable pain, loneliness, shame, guilt, and regret on a person. Many times, these ultimately render one brokenhearted. Of course, most of these wounds are the self-inflicted kind. We are often our own worst enemies. But there is good news.

The self-imposed injuries that leave us emotionally and spiritually handicapped need not be fatal because we have a merciful God who is all powerful and whose understanding is beyond measure. He has promised us in His Word that He is "near to the brokenhearted and saves the crushed in spirit" (Ps 34:18). Moreover, the Lord is the definitive healthcare provider. He hears the cries of His people and provides much more than non-aspirin and a Band-Aid. When we put in a sick call request to Him, we can take solace in His steadfast love and know our internal wounds will be bound up and healed. –Blevins

Morning: Deut 17; Ps 104 — *Evening:* Isa 44; Rev 14

RENEW YOUR MIND

"Do not be conformed to this world, but be transformed
by the renewal of your mind, . . ."
ROMANS 12:2

I n the past decade, there has been a rising phenomenon called "cognitive intervention" within our nation's prison systems. The driving force behind cognitive intervention is the idea that behavior follows in the wake of thought. If you can change the way a man thinks, you can change how he behaves. In other words, renew the mind, and you transform the behavior. In hopes of reducing crime, penologists have instituted some type of cognitive intervention class in almost every prison in America.

Yet, the renewing of the mind is not some novel concept recently discovered by behavior therapists. It has been passed down to us from century to century in the writings of the apostle Paul. In Romans 12, Paul instructs us not to be conformed to the world but to be transformed by the renewing of our minds. When we do so, we will be able to discern the will of God. Yet, how do we renew our minds: by learning how to take a deep breath and count to ten before we act or by asking ourselves if what we are doing will meet our needs over time? No, that is just a temporary fix. Our minds are truly and permanently renewed by meditating on and studying the Word of God. The more we abide in the Word, the more the Word will abide in us, renew our minds, and transform our lives from the inside out.

Reading and mediating on the Word of God is the most effective cognitive intervention therapy. If you really want to change, immerse yourself in God's Word, and let Him renew your mind and transform your life. –Solley

Morning: Deut 18; Ps 105 — *Evening:* Isa 45; Rev 15

LAY DOWN THE LAW

*"For Christ is the end of the law for righteousness
to everyone who believes."*
ROMANS 10:4

Apostle Paul writes about an eagerness to please God through an attempt to establish our own personal righteousness. He relates this eagerness to how Israel had a zeal for God, yet it was not supported with a real understanding of what actually pleases God. Any attempt to establish our own righteousness comes from a misunderstanding of what God requires of us and is a result of an ignorance of the righteousness of God.

Those of us in prison are here because, to one degree or another, we were butting heads with the law. When it came time for judgment, it was the charge of the law that condemned us. In the same way, as sinners, we spend our lives butting heads with the law of God. As lawbreakers, through the law we can never establish a righteousness of our own. Yet, as Christians, even after we have been set free from the condemnation of the law, we still have a propensity to seek a righteousness of our own. Through the lens of the law, we measure our own lives against those who may not have it as together as we do, and by this we attribute to ourselves a righteousness of our own. This neither pleases God, nor is it representative of His righteousness. Essentially, we end up butting heads with the law all over again.

The righteousness of Christ has been attributed to us, and in Him we have our righteousness. Paul tells us that *Christ is the end of the law for righteousness*. We cannot add to His righteousness. All God requires of us in this respect is to lay down the law—give it up! Allow the righteousness of Christ to work through you in a way that pleases Him. –Karch

Morning: Deut 19; Ps 106 — *Evening:* Isa 46; Rev 16

A REAL MAN

"Be watchful, stand firm in the faith, act like men,
be strong. Let all that you do be done in love."
1 CORINTHIANS 16:13–14

I f you are like me, you know what it was like growing up without a father. For whatever reason, Dad just wasn't there. Learning how to become a man was sometimes a painful process. Mom did her best, but there were just some things we needed Dad to teach us. Many of us had to learn those things the hard way, and again if you're like me, those things didn't sink in until you came to prison. However, that is the great thing about the Scriptures: the Word of God has timeless truths for wayward sons searching for the meaning of manhood.

Paul was a great instructor to the men of the churches he started and later corresponded with, teaching them how real men behaved. He taught them to be watchful because they needed to be aware of the dangers they faced in life and not broadsided by worldly opposition. He encouraged them to stand firm in their faith in Jesus Christ to overcome opposition, not turn and flee, but to stand their ground. He instructed them to act like men by being strong, not implying mere physical strength, but a spiritual vitality—a passive increase in vigor. Finally, and most importantly, he taught them to do everything in love, not in anger, jealousy, malice, or frustration—but in *love*.

Growing up without our fathers was a poor hand to be dealt in life, but it in no way justifies the choices we've made. Consider this a fresh start; it is not too late to demonstrate that you're not a product of your circumstances. Even incarcerated, you still have the ability to act like a real man. What are you going to do? –Blevins

Morning: Deut 20; Ps 107 — *Evening:* Isa 47; Rev 17

A LOVE WITHOUT END

"but God shows his love for us in that while we were still sinners, Christ died for us."
Romans 5:8

In the late 1980s, George Strait recorded, "Love Without End, Amen," a song about a father's love for his child. In a rare letter my father wrote to me from Angola when I was thirteen years old, he included the lyrics to this song. I have loved it ever since. However, as a man with a troubled past, the last verse referring to standing at the gates of heaven hoping no one on the other side knew half the things I have done, takes on a whole new meaning.

Many of us have a very troubled and dark past and are now ashamed of the lives we lived. Often times, we believe if God only knew half the things we have done, He surely would not let us enter into His eternal kingdom. However, the beauty of the cross is that God does know everything we have done in life—even the deep, dark secrets we hide inside. Nothing escapes the eyes of God. Yet, as Romans 5:8 tells us, in His love, Christ still died for us. It was in our depraved sinful state that God sent His son to be the propitiation—the appeasing sacrifice—for the very sins we are now ashamed of—the sins that make us cry out like the man in the song, "If they know half the things I've done, they'll never let *me* in."

We can rest assured our Heavenly Father's love is a love without end. Not only will He allow us past those pearly gates, He will be waiting there to escort us through them. –Solley

Morning: Deut 21; Ps 108, 109 — *Evening:* Isa 48; Rev 18

EPHRAIM

"The name of the second he called Ephraim, 'For God has made me fruitful in the land of my affliction.'"
GENESIS 41:52

J oseph was betrayed and sold into slavery by his own brothers, lied on by Potiphar's wife, and forgotten by those he had helped while in prison. He was a man who had many things to be bitter and vengeful about as a result. However, toward the end of his troubles when he named his sons, the name he chose for the second boy sounds like the Hebrew word for *fruitful*. It almost defies reason how a man in his position could retain such an attitude.

There is a great lesson in the name *Ephraim*. Even in the land of his affliction, Joseph knew the Lord had made him fruitful. While in prison many of us view our experiences as if time itself has been suspended and nothing fruitful can come from any of it. We spend day after day focused on little else besides some future parole date. Had Joseph done the same, had he only focused on the time when he would leave Egypt, the country would have been destroyed by famine. The famine would have also affected all the outlying areas, including Joseph's own home.

Joseph sought to serve the Lord even in Egypt, his land of affliction. Likewise, we too can look to serve the Lord right where we are. As we do, we can know He will make us fruitful in our lands of affliction. Like Joseph, we can never understand how being fruitful in our land of affliction may bless others. We never know the extent of the ripple or how it affects others, as the Lord makes us fruitful in this way. –Karch

Morning: Deut 22; Ps 110, 111 — *Evening:* Isa 49; Rev 19

COLOR BLIND

"After this I looked, and behold, a great multitude that no one
could number, from every nation, from all tribes and peoples
and languages, standing before the throne and before the Lamb,
clothed in white robes, with palm branches in their hands,"
REVELATION 7:9

An aunt of mine was born with diabetes. The disease has plagued her with many medical issues throughout her life, including an almost fatal attempt at child birth. My cousin was born healthy, but the complications during the delivery resulted in my aunt almost completely losing her eyesight. Instead, she became color blind. Unable to determine hues or shades of colors, the best she could hope for was discerning lights from darks. This was especially amusing when she attempted to match my cousin's socks. Purples were paired with blues, oranges with reds.

In prison, color is a *big* deal. Whether you like it or not, racial barriers abound. You can't go far without being treated differently because of the color of your skin. Dayrooms are often segmented, certain tables are cordoned off, and even televisions are controlled by one racial group or another. But, these differences in skin pigmentation shouldn't serve to separate us, nor should they determine our worth in each other's eyes.

In the Revelation of John, we get a small glimpse of God's plan for His people. We see it's not a throne room divided by ethnic or cultural barriers but one alive with diversity. It's a place where people from every nation and tongue can worship the one, true God together. It's a place where we can effectively be color blind. –Blevins

Morning: Deut 23; Ps 112, 113 — *Evening:* Isa 50; Rev 20

SEVENTY TIMES SEVEN

*"Lord, how often will my brother sin against me, and I
forgive him? As many as seven times? Jesus said to him, 'I
do not say to you seven times, but seventy-seven times.'"*
MATTHEW 18:21–22

When I walked into visitation and saw my little brother standing there, many different emotions overwhelmed me. Part of me wanted to hug him and part of me wanted to punch him right in his mouth! I had not heard from him in several years; during which time, I had written him numerous letters that went unanswered. On top of that, in a very real sense, I was doing time for both of us. Because of this, I felt he wronged me by turning his back on me when I came to prison.

The feelings I had are common to those of us incarcerated. We've all felt at some time or another that someone close to us has abandoned us and turned their backs on us when we needed them the most. Then, out of the blue, we will get a letter or a visit from them. And, because we love them, we are quick to forgive, only to have them turn around and abandon us again. Eventually, we get tired of forgiving and become bitter. Yet, Jesus made it clear that there should be no limitations on forgiveness. We should always be willing to forgive those who wrong us, no matter how many times they do so. We should never withhold forgiveness from anyone for any reason, even if it means forgiving as often as seventy times seven.

Have you forgiven someone who has wronged you, only to have them turn around and wrong you again? Maybe you are tired of forgiving and have become bitter. If so, meditate on Christ's words today and let them speak to your heart. –Solley

Morning: Deut 24; Ps 114, 115 — *Evening:* Isa 51; Rev 21

SOMEBODY ELSE?

"Are you the one who is to come, or shall we look for another?"
MATTHEW 11:3

J ohn the Baptist was in prison. While many of us can relate to the emotional and psychological strain that comes with incarceration, John's circumstances were a little more strenuous. As John experienced the strain of his situation, he sent his disciples to Jesus to ask outright if He were the Messiah, or should he be expecting help from somebody else?

Inasmuch as prison conditions today are not what they were in first century Palestine, we still find ourselves asking similar questions at times. When the Lord does not seem to be responding to our prayers the way we think He should or in the time frame we think He should, we naturally begin to question both ourselves and the Lord. We wonder if there is indeed somebody else—or some other way—through which we can find relief or sustenance in the midst of our trials and difficulties. As the scene unfolds for John, Jesus' response almost causes us to hold our breath in anticipation. Jesus simply instructs John's disciples to report all the good that is happening for people who need help.

Today we are bombarded by messages that Jesus is still helping the people who need it. We hear numerous testimonies of people whose relationships with their families are restored, who are released from prison, and more. The problem is these testimonies are so prevalent we become numb to them and largely ignore them, primarily because we don't see these things happening for us. So the next time you find yourself contemplating questions similar to John's, look beyond your immediate circumstances and think of the last time you heard or witnessed Jesus helping someone who really needed His help. As you hear of these things, know that Jesus is the One and there is nobody else. –Karch

Morning: Deut 25; Ps 116 — *Evening:* Isa 52; Rev 22

171

FROM VICTORY

"For everyone who has been born of God overcomes the world. And this is the victory that has overcome the world—our faith."
1 JOHN 5:4

Have you ever felt like giving up, just throwing your hands up in the air and saying, "I quit. I'm tired of fighting. Why am I trying so hard and believing in God so much when life just does not seem to work? Every time things start looking up and life seems to be coming together, something happens and I am right back down, flat on my back, wondering what just hit me. So, what's the use trying? The *old life* was so much easier." I have felt like this many times.

The Christian life gets hard, especially in prison when very few things go our way. It often gets very frustrating because we needlessly try to fight a battle that has already been won. We rely on our own strengths, our own fortitude, or our own determination to overcome the world that is against us. And when we are not successful, we want to give up. However, we must understand that what sustains us is not our power or anything of our doing. It is the faith that God had given us. A faith that says, "No matter what, I will not give up because the battle has already been won."

On the cross, Jesus said, "It is finished" (John 19:30). That's it. He won the victory over sin and death and overcame the world. Consequently, as believers in Christ, we cannot be defeated because we do not fight *for* victory but *from* victory—a victory that has been given to us by our faith in Christ. So when the battle gets hard, and it will, don't give up. Let the faith God has given you overcome the world. –Solley

Morning: Deut 26; Ps 117, 118 — *Evening:* Isa 53; Matt 1

KORSAKOFF'S SYNDROME

"They forgot his works and the wonders that he had shown them."
PSALM 78:11

Korsakoff's syndrome is a condition, induced by severe alcoholism, which causes people to lose their memory. In extreme cases, people lose the most basic elements of memory to where they cannot identify things they have known all of their lives. For instance, a man may remember the word *hat* and the word *wife,* but his memory fails him to the point to where he cannot differentiate between his hat and his wife. This is the image we get from the psalmist as he recounts the faithfulness of God from generations past. He bemoans how Israel forgot God's works and miracles through which He had demonstrated His faithfulness throughout history.

Think about the relevance of this passage for us today. How often do we display signs of Korsakoff's Syndrome when it comes to remembering the deeds that God has done in our lives, not to mention the towering miracle of saving us from destruction? Too many times, we catch ourselves wondering where God is at work in our lives. In some instances, we question if He is even at work at all in our lives. We feel abandoned, isolated, and alone. The psalmist says the Israelites could not see where God was at work in their lives, and they forgot His works altogether. Just like the Israelites, we too forget the faithfulness of God.

If you find yourself in one of those inevitable places in your spiritual development where you cannot quite discern where and how God is at work in your life, think about how He has been faithful in the past. Hear the admonition of the psalmist, and do not forget who God is and what He has accomplished for you already through the person and work of our Lord Jesus Christ. –Karch

Morning: Deut 27, 28:1–19; Ps 119:1–24 — *Evening:* Isa 54; Matt 2

GENIE IN A BOTTLE

*"Whatever you ask in my name, this I will do, that
the Father may be glorified in the Son."*
JOHN 14:13

A puff of smoke, dazzling lights, and a turban wearing genie: Is this what we expect whenever we read a passage like John 14:13? So often we hear God's will is for us to be prosperous and to be financially well-off. To have all the finer things in life and cater to our own self-centered desires is usually the meaning we force into a text like this, but are we correct?

In this passage, Jesus had been dialoguing with His disciples and explaining His connection to the Father. He chided Philip for asking to see the Father in order to validate his faith. Jesus emphasized that His words and deeds were not His but those of the Father. He tells them that the works He'd been doing were all according to God's will and thus speak for themselves. He explained that those who believe in Him will do works similar, if not greater.

So is Jesus really telling His disciples that they can ask for whatever they want and He will give it to them? Of course not, He's telling them that by believing in Him they, too, will be carrying on the works of the Father so that the Father may be glorified in the Son. Then, as though anticipating their next question, He tells His disciples of the Helper He's going to send them to accomplish all of this. Jesus didn't give them a magic lamp to obtain selfish objectives; He gave them a guideline to follow for doing the Father's will.

Too often we doubt our faith because we treat God like a genie in a bottle and our prayers go unrealized. Maybe it's time to start seeking His will and looking to do work for His kingdom. –Blevins

Morning: Deut 28:20–68; Ps 119:25–48 — *Evening:* Isa 55; Matt 3

BE OF GOOD SENSE

*"Good sense makes one slow to anger, and it
is his glory to overlook an offense."*
PROVERBS 19:11

Anger and violence are familiar to the majority of us. No matter how passive we may seem at times, when we feel the slightest offense toward us, we often lash out in anger. We make the other person "pay" for the perceived disrespect. Our pride will allow no offense to go unchallenged or unpunished, no matter how minor it might be. Inside these walls, anyone that overlooks an offense is often looked upon as weak, even though he is far from it.

However, Proverbs 19:11 teaches us that good sense makes one slow to anger, and it is a person's glory to overlook an offense. The unspoken part of this proverb is that only a fool is quick to anger and unwilling to overlook an offense. When we react in anger and violence to the slightest perceived disrespect, we are essentially telling those around us that we lack good sense and are controlled by our emotions and what others think about us. Yet, prudence, insight, understanding—good sense—changes a formerly quick temper to one slow to anger. Even when you do not necessarily have to overlook the offense, you now have the choice to overlook it in a responsible and mature manner.

The next time you feel disrespected or offended, remember the proverb discussed here. When you seek to protect some misguided sense of honor or status inside these walls by responding in anger to the slightest offense, you lose the most. It just makes good sense to be slow to anger and to handle every situation you face in the appropriate manner. So, be of good sense. –Solley

Morning: Deut 29; Ps 119:49–72 — *Evening:* Isa 56; Matt 4

BABYLON

*"O you who dwell by many waters, rich in treasures, your end
has come; the thread of your life is cut. The LORD of hosts has
sworn by himself: Surely I will fill you with men, as many as
locusts, and they shall raise the shout of victory over you."*
JEREMIAH 51:13–14

In Jeremiah's day, Babylon was an empire that devoured people. It
was being used as God's instrument to punish a disobedient people. As an instrument of God's wrath it served to enslave people from
many different nations, to destroy families and heritages with no regard for anyone. Yet, inasmuch as Babylon did serve in this capacity,
once it had served its purpose, it would no longer be needed as God's
instrument of judgment for His people. Much the same can be said
for the institution of the penitentiary in America today. It can be said
that these institutions serve as instruments of God in a similar capacity.

In light of the words of God to Jeremiah, here we see how God has
cut the life of the great empire. In doing so, He will first fill Babylon
with men. With rising prison populations throughout the world, we
can easily see the correlation between Babylon and the modern day
prison system. As prisons are being filled, we can begin to understand
this as a preparation of its coming end—its thread of life preparing to
be severed. Once people inside prisons turn to God, we too can raise
a shout of victory as the purpose of the prison will have run its course,
and prison will no longer be needed.

This victory, however, is gained only in the cross of Jesus Christ.
In trusting Him, our lives necessarily are transformed; so there is no
longer a need for us to be housed in such conditions. We will attain a
freedom that transcends all walls and fences. –Karch

Morning: Deut 30; Ps 119:73–96 — *Evening:* Isa 57; Matt 5

THE HEART OF THE KING

*"Blessed be the LORD, the God of our fathers, who put
such a thing as this into the heart of the king, to beautify
the house of the LORD that is in Jerusalem."*
Ezra 7:27

O ne of the most common prayers I hear from fellow inmates is
the plea to go home. They want out of prison and fully believe
God is going to perform some miracle to make it so. They often cite
such miraculous interventions as Peter's release from prison in Acts 12
or Paul and Silas' supernatural release in Acts 16.

However, while busy sitting back hoping for a miracle, these individuals just might miss what God is really doing. In the Old Testament,
whenever God moved to bring His people out of exile, He did so by
moving the heart of the king. Most people are familiar with the story
of Moses and Pharaoh, but God also moved on behalf of His people
during the Babylonian captivity. After the appointed time of exile, God
moved on the heart of Cyrus, King of Persia, to issue a decree for the
Israelites' release. Later, the heart of Darius was moved by God to complete the rebuilding of the temple.

The next time you catch yourself praying for an angel to come and
open your cell door, or an earthquake to bring down the walls of the
prison, remember, "The king's heart is a stream of water in the hand
of the LORD; he turns it wherever he will" (Prov 21:1). Don't overlook
other ways God may be working. Instead, start praying for God's will
to be enacted in the hearts of those in authority. Perhaps that's the
miracle you've been searching for all along. –Blevins

Morning: Deut 31; Ps 119:97–120 — *Evening:* Isa 58; Matt 6

A NEW WAY

"There is a way that seems right to a man,
but its end is the way to death."
PROVERBS 14:12

As prisoners, we have walked down many different paths in life that seemed right to us but only ended up in death. Some led to physical death, but all led to eternal death. Because of the lives we have lived, we often look back on our pasts with many regrets. We have wasted many years following ways of life that seemed right to us at one point, but in the end, only brought us misery and sorrow. Along this misguided way, we have seen our friends die and many lives destroyed, and we have hurt the ones we love the most—our families.

The prices we eventually pay for our actions, no matter how right they seem, are eternal. We cannot escape the consequences. But in His love, God provided us a new way, an eternal way. He provided His son, Jesus (John 3:16). Jesus is the way, the truth, and the life (John 14:6). He came to seek and save those who were lost and held captive by ways which seem right but end in death (Luke 19:10). Because of His death, we have been set free from the chains of our pasts that hold us in bondage and fill us with deep regret and sorrow. Our feet have been set on a new path, a path that ends in eternal life.

If you look back on the roads you have traveled with deep regret, and you seek a better way, an eternal way, God will set you free today. He will put your feet on the path that ends in eternal life, the path of His son, Jesus. All you have to do is trust in Him. –Solley

Morning: Deut 32; Ps 119:121–144 — *Evening:* Isa 59; Matt 7

SUPERMAN

*"No, in all these things we are more than
conquerors through him who loved us."*
ROMANS 8:37

In 1901 the German philosopher Fredrich Nietzsche died. Ironically, he spent the final years of his life under the constant supervision of his mother and sister because he was mentally incapacitated. It is fascinating how such a brilliant individual ended up as a raving madman. I've often wondered what brought about the cause of his mental breakdown. Some biographers say he had contracted Syphilis, while others attribute his illness to a brain tumor. Then, there are some who see something deeper and more subtle that contributed to his insanity.

Throughout Nietzsche's philosophy, he promoted the idea of a will to power. He built this idea on the concept of a Superman (*Übermensch*, or "Overman"). He struggled to identify social and philosophical conditions which lead men to weakness. In his mind, the main culprit for this weakening of mankind was Christianity. However, centuries before Nietzsche, the Apostle Paul informed Christians in Rome that they were more than conquerors through Christ. It is fascinating that in both Greek and in Latin, it is a single word which signifies those in Christ as being the "conquerors of all conquerors." In Christ we are the supermen Nietzsche longed for.

Underneath Nietzsche's madness was a bankrupt philosophy, an empty worldview that could not sustain a complete vision for the totality of life. Because of it, he went crazy. Christ, on the other hand, has given us a platform both positionally and practically from which we exist as conquerors. As you come to Him today, ask Him to renew your vision of what He has made you to be and to re-centralize your appreciation for what He has done for you in making you more than a conqueror. –Karch

Morning: Deut 33, 34; Ps 119:145–176 — *Evening:* Isa 60; Matt 8

BE WATCHFUL

"Be sober-minded; be watchful. Your adversary the devil prowls
around like a roaring lion, seeking someone to devour."
1 PETER 5:8

Being incarcerated teaches you one thing really quick—be aware of your surroundings! When we arrive on a new unit or walk on a new cell block, the first thing we do is take stock of our surroundings and identify those we automatically register in our minds as predators—those who will devour us if we allow them. This process is instinctual. We do not have to think about it; we do it naturally out of self-preservation.

Just as we are instinctively aware of the physical predators around us, we must also be aware of the spiritual predators around us—the hidden enemy who does not want to see us succeed in our Christian walk. This is why Peter instructs us to be watchful, because the devil prowls around like a roaring lion, seeking whom he may devour. That's you and me! If we let our spiritual guard down, the devil will pounce on us and destroy us. And, as most predators do, he will wait until your weakest moments, when you are all alone, and hit you in the spot that hurts the most. Yet, we are not defenseless against the spiritual enemy. We are given the ultimate weapon to defeat Satan—our faith in Christ (v. 9). Our faith ensures us that we, too, ultimately have the victory in and through Christ's defeat of Satan on the cross.

As Christians, we must never underestimate the spiritual battle we are in and grow complacent in our faith. We must continuously be watchful, knowing that we have an unseen enemy who will devour us at the first opportunity we give him. –Solley

Morning: Josh 1; Ps 120, 121, 122 — *Evening:* Isa 61; Matt 9

ETHNICITY

*"Now this I say and testify in the Lord, that you must no longer
walk as the Gentiles do, in the futility of their minds."*
EPHESIANS 4:17

C hristians are no longer to walk the way they used to or to identify with the things they did as unbelievers. Thus, in Paul's mind, there is a before and after—an old and new—when it comes to how a person walks before they become a Christian and after they become a Christian. As Christians, there is a line of demarcation drawn across our entire lives that sets us apart from the lives we once lived and distinguishes how we used to walk from how we walk today as believers in Christ.

The word translated as Gentiles comes from the Greek word *ethne*. It is where we get our English word "ethnic." The connotations cover a lot of ground. It deals with a group of people who have common customs, characteristics, language, and the like. In our old lives—the time before we were Christians—we had many things in common with unbelievers. Yet, as Christians, this ought not to be the case. We should be distinguished from the ethnic group of unbelievers and be identified with the ethnic group of believers.

There are many ways in which the world encourages us to be ethnically identified with some group of people. The world encourages us that this is the way it ought to be. In one sense, the world is right, but as always, the world twists it. Our ethnicity ought to be in Christ. We should identify with Him and those who have been saved by Him. This is our Christian ethnicity, and whatever we identified with prior to our salvation no longer has bearing on our lives. We can no longer walk as the world does. –Karch

Morning: Josh 2; Ps 123, 124, 125 — *Evening*: Isa 62; Matt 10

BUT GOD!

*"but God shows his love for us in that while we
were still sinners, Christ died for us."*
ROMANS 5:8

T he prevailing worldly wisdom will tell you that if somebody
wrongs you, the right thing to do is to wrong them back. Most of
us in prison understand that sense of justice: an eye for an eye, a tooth
for a tooth. We're taught, unless you stand up for yourself, other folks
are going to walk all over you. Forgiveness is a foreign concept to most
of us doing time.

However, for those of us who've been redeemed, forgiveness is
to be the *modus operandi.* Our heavenly Father has demonstrated His
love for us by sending Jesus to die for our sins, but the truly remarkable thing is He did it while we were still sinners. We were all, at one
time, hostile to the Creator of heaven and earth, but God in His infinite loving-kindness had mercy on His lost children. Jesus provides
detailed instruction regarding our treatment of our fellow man when
we're assaulted: "But I say to you, Do not resist the one who is evil. But
if anyone slaps you on the right cheek, turn to him the other also"
(Matt 5:39).

One of the hardest things we will ever have to do as Christians is
love our enemies. Part of loving them entails forgiving them of their
transgressions against us. The next time a situation arises and you want
to give somebody exactly what they deserve, remember you were once
a sinner headed for destruction—but God! –Blevins

Morning: Josh 3; Ps 126,127, 128 — *Evening:* Isa 63; Matt 11

GLORIOUS DAY

*"He will wipe away every tear from their eyes, and death shall
be no more, neither shall there be mourning, nor crying, nor
pain anymore, for the former things have passed away."*
REVELATION 21:4

I heard a man speak recently about growing up with a very physically
abusive father. He talked about times when he and his younger
brother would lie in bed together at night in their small 10-foot by
10-foot room, listening through the thin walls to their drunken father
beat their mother. His younger brother would take comfort in his arms,
crying over and over, "When is this going to end?" The only answer he
could give his brother was, "Someday. I promise you, someday."

Like this man's little brother, many of us asked ourselves the same
question when we go through the heartaches and difficulties of life:
When is this going to end? And many times, the answer seems elusive.
All we can tell ourselves is, "Someday. I promise, someday."

Unfortunately, the pains of life do not go away. They lessen but
never end. Because of the fallen world we live in, pain, sorrow, mourning, crying, and even death are factors of everyday life. Sometimes, we
have no choice but to share in those things. However, God does promise that someday all of the heartaches we experience living in a fallen
world will pass away. Someday, He will wipe away every tear from our
eyes, death shall be no more, neither shall there be any mourning, crying or pain. On that day, children no longer will be listening to their
fathers beating their mothers, wondering, "When is this going to end?"

I do not know about you, but I look forward to that day. Oh, what
a glorious day that will be! –Solley

Morning: Josh 4; Ps 129, 130, 131 — *Evening:* Isa 64; Matt 12

JULY 3

IF NOT TODAY, FOR SURE TOMORROW

> *"I wait for your salvation, O LORD."*
> GENESIS 49:18

Years ago there was an old man on the unit I was on whom everyone mocked. We would always ask him: "When you going home, Old School?" He never missed a beat: "If not today, for sure tomorrow." Nobody knew how long he had been down or how much time he had, but we all thought that he was a little crazy. However, there was also something strangely real about him—there was a confident expectancy in him when he said those words. He acted as if he knew something the rest of us did not. Likewise, Jacob was an old man when he spoke the words of our text. Shortly after he blessed Joseph's sons, far from his homeland, he died. Yet, he had a confident expectancy of the Lord's blessing on him and his family.

As I remember the old guy from my unit, his expectancy was something none of us who mocked him had. However, now that I am a Christian, I can understand that type of expectancy a little better. Still, our waiting on the Lord for His salvation and deliverance is sometimes riddled with anxiety, panic, or despair. We know what it's like to wait for mail, a long expected visit, or a parole date or answer. We also know just how fickle those hopes can be. Yet, the capabilities of our God far transcend any of that.

As we ask the Lord to deliver us from strongholds or to restore shattered relationships—whatever the case may be—let us express the same confident expectancy as Jacob and Old School had while we wait on the salvation of the Lord. For if it's not today, then it's for sure tomorrow. –Karch

Morning: Josh 5, 6:1–5; Ps 132, 133, 134 — *Evening:* Isa 65; Matt 13

FREED!

*"To him who loves us and has freed us from our sins by his
blood and made us a kingdom, priests to his God and Father,
to him be glory and dominion forever and ever. Amen."*
REVELATION 1:5B–6

July Fourth is the day when the entire country celebrates its independence from British rule. It is a day when fireworks are set off and colonial reenactments are produced in force to help us remember we are free from imperialist oppression. Countless crowds huddle together to watch the "bombs bursting in air," commemorating our country's liberation from foreign authority. What a sight to see.

All those festivities seem to lose their luster, however, once you've experienced a Fourth of July behind bars. Gone are the colorful explosions and ponderous parades; now it's prison whites and a sweltering chow hall. The celebration of the freedom of our country doesn't evoke the same response when we've given up our personal freedom, but, oh, what a gracious God we serve!

While our nation's freedom from tyranny is a good thing, our freedom from sin is so much better. The best freedom came at the highest price, and it was paid for by the precious blood of our Lord Jesus. He has redeemed us and freed us from the tyranny of Satan and made us a kingdom of priests to God the Father. So, this year, instead of treating the Fourth of July like just another irrelevant holiday behind bars, rejoice in the freedom you have in Christ. May to Him be the glory and dominion forever and ever. –Blevins

Morning: Josh 6:6–27; Ps 135, 136 — *Evening:* Isa 66; Matt 14

BE STILL

"Be still, and know that I am God."
PSALM 46:10A

I have spent many years fighting my conviction. As a *pro se* petitioner,
doing it myself, I have felt like I am up against a gigantic legal system of trained lawyers and judges with absolutely no help at all. When
things did not go as I prayed or I received a negative response from
the courts, I would get stressed and worried and immediately fire off
some type of rebuttal in hopes it would be read. I was obsessed! All I
could think about was that I had to get my conviction overturned. A
reversal was the only way my wife would be okay; I could be a father
to my daughter, and we could have a normal life. It was the only way
I could fix what I had broken. Then it dawned on me one day: all of
my stress and worry demonstrated a lack of trust in God. I was so busy
being busy that I had forgotten who was ultimately in charge of my life
and my circumstances.

Being still when you want to do something is never easy. However,
because we are incarcerated and face situations beyond our control,
we tend to stress and worry. Yet, it is during these times that we must
be still and trust in God. This surrender does not necessarily mean
everything will work out in our favor; but rather, that no matter the
circumstances or the outcome, we trust that God will work all things
out for the good for those who love Him and are called according of
His purpose (Rom 8:28).

When you find yourself stressing or worrying over something beyond your control, don't panic; and don't become obsessed. Simply be
still, and let the Lord take care of it. It is so much easier. –Solley

Morning: Josh 7; Ps 137, 138 — *Evening:* Jer 1; Matt 15

GONE CRAZY

"For if we are beside ourselves, it is for God; . . ."
2 CORINTHIANS 5:13

A fter my conversion to Christ, people who had previously known me thought I had gone, or, at the very least, was going crazy. I changed radically. This is a stereotypical image ascribed to most committed Christians in prison. The lifestyles many of us once embraced were diametrically opposed to Christianity. When we are being conformed to the image of Christ, we stick out and are somewhat at odds with the cultural norms. However, this is not a unique experience to those of us inside prison. The apostle Paul knew it well, also.

The Greek word that is translated "beside ourselves" literally carries the idea of being out of your mind, being mad, or crazy. As false teachers and unbelievers accused Paul of being crazy, he basically tells the Corinthian church, "So what? If we are crazy, it is for God. They can think what they will—we are who we are by the grace of God—crazy or not." While those around us continue to see the cross as foolishness, it is likely they will count us as fools for Christ and think we are crazy.

Paul's own life shows us there will be times when we will feel ostracized from others because of our stance for Christ; or, we may feel a little crazy because we are now so different than everybody else around us. Nevertheless, when standing for Christ over and against the cultural norms of prison life, remember that Paul says, "If we are [crazy], it is for God." I can think of no better reason to be crazy than for God. –Karch

Morning: Josh 8; Ps 139 — *Evening:* Jer 2; Matt 16

AMAZING GRACE

"But God, being rich in mercy, because of the great love with which
he loved us, even when we were dead in our trespasses, made us
alive together with Christ—by grace you have been saved."
EPHESIANS 2:4–5

O n March 21, 1748, a slave trader named John Newton awakened in the middle of the night only to discover that the ship he traveled on was caught in a horrific North Atlantic storm. One man had been washed overboard, and everyone else on the ship feared the same fate. In the midst of the driving rain, crashing waves, and pounding seas, Newton found himself uttering a prayer to God for mercy. When his ship safely reached the coast of Ireland, John Newton's life was changed. Years later, John Newton, the *former* slave trader, published "Amazing Grace," one of the most well-known and heartfelt Christian hymns of all time.

Like many people in prison, John Newton had a very disturbing and troubled past. Yet, the lyrics to the hymn, "Amazing Grace," reveal John Newton's understanding that even though the things he had done in his past were wretched, God's loving grace surpassed them all. This is why he could so confidently pen the words, "Amazing grace, how sweet the sound that saved a wretch like me. I once was lost but now I'm found, was blind but now I see."

Yes, our pasts are far from perfect; but even when we were dead in our trespasses and sin, God, being rich in mercy, offered us grace. I believe that is why, as people with troubled pasts, we appreciate the gift of His grace all the more. Like Newton, we know where God has brought us from and who we once were. It is by God's amazing grace alone that we have been saved. –Solley

Morning: Josh 9; Ps 140, 141 — *Evening:* Jer 3; Matt 17

EYE TO EYE

"Do two walk together, unless they have agreed to meet?"
AMOS 3:3

Have you ever tried to live or work with someone you simply could not get along with? If so, then you know how even the most friendly conversations can revert to some form of disagreement. No matter how hard you try, situations like this simply do not seem to work.

The prophet Amos lists several rhetorical questions, all of which have "no" as the implied answer. Amos' questions are in reference to Israel's relationship with the Lord. We know the Lord will not look upon or be in agreement with sin. We are, therefore, at definite odds with God. As conflict was the condition of Israel's relationship with the Lord, it is also descriptive of the relationship we have with God as sinners. Relationally speaking, we are in a situation that can never work—we can never walk in agreement with God, given our condition as sinners. Nor can we see eye to eye with God. The good news is we have a mediator in Jesus, through whom we have agreement with God. Now we can walk with the Lord in agreement and harmony. Because of Jesus' sacrifice on the cross, our relationship with Him is reestablished. As a result, now that we have a right relationship with God, we are also called to have a right relationship with one another.

Remember what has been accomplished for you in Jesus' sacrifice and how He has made you to be in a right relationship with the Lord. As you do so, think of a brother or sister with whom you often find yourself at odds and make a sincere effort to reconcile a right relationship with that person. A right relationship with the Lord calls us to make that effort. Because of our relationship with Him, we are called to see eye to eye with others (Rom 12:18). –Karch

Morning: Josh 10; Ps 142, 143 — *Evening:* Jer 4; Matt 18

MOVING FORWARD

*"I press on toward the goal for the prize of the
upward call of God in Christ Jesus."*
PHILIPPIANS 3:14

Reflecting back on past mistakes in order to avoid them again is helpful. Our contemplating old decisions that went awry so as not to repeat them is a huge part of learning and growing. But there comes a time in everyone's life when you have to stop looking back and move forward, a time when you have to actually put to use what you have learned and push toward the goal in front of you.

We face challenges daily, and walking according to God's Word makes those challenges no easier. The difference is, not only do we have a new objective, we have a Helper as well. From the moment God grabbed ahold of you, He set before you a higher calling, but He also provided the means to get there. We are not running this race alone. We no longer have to fret or worry about the difficulty of the challenges we face because "the sufferings of this present time are not worth comparing with the glory that is to be revealed to us" (Rom 8:18).

I've never seen a race where the runners were constantly looking back over their shoulders. They may take a quick glance, but their focus is on the finish line. We too are racing toward a goal, so keep your head up, eyes forward and press on. –Blevins

Morning: Josh 11; Ps 144 — *Evening:* Jer 5; Matt 19

GOD'S STRENGTH

*". . . I have learned the secret of facing plenty and hunger, abundance
and need. I can do all things through him who strengthens me."*
PHILIPPIANS 4:12B–13

T he apostle Paul faced many obstacles in his endeavor to spread the
gospel of Jesus Christ. He was beaten, imprisoned, shipwrecked,
and abandoned by friends. Yet, through it all, Paul stayed true to the
calling God set before him. This endurance was not because he was so
tough he could face anything that came his way. It was because Paul
discovered a secret: no matter the situation or circumstance he faced,
he could do all things through Christ who strengthened him. Paul
understood that relying on his abilities was useless. He knew the only
way he would make it was by relying on God for the strength needed
to see him through.

As prisoners, we often experience times when we doubt we can
make it. We grow weary of living inside these walls, of never hearing
from home, of hoping and praying for parole, only to be shot down
time and time again. Eventually, the hardships of prison take their toll
on us, and we simply want to give up and turn back to our old ways of
life. Yet, just as Paul discovered long ago, when we feel this way, we are
not helpless or hopeless. We can face these trying times head on when
we learn to lean on God's strength and not our own.

When times get rough and you feel like you cannot make it one
more day, remember the secret Paul shared with the church at Philippi:
"I can do all things through Christ who strengthens me." –Solley

Morning: Josh 12, 13; Ps 145 — *Evening:* Jer 6; Matt 20

ALL THE TIME

"Have I not commanded you? Be strong and courageous.
Do not be frightened, and do not be dismayed, for the
LORD your God is with you wherever you go. "
JOSHUA 1:9

J oshua received his commission on the plains of Moab to lead Israel
into the Promised Land. Anyone, no matter how skilled in leader-
ship, would have considered such commission a daunting responsibility. For that reason, God addressed those reservations and commanded
Joshua to be strong and courageous.

I recall the naysayers when I was accepted to a brand new seminary
program inside prison. People tried discouraging me from going because the school was located on a unit that had a longstanding reputation for being a very dark and violent place. I was often confronted
with the question: Why would anybody want to go there? Truthfully, I
didn't want to go to that unit, but I did want to attend the school. By
virtue of being selected to go, I had the distinct impression that the
Lord had clearly called me to go. As I prepared myself for relocation,
these words the Lord spoke to Joshua became a very real comfort to
me. I knew that no matter what kind of unit the school was in, the Lord
would be with me while I was there.

These same sentiments may resonate with us for any number of
reasons—particularly if we are going to another institution or, more
importantly, if we are preparing to transition back into society. No matter what situations we are confronted with, or whatever reservations we
may have as believers, we can take comfort knowing that God is with us
all of the time. –Karch

Morning: Josh 14, 15; Ps 146, 147 — *Evening:* Jer 7; Matt 21

NO SUBSTITUTE, NO REPLACEMENT

*"I am the LORD, and there is no other, besides me there is
no God; I equip you, though you do not know me."*
Isaiah 45:5

Do you remember when you were in grade school and your teacher was sick? They didn't cancel class, but instead, called in a substitute teacher. What about when you were playing sports and one of the starters was injured, what did the coach do? He put in the back-up, the replacement. It seems like for most things in this world there's always an alternative or a back-up plan. However, as God is infinite and eternal, having no beginning and no end, He does not have a replacement. No one is like God.

The Israelites found that out the hard way. They kept trying their hardest to find a replacement for the Lord who brought them up out of the land of Egypt. Even with signs and wonders that left no doubt about God's power and might, subsequent generations lost sight of His uniqueness and loving care. They chased after foreign gods who weren't really gods at all but simply idols of false hope.

What about us? Do we not still try to put things in the place of God? Don't we tend to worship the creation rather that the Creator (Rom 1:25)? Aren't we constantly trying to substitute something else for the Almighty God? Even though God reveals Himself to us in so many ways, we are just like the ancient Israelites in that we quickly forget how gracious and good He has truly been to us. We continuously need to be reminded that God is real when all we have to do is open our eyes to see Him at work all around us. Think about it; there really is no substitution. So, open your eyes, and stop trying to replace the irreplaceable. –Blevins

Morning: Josh 16, 17; Ps 148 — *Evening:* Jer 8; Matt 22

LOVED BY THE FATHER

*"Jesus answered him, "If anyone loves me, he will keep
my word, and my Father will love him, and we will
come to him and make our home with him."*
JOHN 14:23

Many people incarcerated, including myself, have one thing
in common, we lacked one of the most important factors for
healthy childhood development—we lacked active, loving fathers. We
were forced to grow up without our father or with a father who was
present but dysfunctional. As a result, we never knew what it felt like
to be loved and cherished by our father, and we never experienced
the security of knowing our father was there when we needed him.
Consequently, we grew up to be dysfunctional adults who still needed
to be loved by a father.

The lack of experiencing the real love of a father is why I am always
amazed by the depths of the relationship Christ has with the Father
when I read John 14–17. Christ intimately refers to God as Father almost fifty times in four chapters. Obviously, Christ has no doubt that
he is loved by His Father and He rests in the security of that love. Yet,
the most awesome thing is that we also can enjoy the same relationship
with the Father that Christ has. Christ Himself assures us that we are
loved by the father just as He is (John 14:21, 23; 16:27). Therefore,
we no longer have to long for the love of a father we never had as
children.

As children of God, we have a Father who loves and cherishes us
like no earthly father can. Let us always take comfort in the security of
that love—a love nothing can separate us from (Rom 8:35–39). –Solley

Morning: Josh 18, 19; Ps 149, 150 — *Evening:* Jer 9; Matt 23

EVERY STEP OF THE WAY

"When you pass through the waters, I will be with you; and through the rivers, they shall not overwhelm you; when you walk through fire you shall not be burned, and the flame shall not consume you."
ISAIAH 43:2

I saiah explains to the Israelites, not if, but when they pass through the waters and when they walk through fire, they will be all right because the Lord will be with them. Prison life possesses the possibility for a myriad of floods and fires and yet we have the same promise that the Lord will be with us as we go through them.

Several years ago, two of the most important people in my life left. While these were separate instances, they happened within two weeks of each other; and I have seen neither of these loved ones since. Serving a life sentence is difficult enough; and as the years accumulate, the potential for those you love to fade away becomes an ever present reality. This is possibly the greatest fear those of us in prison have, seeing those we care about slowly vanishing from our lives. There is really no greater flood or fire we face. Yet, looking back on that time, I can see very distinct ways in which the Lord was present in the midst of it all. Even though it was emotionally painful and exhausting, the Lord brought me through, and He was with me every step of the way.

The floods and fires are bound to come, and you may even be experiencing one of them today. If so, know the Lord is with you. In the thick of things, we often find it difficult to discern exactly the ways in which He is present; but understand from Isaiah's words that He is there every step of the way. –Karch

Morning: Josh 20, 21; Acts 1 — *Evening:* Jer 10; Matt 24

POWER FROM ABOVE

"For this reason I bow my knees before the Father, . . . that
according to the riches of his glory he may grant you to be
strengthened with power through his Spirit in your inner being,"
EPHESIANS 3:14–16

One of the great exemplars of our faith was the apostle Paul, and one of the greatest things he modeled for us was prayer. Paul was never afraid to pray, and he was usually praying for others. But what was Paul usually praying about? What was the content of Paul's prayers?

In the book of Ephesians, we have a written account of a prayer Paul prayed for the believers in the fledgling church he'd started during his first missionary journey. In the prayer, Paul petitioned God to strengthen the Ephesian believers with power through His Spirit. Earlier in the letter, Paul described the power as the very same power by which God raised Jesus from the dead.

Imagine that for a second: Paul asked for the exact same power God used to resurrect Jesus from the grave to be used to strengthen the Ephesian believers. What an extraordinary petition! Paul knew the Christian life wouldn't be all roses, and there would be times when Christians would need supernatural help. Likewise, Paul was acutely aware of where that help would come from, and he wasn't shy about asking for it.

Sometimes we're going to go through some hard times. In fact, many of us are going through something right now. Nevertheless, like Paul, we can pray for our Father to bolster us with that unequivocal power from on high. –Blevins

Morning: Josh 22; Acts 2 — *Evening:* Jer 11; Matt 25

MISSIONARIES

"And He said to them, 'Go into all the world and
proclaim the gospel to the whole creation."
MARK 16:15

N ot long after I became a Christian, I began to read biogra-
phies on missionaries like David Livingstone, David Brainerd,
Adoniram Judson, and Henry Martyn. It is impossible to convey how
deeply the lives of those men influenced me. I wondered about God's
will in respect to their labors. I wondered why some of them lost their
loved ones to illnesses that were indigenous to the places where they
labored, and I wondered why some of them lost their own lives serving
people who were hostile and indifferent to the gospel of Christ. In the
same way, I wondered if it was God's will for us to labor here inside
prison as we live among people who need the Gospel.

It is the will of God for every Christian to participate in the Great
Commission, and prisons are not excluded from the scope of the commission. Thus, somebody must be in prison in order to labor here. Can
we view our incarceration as the vehicle through which we are missionaries for the cause of Christ even if it means laboring here for the rest
of our lives, and like Livingstone, not seeing much tangible fruit for
which we have labored? Can we say our hearts are for those in prison
who desperately need to see what real Christianity looks like?

While it may very well be God's will for some of us to labor in some
other field, the fact we are here now is a strong indicator that we have
work to do right here, right now. Before the Lord moves us to some
other field, we have been commissioned to work in this field while we
are here. Thank the Lord for that opportunity, and ask Him to show
you the work assignment He has for you, right where you are. –Karch

Morning: Josh 23; Acts 3 — *Evening:* Jer 12; Matt 26

PRAISE HER

*"Give her the fruit of her hands, and let her
works praise her in the gates."*
PROVERBS 31:31

A s the Day With Dad event drew to a close, the host went around
the room asking each father if they had anything to say. Father
after father thanked the chaplain, the volunteers, the warden, and the
unit staff. As I sat there holding my daughter and feeling all of my
love and pride for her, I could not help but think of her mother who
had done an amazing job raising our little girl on her own. Looking
around at the smiling faces of the other children there, I knew all of
them were being raised by women who were forced to pick up the
pieces and carry on with us fathers gone. It grieved my heart that while
thanking everyone, not one father cared enough to thank the mother
who was raising their child—alone.

Often, we get so caught up in the struggles of doing time that we
overlook the struggles of the ones in the free-world raising our children. We are quick to berate them when they do not write, bring our
children to see us as often as we would like, or send us money. Yet, how
often do we praise them for the wonderful job they are doing raising
our children? No matter what type of relationships we have with the
women raising our children, we owe them respect and gratitude for
not only doing their jobs, but for doing ours as well. Without them,
where would our children be?

As you think about your children, consider the mother raising them
alone. Thank God for her; and as the proverb instructs us, next time
you have contact with her, praise her for the work of her hands. –Solley

Morning: Josh 24; Acts 4 — *Evening:* Jer 13; Matt 27

SLICK

"Woe to those who are wise in their own eyes,
and shrewd in their own sight!"
ISAIAH 5:21

In the early chapters of Isaiah, the prophet describes the destruction of the Lord's vineyard and pronounces a series of woes against those who have been defying God. In prophetic literature the "woe" is a pronouncement of judgment. One of these woes is against those who see themselves as smarter than everyone else, those who believe they can run game so that nobody else knows what they are up to. Isaiah makes clear the Lord knows what's up and is always a step ahead of the weak games they play.

In the same way, many people inside prison pride themselves on having game or being slick. They see themselves as being smarter than those around them and believe they have more game than Milton Bradley or the Parker Brothers. Being in prison proves that many of us thought the same way to one degree or another in the past. In some instances, we see people who are posing as believers running this same style of game. They believe they are even wise enough to run game on the Lord. Isaiah pronounces a stern woe against those who are wise and cunning in their own eyes. They are not getting away with anything in the eyes of God and are actually subject to judgment.

While it is easy to see everybody else trying to be slick, it is difficult to see it in ourselves. As we see how this series of woes unfolds against God's people, we should take seriously the prophet's warning. It is always beneficial to examine our own lives to make sure we are being real with those around us, with ourselves, and with the Lord. In the long run, it does not pay to run game and try to be slick. –Karch

Morning: Judg 1; Acts 5 — *Evening:* Jer 14; Matt 28

NEVER TOO LATE

"But God chose what is foolish in the world to shame the wise;
God chose what is weak in the world to shame the strong."
1 CORINTHIANS 1:27

"I'm a drop out," were Annette's first words to us. She was pushing sixty, wore glasses, and looked as if life had not treated her kindly. Nonetheless, she had a smile that lit up the room and a precious heart for God. As she began talking, her story unfolded. In her early twenties, she lost a child in a horrific accident. Unable to deal with the pain, she turned to the bottle where she lost herself for three decades. She sank into her own living, alcoholic hell. At fifty, she found herself in a hospital bed on the brink of death. There, she cried out to God, telling Him that if He would let her live, she would spend the rest of her life serving Him—if it was not too late.

Annette has kept her promise. She is now the chaplain for Wharton County Jail and has worked in coordination with several ministries to open a 28,000 square-foot facility for runaway girls and pregnant teens. At fifty years old, her life became a living example of how God often takes the foolish things of the world to shame the wise, and the weak to shame the strong. God is now using Annette mightily for His honor and glory.

Maybe you have reached a point where you believe it's too late, that you have made such a mess of your life that God could never use you. Or maybe you feel you are too old and frail to be of any use to God. Let Annette's example be an encouragement to you. With God, it is never too late! –Solley

Morning: Judg 2; Acts 6 — *Evening:* Jer 15; Mark 1

EVEN IN THIS

"yet I will rejoice in the LORD; I will take
joy in the God of my salvation."
HABAKKUK 3:18

H uman nature is quite capricious. We're fickle with our loyalties and often let our unsatisfied selfish desires dictate who or what we place our faith in. We cry and whine when we don't get things our way, and once we do, we find something else to complain about. This seemingly never-ending cycle of discontent demoralizes us and greatly disheartens those who look to us for righteous living.

What exactly does God demand of us? Does He give us a free pass during tough times or when things don't work in our favor? Is your faith small or strong? Will your faith waver at the first sign of trouble? Paul encourages us to examine ourselves to see whether we are in the faith (2 Cor 13:5). Can your faith stand under the pressure of hard times? Will it crumble and fall apart when a strong wind blows?

Habakkuk witnessed some difficult times as the Babylonians came to conquer, destroy, and capture his people. Although they plundered and destroyed entire cities, Habakkuk soon realized after a short dialogue with God, that He was still sovereign. God was still in full control even in the face of adversity. Thus, Habakkuk rejoiced amidst all the turmoil and was able to take joy in the God of his salvation.

What about you? Will your faith stand strong during your incarceration? Will you praise Him even in this? –Blevins

Morning: Judg 3; Acts 7 — *Evening:* Jer 16; Mark 2

DON'T LOOK BACK

"Jesus said to Him, 'No one who puts his hand to the plow and looks back is fit for the kingdom of God.'"
LUKE 9:62

I was in the dayroom the other day, kicking back talking to a few guys; and like always, the conversation turned to the "old days." Before I knew it, I was talking about my past, the things I had done, the lifestyle I was once part of, and even the many years I had spent in solitary confinement. For over an hour, my past held me captive. I sat there reminiscing and glamorizing my sinful life—temporarily oblivious to the hurt I caused along the way. When the conversation ended, I walked back to my cell, mentally lost in the past. Yet, it was not long until the Holy Spirit reminded me of a vital aspect of being a follower of Christ: "No one who puts his hand to the plow and looks back is fit for the kingdom of God."

We all get caught up in our war stories, reminiscing about the past and glamorizing the lifestyles we once lived—destructive lifestyles from which Christ has redeemed us. We have put our hand to the plow but cannot see what is in front of us because we are too busy looking back. However, as followers of Christ, we must let go of the things in our pasts that hold our thoughts captive and allow our minds to become renewed by the Word of God (Rom 12:2), forgetting what is behind and straining forward to what God has ahead of us (Phil 3:13).

When you find yourself viewing the past through rose colored glasses, remember where Christ has brought you from and the truth behind the life you once lived. Remember that no one who puts his hand to the plow and looks back is fit for the kingdom of God. –Solley

Morning: Judg 4; Acts 8 — *Evening:* Jer 17; Mark 3

WEIRDOS

"Enter by the narrow gate. For the gate is wide and the way is easy that leads to destruction, and those who enter by it are many. For the gate is narrow and the way is hard that leads to life, and those who find it are few."
MATTHEW 7:13–14

T hose who stray from the beaten path are seen as weird. In the past, when Christianity dominated Western culture, those who differed from the norms of Christianity were seen as weird or strange. It was Nietzsche who condemned this attitude as the "herd mentality." He viewed people as being unable to break away from the constraints of what was normal. Today, the norms of society are not necessarily Christian. Western culture, as a whole, is more representative of the wide gate discussed in Matthew.

This is particularly true inside prisons. Those who follow Christ and walk through the narrow gate are looked at as weird. If a person does not get in where they fit in they become targeted for mockery or scorn. In many ways, being a Christian inside prison opens us up to being viewed in this way, and therefore, mocked or scorned for our attempts to be Christ-like. Unfortunately, for many of us, there were times in the past when we were the ones doing the mocking.

While it may create problems for us, those who have entered by the narrow gate, it is all right to be weird. So long as we are being weirdos for Christ, He is pleased with us for stepping outside the norms of the prison culture. Whatever ridicule or mockery comes our way, it is a passing thing; and we have the promise of being delivered from the destruction which awaits a world that refuses to be weird for Christ. Embrace the way that is hard and live for the Lord right where you are. –Karch

Morning: Judg 5; Acts 9 — *Evening:* Jer 18; Mark 4

SUPPORTING CAST

*"Who would listen to you in this matter? For as his share
is who goes down into the battle, so shall his share be
who stays by the baggage. They shall share alike."*
1 SAMUEL 30:24

The spotlight is a unique place, and not everyone is suited to be in it. Speaking to large crowds, preaching to a huge congregation, or giving TV or radio interviews is not something everyone is comfortable with or even passionate about doing. Whether it's in a more low-key ministry like writing or supporting another's ministry, some people employed in God's kingdom are better equipped to serve unnoticed behind the scenes.

Have you ever struggled to find your place or purpose in God's kingdom? Have you ever had difficulty figuring out exactly what God is calling you to do? The front-line offices of evangelism, preaching, or doing missionary work may not be what God has in store for your life. He may be calling you to a supporting role. For every evangelist or preacher or missionary, dozens of folks work behind the scenes to help them be as effective as possible. Even King David recognized the value of such people and refused to look down on their less glamorous work. He realized that in order for his men to be successful in battle, someone had to guard the equipment; someone had to support the troops.

God has a perfect place for each one of His children. Do not feel discouraged or inadequate because your calling does not garner as much attention as someone else's. Your place in God's glorious kingdom is just as important as the next man's. God loves us all equally, including the supporting cast! –Blevins

Morning: Judg 6; Acts 10 — *Evening:* Jer 19; Mark 5

THE DEVIL MADE ME DO IT!

"But each person is tempted when he is lured and enticed by his own desire. Then desire when it has conceived gives birth to sin . . ."
JAMES: 1:14–15

T he devil made me do it! How many times have you used those words? Or how many times have you tried to justify your actions by blaming someone else? I am guilty as charged. Been there, done that—many times. Blaming others to lessen our guilt is a natural reaction to sin. After partaking of the forbidden fruit in the Garden of Eden, Adam and Eve set the standard of blame. Adam blamed God, and Eve blamed the serpent (Gen 3:12–13). Likewise, we are quick to blame others, including the devil, when we stumble and fall.

Satan, and those working on his behalf, cannot make us sin. We sin when we are drawn away by our own natural desire and lust. When we give in to our own desire, we give birth to sin. And, as we all have experienced, sin is devastating. Sin abandons our children and destroys our homes, our marriages, and our lives. All we have to do is take a long look around us to see the effects of sin on our lives and on the lives of those we love. And the truth is, no matter how much we want to deny it, we are the only ones responsible.

Have you been blaming others for your mistakes—for your sin? Do you consider yourself a victim of circumstance? If so, decide today to take a closer look at your actions to determine who is really responsible. If you find that person is you, then confess the sin in your life. Allow God to forgive you and to set your feet on a path of healing and restoration. –Solley

Morning: Judg 7; Acts 11 — *Evening:* Jer 20; Mark 6

ON A MISSION

"And I heard the voice of the Lord saying, 'Whom shall I send,
and who will go for us?' Then I said, 'Here I am! Send me.'"
ISAIAH 6:8

T he vision of the Lord from Isaiah 6 is a well-known section of
   Scripture. However, it is often overlooked how, as Isaiah realized
his own sinfulness, he also realized the sinfulness of the people around
him. Isaiah understood that if the holiness of the Lord demands forgiveness and redemption, then those around him needed the Lord's
forgiveness and redemption, as well. The question for Isaiah became:
"Who will go and tell them?"

Far too often salvation inside prison is a private thing. As we meet
the Lord and understand the demands His holiness places on us as sinners, we realize our need for forgiveness and that redemption comes
only from Him. Once we receive forgiveness and redemption, we can
become somewhat isolated, or at the very least insulated, from those
who we come into contact with on a daily basis. As our need of Him
allows us to see the need of those around us, the question for us becomes: "Who will go and tell them?"

In your quiet time with the Lord today, ask the Lord if there is any-
one around you who needs to hear the redemptive message of Jesus
Christ. If the Lord brings someone to mind, respond like Isaiah: *Here
I am! Send me.* –Karch

Morning: Judg 8; Acts 12 — *Evening:* Jer 21; Mark 7

STRAPPED UP

"Put on the whole armor of God, that you may be
able to stand against the schemes of the devil."
EPHESIANS 6:11

I sat in the dentist chair listening to the soft elevator music in the background as I waited patiently for the dentist to make his way over to me. When my turn came, his assistant laid out all of the medical equipment piece by piece. She then turned her attention to her own safety. She quickly donned her apron, expertly snapped on her gloves, blindly tied her mask in place, and put her face shield on her head, then reached up and slapped it down into place. Then she looked at me, ready. She was now strapped up!

As I watched the dental assistant strapping up for battle with my stubborn tooth, I could hear Paul's words echoed in my mind: "Put on the whole armor of God." It was one of those moments when the Word of God comes to life right before your eyes, and you understand it in a way you never have before. Just as the dental assistant prepared herself for the battle ahead, we, too, must prepare ourselves for battle against our enemy. However, our armor is not merely a routine checklist we go through every day. Nor is it protective equipment we put on in the morning and take off at night. We are playing for keeps when we put on the belt of truth, the breastplate of righteousness, and the helmet of salvation, ready our feet with the gospel of peace, take up the shield of faith and the sword of the Spirit, and pray at all times in the Spirit. (Eph 6:14–18). Our armor becomes part of who we are as soldiers of Christ, and we never remove it for any reason. We stay strapped up and ready to stand against the enemy at all times.

So, how about you? Are you strapped up, or will you be caught unprepared by the enemy? –Solley

Morning: Judg 9; Acts 13 — *Evening:* Jer 22; Mark 8

SCHOOLED IN BAD

"Can . . . the leopard [change] his spots? Then also
you can do good who are accustomed to do evil."
JEREMIAH 13:23

A s Israel was threatened with exile, Jeremiah asked the rhetorical
question: *Can the leopard change his spots?* In the same way, those
who are accustomed to doing evil cannot amend their ways any more
than a leopard can change its spots. Those accustomed to doing evil
cannot just stop doing what they have been schooled to do.

The Hebrew word translated *accustomed to* literally means "trained
in" or "discipled." Because of sin, we have inherited a nature that is
schooled in bad. We are born sinners. Like the leopard who cannot
change his spots, we cannot stop doing wrong—we cannot change our
sinful nature. Nevertheless, we still have a responsibility toward God to
do what is right. So how do we do what is required of us if we are unable to do it? That is the beauty of what is offered to us by Jesus: what
we could not do for ourselves, He did for us. Now, because of what
Jesus has accomplished for us, there has been a fundamental change
in our schooling. We are now in the school of Christ.

In short, as believers in Jesus, we no longer have to be accustomed
to doing evil. In fact, the Holy Spirit within us precludes that old
schooling in bad so that, in Christ, we are able to live and act in a new
way. –Karch

Morning: Judg 10, 11:1–11; Acts 14 — *Evening:* Jer 23; Mark 9

LET THE WORLD KNOW

"I have not hidden your deliverance within my heart; I have spoken of your faithfulness and your salvation; I have not concealed your steadfast love and your faithfulness from the great congregation."
PSALM 40:10

Why is it so difficult to tell others about God? Our conversations will take on any subject from sports to politics; but when it comes to telling others about the most important thing in our lives, we clam up. God is relegated to the sidelines when we get around our friends and put on the back burner as soon as we hit the dayroom.

King David was not afraid to let his love for God show. Not only did he talk about God, he sang and danced in honor of Him in front of all Israel. David was not ashamed of the God who did so many wonderful miracles, not only in his own life, but in the life of Israel as well. David felt compelled by sheer gratitude to share what God revealed to him about Himself. God's righteousness, faithfulness, salvation, loving-kindness, and truth were the subjects of David's outpourings and praises.

How has God revealed Himself to you? Has He brought you through some tough times or been patient with you during your rebellious stages? Has He delivered you from bondage or broken down some unholy stronghold in your life? If we are truly honest with ourselves, there are endless reasons in our lives to praise God in front of others. He has revealed Himself to us countless times, through His Word and in our lives, that we can share with others.

The next time you find yourself entering into one of those humdrum conversations about the usual worldly things, try expressing to those around you the manifold goodness of the One who saved you. Try sharing your personal testimony of God's amazing grace. Let the world know who is number one in your life! –Blevins

Morning: Judg 11:12–40; Acts 15 — *Evening:* Jer 24; Mark 10

GOD

*"so that at the name of Jesus every knee should bow, in heaven
and on earth and under the earth, and every tongue confess
that Jesus Christ is Lord, to the glory of God the Father."*
PHILIPPIANS 2:10–11

There is a great deal of loose talk about God in contemporary society. This type of talk is particularly common within the context of prison. People easily make reference to God in the most blasphemous ways. Even those who have some level of reverence toward God often speak of Him only in very broad and general terms. Even Christians lack specificity when they speak about God and what He has done for them.

The apostle Paul affirms that in the end, all will acknowledge and worship Jesus Christ. All creation will bow to Him. In the end, those who speak of God in vain and those who have a sense of reverence toward Him, will all bow and worship Jesus Christ. Those who know Him will do so acknowledging their debt to Him for their salvation; while those who have rejected Him will do so acknowledging the justification of their own condemnation. With this understanding, it should shore up loose talk about God for the Christian. If we are to confess Jesus as Lord in the end, then we should also do so specifically today. All of our talk about God should be carried out with specific reference to Jesus Christ.

As you go through the day, pay attention to how people around you make reference to God, particularly other believers. In doing so, take the initiative to speak of God in reference to Jesus as Lord with the realization it clarifies our witness of Jesus and brings glory to the Father. –Karch

Morning: Judg 12; Acts 16 — *Evening:* Jer 25; Mark 11

THE MASTER'S TOUCH

"And God saw everything that he had made,
and behold, it was very good."
GENESIS 1:31A

S everal years ago, I was given the privilege of building a doll cradle for Toys for Tots.

Because I couldn't be there for my own daughter, I was determined to make some little girl's Christmas special. I painstakingly drew the designs, cut out each piece, and carefully put the cradle together. As a final touch, I painted the cradle pink and white, and scrolled *Princess* in fine print on both sides. When I finally stepped back to look at the finished product, I realized my hard work had paid off—the cradle was beautiful! I knew it would fulfill the purpose for which it was created: to put a smile on the face of an underprivileged child.

Building that cradle taught me a lot about God and even more about man. When I think about how satisfied I was upon completing that cradle, I am reminded that God felt the same way when He created man. The Master reached down, took the dust from the ground, and formed man. Then He put the final touch, the breath of life, into man and he became a living being (Gen 2:7). When God took a step back and saw all He had created, He said it was very good. God was pleased with His creation. He was pleased with us! He knew that man would fulfill the purpose for which he was created. And, as Paul tells us, we are God's workmanship, created in Jesus Christ for good works (Eph 2:10).

Today, think about that. You are created by the Master Builder, the Ultimate Designer, the Most Skilled Artisan. You are a pleasing product of the Master's touch. –Solley

Morning: Judg 13; Acts 17 — *Evening:* Jer 26; Mark 12

ALL OF A SUDDEN

*"And Hezekiah and all the people rejoiced because God had
provided for the people, for the thing came about suddenly."*
2 CHRONICLES 29:36

O nce Hezekiah had restored temple worship to the nation of
Israel after a long time of living under the rule of evil kings,
good things began to happen. However, the response of God to this
new obedience to His order of worship was far from reactionary. The
Chronicler tells us God had prepared those good things for the people. God having prepared what began to happen implies that those
things had been stored up by Him in anticipation of bringing them
about for His people. Most interesting, when those things God had
prepared began to happen, they happened *all of a sudden.*

As it was with Hezekiah and the Israelites, we too can believe the
Lord has things prepared for us as well. We do not serve a reactionary
God who is caught by surprise by our actions. He has things stored up
for us and anticipates the opportunity to pour them into our lives. As
we continue to serve Him, we should also anticipate the sudden in-
breaking of these blessings into our lives.

So, as you go about your day, continue to serve the Lord under
the order which He has designed—to worship Him in spirit and in
truth. When we do so, we begin to see clearly the promises He has for
those who belong to Him. In view of those things promised to us in the
Scriptures, we can begin living by faith in anticipation of them breaking into our lives all of a sudden. –Karch

Morning: Judg 14; Acts 18 — *Evening:* Jer 27; Mark 13

PATIENCE

*"Wait for the LORD; be strong, and let your
heart take courage; wait for the LORD!"*
PSALM 27:14

I f there is one thing prison has ingrained in me, it's patience. We have to wait for everything—chow, showers, medical, mail call, just to name a few. There's never an instance where patience isn't needed. Likewise, patience is the fruit by which the Holy Spirit allows us to handle the pain of difficult times calmly and without complaining. This wasn't always the case with me. I can remember having to develop patience—sometimes painfully. I eventually realized that being impatient took me nowhere fast and only left me frustrated and angry.

For many of us, time is more a foe than a friend. The days, months, and years can't come fast enough; and our sentences grow heavy. We repeatedly pray for God to let us out soon, but we continue to rage against the hands of the clock. Because our narrow focus is on the wasted years we have spent behind bars, our impatience only grows.

Godly patience, though, is often cultivated through the hardship of waiting for something you cannot rush. There is a cliché that says, "The best things in life come to those who wait." As a Christian, I would have to add that "The best life is yet to come!" We endure the waiting by knowing our patience is a direct result of God's sanctifying work within us. As the Lord reminds us through James 5:8, "the coming of the Lord is at hand." As we wait, we just need to have a little patience. –Blevins

Morning: Judg 15; Acts 19 — *Evening:* Jer 28; Mark 14

SENTENCED TO DEATH

*"Therefore, just as sin came into the world through
one man, and death through sin, and so death
spread to all men because all sinned—"*
ROMANS 5:12

I sat next to my lawyer, listening to the district attorney give her closing arguments during my trial for bank robbery. As she wound down, she paused to look every juror in the eye, then turned to me and said, "That's why I ask for life." *Life?* My heart dropped. I looked at my lawyer, and then turned to my wife and sister sitting in the audience several rows behind me.

"Life?" I was stunned. Though the jury did not return a verdict of life, the idea that I could have been sentenced to life still troubles me today.

We all know that heart sinking feeling: the feeling of being found guilty and facing long sentences for our crimes, sentences that seem too hard to bear. However, what many of us do not realize is that, as much as we fear the harsh punishments of the judicial system, our crimes against God carry only one penalty: death. Because of our sin, we have already been justly convicted and sentenced to die. And in God's court, there is no such thing as mitigating circumstances to alleviate the punishment we deserve. However, in Christ we have the perfect advocate, a lawyer as none other. He not only intercedes with the Father on our behalf, but took our sentence of death upon himself. Because of His love for us, He paid the penalty for our crimes. *He* died in *our* place.

Today, think about what this means. Meditate on what Christ has done for you. Because of Christ, your sentence of death has been commuted to everlasting life. –Solley

Morning: Judg 16; Acts 20 — *Evening:* Jer 29; Mark 15

PUT IT ON SOMETHING

"By myself I have sworn; from my mouth has gone out in righteousness a word that shall not return: 'To me every knee shall bow, every tongue shall swear allegiance.'"
ISAIAH 45:23

O ften in heated arguments, the determining factor settling some statement as true occurs when somebody steps up and says, "Put it on [something]." Somebody swears to the statement's truth by putting it on their skin, their set, their hood, their momma. The idea is that they are swearing by something higher or more important than themselves—something they would not tarnish with a lie.

In today's world, the human response toward God is that He must prove Himself. There seems to be an implicit challenge for God to substantiate His existence and His Word by putting it on something. Through Isaiah, the Lord God swears by Himself—there is nothing higher or more important to swear by. Nothing existed prior to Him and His existence and attributes cannot be tarnished because He cannot lie or deal falsely. God has spoken. The Word has gone out. He swears by *Himself* that every knee shall bow and every tongue shall swear allegiance.

All of us experience trying times when we find ourselves questioning how and when things will take a turn for the better. Inevitably, there will be times when we begin to ask the Lord when He will make things right and bring us to a place where we no longer have to endure the alienation and dehumanization of prison life. In those times, we can know in the face of it all that the Lord has put it on Himself. While people of the world continue to demand their proof, we have the confidence that the Lord has sworn by Himself, and there is no higher by which or by whom to swear. –Karch

Morning: Judg 17; Acts 21 — *Evening:* Jer 30, 31; Mark 16

REMEMBER ME

"And he said, 'Jesus, remember me when
you come into your kingdom.'"
LUKE 23:42

He hung there in agony, beaten and bloody, as the angry spectators looked on, viciously mocking and sneering. He leaned his head back, struggling for breath, as pain wracked his body. All was lost. Life was over, so why couldn't he just die? Once again his insane fall partner mocked the man hanging between them; he cringed as he heard the vile words. He could not believe he partnered up with this madman. Now they would both die for it. How could he have been so foolish? In rage and frustration and with all the strength he had left in his body, he screamed, "Do you not fear God . . . this man has done nothing wrong!" (Luke 23:40–41). His head fell to the side, and he looked into the kindest eyes he had ever seen: "Jesus," he whispered, "remember me when you come into your kingdom." Struggling for breath, Jesus answered, "[T]oday you will be with me in Paradise." The thief's eyes flared with hope.

I love that one of the first people to place their faith and trust in Jesus Christ was a thief—someone just like us. He was an outcast from society who lived a hard and destructive life, a criminal who had been tried, found guilty, and sentenced to death. Jesus' response to the thief on the cross should give us all hope. It should be a constant reminder that Jesus Christ came to save hopeless wrecks like us. And when all hope seems gone, Christ offers us His hope—just as He did to the thief on the cross.

Be assured that when Christ looks on you, He does not see your sins or the crimes you committed. Christ sees someone who has placed their faith and trust in Him, and He will remember you. –Solley

Morning: Judg 18; Acts 22 — *Evening:* Jer 32; Ps 1, 2

HEROES

*"Remember your leaders, those who spoke to you the word of God.
Consider the outcome of their way of life, and imitate their faith."*
HEBREWS 13:7

I once heard a preacher mention the importance of role models. He said we should find "heroes of the faith," our predecessors in the Christian faith whom we can study and from whom we can learn. The author of Hebrews encourages this same thing. We are to remember those who have gone before us in the faith, consider how their Christian life and faith has impacted the world around them, and imitate them.

Inside prison, it is difficult to find good role models because it is hard to find those who have established an actual outcome in a life of faith which we can emulate. Too often our role models tend to be epitomized in people who have no faith at all—such as movie stars, musicians, or professional athletes. We tend to imitate them as they capture the attention of the world. Realizing this, I took the preacher's advice and found a couple of men who have left lasting impressions on the world through their lives because of the outcome of their faith in Jesus Christ. As I studied their lives and writings they left behind, I see how I have been shaped by them. I understand I would not be who I am today without their influence in my life. This influence is something the author of Hebrews understood as well.

Who are your heroes? Who are the role models influencing and shaping you at present? Find one or two who have gone before you in the faith; remember them, and consider the outcome of their lives. Then learn from them, and imitate their faith with the same faith given to you by our Lord. –Karch

Morning: Judg 19; Acts 23 — *Evening:* Jer 33; Ps 3, 4

REST ASSURED

*"I know that you can do all things, and that
no purpose of yours can be thwarted."*
JOB 42:2

W e all must face obstacles in life. Nobody has been blessed with
a carefree existence. Trials and tribulations are commonplace,
especially considering we live in a fallen world. Some of these obstacles
occur for seemingly no reason while others, like our present situation,
are self-inflicted. Obstacles are excellent opportunities to rest in the
sovereignty of God. Knowing that He's in complete control reassures
us when our obstacles entice us to quit.

When Job went through his ordeal before God, he was confronted
by all kinds of negative advice. His friends who counseled him amidst
his troubles grossly misled him, and his own wife advised him to curse
God and die (Job 2:9). After a lengthy rebuke by the Creator of heav-
en and earth, Job repented; and God restored his fortunes. Lesson
learned.

How easy it is to forget that God runs the show. To think our earthly
well-being is somehow a result of chance or mere coincidence is a griev-
ous mistake. We take for granted the blessed life, but less fortunate times
drive us to confusion and despair. When we consider the wonderful sovereignty of God, we can breathe easy in times of trouble. We can take
comfort in His awesome power and goodness which serves to chase the
shadows of doubt from our hearts and minds. Be confident that God
has a perfect plan. He is bringing it to fruition even now. Take heart in
the midst of trouble, and know that our God is greater than our circumstances. Rest assured in His divine sovereignty. –Blevins

Morning: Judg 20; Acts 24 — *Evening:* Jer 34; Ps 5, 6

FORGIVENESS

"For if you forgive others their trespasses, your heavenly Father
will also forgive you, but if you do not forgive others their
trespasses, neither will your Father forgive your trespasses. "
MATTHEW 6:14

Have you ever been deeply hurt in life? Odds are you have. We all can close our eyes and think about a time when we felt betrayed, abandoned, or abused by someone close to us. And no matter how long ago the incident occurred, we still feel the lingering pain of and anger toward being treated the way we were, especially by someone we love. Many times, there is nothing more difficult in life than forgiving someone who has hurt you. We cringe when we hear the F-word: Forgiveness.

Forgiveness, however, is an essential part of being a follower of Christ. Our willingness to forgive others is not only a mark of our maturity as believers but is tied directly to God forgiving us. Jesus emphatically states we are to forgive others so that our Heavenly father will forgive us. Stated simply, when we do not forgive, we are not forgiven. One is reliant upon the other. Our forgiving others is conditioned upon God first forgiving us. By harboring unforgiveness in our hearts, we demonstrate that we have not been forgiven by God and are separated from a proper relationship with Him.

Forgiving is never easy. But as believers in Jesus, we are commanded to do so. So when you find yourself struggling to forgive someone for the wrong they have done to you, pray that God would forgive your unwillingness to forgive. –Solley

Morning: Judg 21; Acts 25 — *Evening:* Jer 35; Ps 7, 8

THE FIRST AND THE LAST

"When I saw him, I fell at his feet as though dead. But he laid his right hand on me, saying, 'Fear not, I am the first and the last,'"
REVELATION 1:17

As days turned into weeks and weeks into months, the Apostle John had little hope for relief from his situation. He had been sentenced as a prisoner of exile to the isle of Patmos under the tyranny of Rome. Yet, in the midst of being cast away from all he loved on that desolate rock, the glorified Christ revealed Himself to John in a special way. For centuries, this same revelation has lent to people the same comfort and hope that it did to John. History attests to how early martyrs in the first centuries of the Christian church went to their deaths reciting sections of the book of Revelation. It was not some mysterious and undecipherable jumble of prophecy but a clear and exalted picture of our Lord.

In the text, John finds himself prostrate before Jesus, whose glory had knocked John onto his face as though he were dead. The comforting words of Christ are stunning. Harkening back to Isaiah 44:6, Jesus says, "I am the first and I am the last"—language used only by God Himself. In the midst of John's terror, Jesus' assertion is one we would do well to ponder deeply. Jesus comforts John by telling him that, as all things begin in Him, they will also terminate in Him.

Those of us in prison have as much reason as John to be encouraged by Jesus' words—to know when things look bleak, Jesus is in control. Take time to think about Jesus' words today. He truly is the first and last of all things. –Karch

Morning: Ruth 1; Acts 26 — *Evening:* Jer 36, 45; Ps 9

SET YOUR MIND

*"For you are not setting your mind on the things
of God, but on the things of man."*
MATTHEW 16:23B

During His short earthly ministry, Jesus taught His disciples many things. An important principle He imparted to them was for them to set their mind on the things of God. Jesus reinforced this teaching while explaining to His disciples about His impending death and resurrection. However, Peter couldn't believe God's plan would include something so difficult. How could God send His sinless Son to die for the world's sin? I'm sure Peter was thinking something along the lines of, "Not fair!"

In prison, we often encounter things we believe are unfair. Undoubtedly, God has allowed you to have to do some things that were difficult to understand. Perhaps it involved being silent when you wanted to speak. Maybe it included sacrificing your time to help someone when your favorite show was on or even giving of your resources to fill another's need. Whatever it was, you were staring in the face of a common decision we all make daily: the decision to serve self or to serve God.

What Jesus told Peter then, and what applies to us today, is true. After a stern rebuke, Jesus instructed Peter to set his mind on God and His will. If Peter had it his way, we would all still be under God's wrath; but thankfully, Jesus had His mind set on doing the Father's will. When you are faced with a decision to either do God's will or serve your self-interests, set your mind on the things of God. –Blevins

Morning: Ruth 2; Acts 27 — *Evening:* Jer 37; Ps 10

NOT OF THIS WORLD

"They are not of the world, just as I am not of the world."
JOHN 17:16

I t is amazing how we can grow so accustomed to being incarcerated that life behind bars seems normal to us. When we were first incarcerated, everything was foreign to us. It was like walking into another world, another time dimension. We did not know anyone, nor did we have any friends. We were strangers in a land we knew nothing about. We were hesitant, we were nervous, and at times, we were afraid. However, as time passed, we started to find our place little by little. We became complacent with our lives inside these walls. We were no longer strangers in a foreign land, but longtime residents—convicts.

Even as Christ is not of this world, neither are we. As followers of Jesus Christ, we are called to be set apart—in the world but not of the world (John 15:19). Because of such, we should never grow complacent with a world that is not our home: in our case, a world of incarceration—our place of exile. Though we live life surrounded by concrete and razor wire, prison is not our home. Heaven is our home; and as we walk through these halls, we must maintain an eternal perspective. We must not concern ourselves with who we are in the eyes of others but who we are in the eyes of God. Are we complacent convicts, or are we unsatisfied Christians whose hope will only be fulfilled in the kingdom of God, our eternal home?

Let us never grow complacent with the life inside these walls. Rather, let us always remember, as Christ expressed: we are in the world, but not of the world. –Solley

Morning: Ruth 3, 4; Acts 28 — *Evening:* Jer 38; Ps 11, 12

DOOR OF HOPE

*"Therefore, behold, I will allure her, and bring her into the
wilderness, and speak tenderly to her. And there I will give her
vineyards and make the valley of Achor a door of hope."*
HOSEA 2:14–15A

Hosea is conveying to Israel the words of the Lord about her restoration. The Lord says He will bring her into the wilderness. The wilderness will be where the Lord will give to her, vineyards. Nevertheless, the wilderness is not necessarily a good place. To understand this a little better, the word *Achor* means "trouble." Yet, it is in the valley of trouble where the Lord makes a door of hope.

Prison certainly can be synonymous with a valley of trouble or a wilderness. How radically would it shape the way we see our prison experience if we would begin to see prison as a place where the Lord has brought us? What if we would see prison as the place where He speaks to us tenderly and gives to us vineyards where He cultivates our relationship with Him and causes it to blossom? What if we would see our place of trouble as the place where He makes our door of hope? To see things in this light would change everything about how we view and understand our prison experience.

Begin to think about prison as our wilderness. As we reside here, as we live in our valley of trouble, let us prayerfully ask the Lord how He is alluring us today. Let us give ear to the tender words He speaks to us. Let us cultivate the vineyard of our relationship with Him and continually look for the door of hope that He has made out of our valley of trouble. –Karch

Morning: 1 Sam 1; Rom 1 — *Evening:* Jer 39; Ps 13, 14

DINNER TIME

"Behold, I stand at the door and knock. If anyone
hears my voice and opens the door, I will come in to
him and eat with him, and he with me."
REVELATION 3:20

E arly in His mission, Jesus established a pattern of breaking bread
with His followers. We find numerous examples of this just in the
gospel of Matthew (12:1, 14:16–21, 15:32–38, 26:20, 26). Obviously,
sharing a meal with another was a customary form of fellowship, one
in which two or more would share food and drink and get to know one
another in an intimate setting.

Fellowshipping with another was meant to bring two or more
people together in a much closer relationship, and dining together
was the best way to accomplish this. This is precisely the illustration
used in the warning to the Laodicean church, described in the book
of Revelation. The imagery of Jesus coming into a person's life and
dining with him was meant to invoke the very same concept of fellowship. The Laodicean church had been warned against complacency
and placing their faith in material things. They had been instructed to
take a stand and repent from their worldly ways. The way they were to
do this was by inviting Jesus in to dine with them, in other words, to be
in fellowship with Jesus and not with the world.

This message, although given to the church at Laodicea, has universal application. Many Christians loathe to give up their worldly ways
or have difficulty trusting in the unseen spiritual working of God. If
we claim to have fellowship with Jesus Christ but continue to be luke-
warm, we're only fooling ourselves.

The table is set, the meal is prepared, and He is knocking at the
door. Make the right decision and dine with Him today. –Blevins

Morning: 1 Sam 2; Rom 2 — *Evening:* Jer 40; Ps 15, 16

BY NO MEANS!

"What shall we say then? Are we to continue in sin that grace may abound? By no means! How can we who died to sin still live in it?"
Romans 6:1–2

In Romans 6, Paul gives us a vivid picture of being dead to sin. Sadly, some Christians believe that because Jesus has freed them from the law of sin and death, they are free to act as they choose. To think Christians are free to sin shows a lack of understanding of who a Christian is. A Christian is not merely a justified believer, but someone who has entered into a personal union with Christ. We have been buried with Christ through baptism into His death and raised from the dead to walk in newness of life (vv. 3–4).

As Christians, death no longer has a hold on us (v. 11). It no longer has lordship over our lives. Consequently, just as Christ lives His life to God, we must also live to God. We must constantly bear in mind that we are no longer who we were, and our lives must demonstrate that. To wallow in sin so that grace may abound demonstrates the opposite. Put simply, if that old man is dead, then why are we still trying to live his life?

Remember, Jesus paid the penalty for sin, and the law's demand of death has been met. Consequently, neither sin nor the law of sin and death has a claim on us. We are no longer prisoners under the law, but children of God under His grace (v. 14; Gal 3:22–24). Therefore, as Paul so eloquently stated, "What shall we say then? Are we to continue in sin so that grace may abound? By no means!" –Solley

Morning: 1 Sam 3; Rom 3 — *Evening:* Jer 41; Ps 17

NOT US

*"Not to us, O LORD, not to us, but to your name give glory,
for the sake of your steadfast love and your faithfulness!"*
PSALM 115:1

Prison is a systematic process of dehumanization. Yet, against this dehumanization is a deep-seated aspect of human nature which desires self-expression and individuation, and men and women who are incarcerated spend a great deal of time finding ways to meet that desire. Far too often it is in destructive ways. For instance, by the time I was twenty-three years old, a large percentage of my upper body was covered in tattoos. Tattoos were one outlet through which I could find self-expression. Another was through gang affiliation. For the most part, a desire for self-expression does not change when we become Christians.

As Christians, we find ways of self-expression through various means of ministry. We may play in the church band, sing in the choir, or preach. All of which is good. But, we have to be on guard against allowing self-expression to become the end or goal of those ministry efforts. The psalmist goes to great lengths to dispel notions of individuation. In the end, it is not about us at all, but it is all about the Lord. To Him belongs all honor and glory, and we simply should be vessels through which His steadfast love and faithfulness are expressed.

As we pursue and grow in our ministry efforts, both behind these walls and when we are on the outside again, we should also grow in the understanding that ministry is not about us. We should prayerfully seek the self-expression of the Lord as He is glorified through our ministry efforts because it is all about Him—not us. –Karch

Morning: 1 Sam 4; Rom 4 — *Evening:* Jer 42; Ps 18

MY APOLOGIES!

*"but in your hearts honor Christ the Lord as holy, always
being prepared to make a defense to anyone who asks
you for a reason for the hope that is in you; . . ."*
1 PETER 3:15

If you haven't had to defend your faith by now, you will. It does not take people long to realize when someone begins to walk differently. The change within our hearts is necessarily going to manifest itself in our outward actions, and the change caused by our newfound hope is going to be evident to those around us. Some will ridicule us, and some will ask questions.

The Greek word used for "defense" is *apologia,* and it is where we get our word apology. But this is not the typical "I'm sorry" we hear every day. Peter encourages us to always be ready to make a defense of our faith, but how we do that is an amazing thing. First and foremost, it should be done for the express purpose of pointing people to Jesus Christ. We should never attempt to defend our faith motivated by hatred or anger. Second, it should be done as Peter reminds us, with gentleness and respect. People will not be convinced of the sincerity of our faith by arrogance or intimidation tactics.

Standing up for our faith is something we are called to do, even when it's hard, but we must do so with wisdom and discernment. So the next time someone asks you to give a reason for the change in your life or to defend your beliefs, remember to gently and humbly offer your apology! –Blevins

Morning: 1 Sam 5, 6; Rom 5 — *Evening:* Jer 43; Ps 19

LIVING ON THE EDGE

*"Therefore let us go to him outside the camp and bear
the reproach he endured. For here we have no lasting
city, but we seek the city that is to come."*
HEBREWS 13:13–14

T he author of the book of Hebrews sums up his work with an encouragement for Christians to follow Jesus to a place "outside
the camp." A camp signifies security and safety—a place where we can
easily become comfortable. Jesus came from the security of heaven
to minister in the midst of the wilderness of the world. His way was
the way of the cross from start to finish. According to the author of
Hebrews, the way of the cross is the exemplary aspect of the Christian
life. We are to forsake the comforts offered by the security of the camp
and venture into the wilderness of the world to minister to those who
need it.

Inasmuch as prison can be thought of as an example of being outside the camp, it is still easy to confine our faith to the more secure
and comfortable places. As a result, following Jesus can easily become
restricted to the privacy of our cell or isolated to the chapel. There is,
however, an excitement—a type of living on the edge—when we follow
Jesus outside the comfort and security of those places. Following Jesus
in this way exemplifies our faith and illustrates that we understand the
comforts and security of this world are passing away.

As we venture beyond the boundaries of the safe and secure places
we find most comfortable, we do so with the realization that we look
for a new city altogether. As we live on the edge in this way, we do so
with the expectation that the wilderness of prison is passing away and
that we have a heavenly city which is to come. –Karch

Morning: 1 Sam 7, 8; Rom 6 — *Evening:* Jer 44; Ps 20, 21

PLUGGED IN

"Abide in me, and I in you. As the branch cannot bear fruit by itself,
unless it abides in the vine, neither can you, unless you abide in me."
JOHN 15:4

I t was summer; it was hot, and we were on lock-down. I had just carried all of my property to and from the gym where it was ransacked
and I was strip searched—again. Upon returning to my cell, I set my
fan on the table next to my cellie's fan, dropped my property on the
bunk, then turned and plugged in my fan. Nothing happened. I flipped
the switch: nothing. I wiggled the cord: still nothing. Frustrated, I un-
plugged and plugged it back in—nothing. Hot, tired, and frustrated,
I closed my eyes, took a deep breath, and prayed, "Lord, I can't afford
another fan. Please don't let my fan be broken." When I opened my
eyes, sitting on the floor between my feet was my fan cord. In my hand
was the cord to my cellie's fan! Nothing was wrong with *my* fan; I just
had to plug it in.

When I think about that incident, I am reminded of Jesus' instruction to His disciples: "Abide in me, and I in you. As the branch cannot bear fruit by itself, unless it abides in the vine, neither can you,
unless you abide in me." Just as my fan was useless because it was not
plugged in to the power source, we are useless if we are not plugged in
to Christ. It is only by abiding in Christ, being plugged in to our power
source, that we will bear fruit for the kingdom of God.

Apart from Christ, we can do nothing. We are useless if we are not
plugged in to Jesus! Therefore, the question remains: Are you plugged
in to Christ? –Solley

Morning: 1 Sam 9; Rom 7 — *Evening:* Jer 46; Ps 22

WITHOUT MASKS

"Let love be genuine. Abhor what is evil; hold fast to what is good."
ROMANS 12:9

T he world has been entertained long enough to recognize a mask when they see one. Consequently, we are not fooling anybody if our love isn't real. Our text today is translated in different ways. Some render it as, "Let love be without hypocrisy" (*New American Standard Bible–NASB, New King James Version–NKJV*). Sincere love is unfeigned, without hypocrisy; it isn't pretentious, does not play a role, and cannot be faked. The Greek word translated to English as *genuine* is derived from the Greek word also translated *without hypocrisy,* and it literally means "without a mask." As Christians we live our lives, literally, without masks.

Genuine love is a direct attestation of our salvation. Paul describes this love's attributes, actions, and reactions here in Romans 12 (and John 3:16–17; 15:13; 1 Corinthians 13; 1 John 4:7–12). He begins by saying that true Christian love must be genuine. Also, the voice of the verb "abhor" and "hold fast" is carefully chosen and tells us more about love. Abhor is *active* and hold fast is *passive.* If love is genuine then, with the help of the Holy Spirit, we actively despise what is evil and are united to and associated with, through Christ, to what is good. Genuine love binds us to what is good. It is a natural outworking of our salvation.

This is why the Roman world was dumbstruck by the early Christian community—they *loved* one another. They wore no masks. Until this same genuine love is made manifest as a result of our salvation, we can never expect those around us—inmate and officer alike—to be struck on any real level. As Christians, it should be our prayer that we can live for and serve the Lord in a way that is genuine. Let us always pray to love without masks. –Karch

Morning: 1 Sam 10; Rom 8 — *Evening:* Jer 47; Ps 23, 24

THE REAL SUPERHERO

". . . for I did not come to judge the world but to save the world."
JOHN 12:47

When I was young, I loved superheroes. My little brother and I tied towels around our necks and "flew" around the house saving the world from the many faces of evil. Of course, I was Superman and he was my sidekick, Batman. For hours we would get lost in play, mesmerized by pretending to be the good guys, the ones who came to rescue the world. We were enraptured by the idea that one man, transformed in a moment to a superhero by simply changing clothes, could save the entire world.

Though the superheroes we idolized as children were birthed in the fertile imaginations of men and brought to life in comic books, cartoons, and movies, there is a real Superhero who came to save the world—Jesus Christ. John 1 tells us, "In the beginning was the Word, and the Word was with God, and the Word was God" (1:1), and "the Word became flesh and dwelt among us" (1:14). Transformed in a moment, Christ, the God-man, left His home in heaven to come to earth to save a lost and dying world, not merely from temporal evils but from everlasting damnation. Because He loved us, Christ came so that those who believed in Him would not perish but have everlasting life (John 3:16). He did not accomplish our salvation through fictional superpowers, but through His death on the cross. Dying, He saved us.

In prison, we live among a lost and dying world. We are surrounded by those who are in dire need of a superhero, someone who, transformed in a moment, can give them life. Why don't you introduce them, today, to the real Superhero, Jesus Christ. –Solley

Morning: 1 Sam 11; Rom 9 — *Evening:* Jer 48; Ps 25

IT'S ALIVE! IT'S ALIVE!

*"For you formed my inward parts; you knitted me
together in my mother's womb. I praise you, for
I am fearfully and wonderfully made."*
PSALM 139:13–14A

Existence. What an often overlooked concept. To *be* is something we take for granted each and every day; but if we truly understood what a complete miracle existence actually is, we just might have a different perspective on life itself.

Science has demonstrated that humans, and all living creatures for that matter, are composed of the same basic carbon, hydrogen, oxygen, and nitrogen atoms found throughout nature. In fact, science has even conducted elaborate experiments to try and mimic Earth's early conditions in order to try and create life. Scientists have not been able to manipulate these basic elements and come up with amino acids—the basic building blocks of life. Scientists have not been able to give those amino acids life. They can't give them sentience. The basic elements simply remain inanimate objects.

The Bible tells us that it is God who puts us together and gives us life (Gen 2:7). Each and every one of us has been brought into existence by His mighty hand. Sure, we have moms and dads who provide the genetic material, but that inner part, our very soul, is a miraculous creation of God. Consider the fact that you're reading these words and thinking about them right now. We are more than just some basic elements randomly stacked together. We are alive. Praise God for His graciousness and creativity because we are fearfully and wonderfully made. –Blevins

Morning: 1 Sam 12; Rom 10 — *Evening:* Jer 49; Ps 26, 27

LEAVE IT ALL BEHIND

*"And when they brought their boats to land,
they left everything and followed him."*
LUKE 5:11

W hen Jesus walked into His disciples' lives, their entire world changed. Everything they identified with became a shadow compared to who Christ became to them. When He called, they answered. In a moment, He became the center of their existence, and they left it all behind to follow Him: families, friends, jobs, *everything*. And though they stumbled and fell along the way, they followed Christ for the rest of their lives. Discounting Judas, all but the disciple John were martyred for their faith in Christ. Not even their own lives were more important to the disciples than Christ.

When I think about how committed the disciples were to their faith and belief in Jesus Christ, I am forced to evaluate my own commitment to Christ. Has Jesus become the center of my existence like He was for the disciples? Have I left everything behind and made Christ everything, or am I still clinging to things in my life that are more important to me than Him? Are there relationships in my life more important to me than my relationship with Christ? Are there material things in my life that mean more to me than Christ? Are there sins in my life I am not willing to give up for the sake of Christ? These types of questions force me to take close inventory of my heart.

As you go about your day, think about how committed Christ's disciples were to Him. Think about your relationship with Christ and your commitment to Him. Like the disciples, are you willing to leave it all behind and follow Him? Are you willing to make Christ your everything? It is an honest question that demands an honest answer that only you can give. –Solley

Morning: 1 Sam 13; Rom 11 — *Evening:* Jer 50; Ps 28, 29

TRASH

"But whatever gain I had, I counted as loss for the sake of Christ . . .
because of the surpassing worth of knowing Christ Jesus my Lord. For his
sake I have suffered the loss of all things and count them as rubbish, . . ."
PHILIPPIANS 3:7–8

I n prison, a person can be whoever he wants to be. There are self-professed drug dealers who claim to have pushed millions of dollars' worth of one narcotic or another. You also have models, martial arts experts, and a myriad of other professions. That kind of claim is even made among those who profess Christ, as if He were somehow not enough to substantiate one's identity.

To desire an identity beyond the drab sameness among the prison population is, to an extent, understandable. Yet, it is interesting to see how Paul was not merely trying to conjure a past that wasn't real. Paul had been somebody before he came to know Christ; he had been the real deal. Having a past from which Paul could have gleaned a definite identity, he still counted it all as trash. All of who he had been prior to knowing Christ looked like junk compared to who Christ made him. To have his identity in Jesus meant more to him than his past.

Our own identity in Christ should surpass our pasts as well. And, in the context of prison, we should be able to show the worth of Christ Jesus over and against the myriad of fantasies with which people so desire to identify. When asked what we did in the world, we should honestly count those things as loss—as trash—compared to who Christ has made us today. –Karch

Morning: 1 Sam 14; Rom 12 — *Evening:* Jer 51; Ps 30

SURVIVAL

*"Two are better than one . . . For if they fall, one will
lift up his fellow. But woe to him who is alone when
he falls and has not another to lift him up!"*
E CCLESIASTES 4:9–10

W hen we were growing up in low-income, rundown neighbor-
hoods, my two brothers and I had an unspoken agreement
which guaranteed our survival: If you beat my little brother up, I will
beat you up. If you beat me up, my older brother will beat you up. If
you beat him up, we will all beat you up! You may have been able to
whip one of us, but there was no way you were going to whip us all.
We took comfort in knowing we were not alone, and we had one another's back. It gave us each more confidence when times of trouble
did come.

My brothers and I learned at a young age that two (or three) are
better than one. When one falls, the other will be there to lift him up.
As Christians, the same rules apply. God never intended us to walk
through life fighting spiritual battles alone. He gave us fellow believers to stand with us. Though many, we are one body (1 Cor 12:12).
As brothers and sisters, we are fellow soldiers in God's army. We take
strength from one another when we are weak. We lean on each other when times get rough. We take confidence in knowing we are not
alone.

We Christians have an unspoken agreement to guarantee each
other's spiritual survival: we will never allow each other to walk alone.
Take a look around you. Are there other believers you can reach out to
whose back you can catch and who can catch yours? If so, yoke up with
them and walk this Christian journey together. –Solley

Morning: 1 Sam 15; Rom 13 — *Evening:* Jer 52; Ps 31

THE HIDDEN GOD

"Truly, you are a God who hides himself, O God of Israel, the Savior."
ISAIAH 45:15

What does it mean for us to confess that God *hides*? There are times when we feel as if God is distant and not working in our lives. We find ourselves in positions where we cry out like the psalmist, "Why, O Lord, do you stand far away? Why do you hide yourself in times of trouble?" (Ps 10:1) This is nothing new in that one of the most pressing problems within contemporary philosophy of religion is defined as "divine hiddenness." Yet, our text today does not present the hiddenness of God as a problem. The context in which Isaiah makes this confession is in regard to the everlasting salvation of the Lord. This comes through the means of hiddenness.

In the sixteenth century, Martin Luther differentiated between the revealed God and the hidden God. Both instances are articulated in the crucifixion of Jesus Christ. In salvation, God is both revealed and hidden in the suffering of Jesus. As those who believed in the salvation of the Lord witnessed the crucifixion, they questioned where God was in the midst of it all. Nobody could see God's eternal salvation wrought in the suffering of our Savior. In the same way, we often find it difficult to see how God is working in the midst of our own suffering and trials. This is what Isaiah means by the God who hides himself.

When God seems distant and it is hard to discern where and how He is working in our lives, we can know that even in the midst of suffering, He is present—those are the places where He hides Himself. Those are the places where He is most at work. –Karch

Morning: 1 Sam 16; Rom 14 — *Evening:* Lam 1; Ps 32

SHOULDER WORKOUT

*"So if there is any encouragement in Christ, any comfort
from love, any participation in the Spirit, any affection and
sympathy, complete my joy by being of the same mind, having
the same love, being in full accord and of one mind."*
PHILIPPIANS 2:1–2

A good shoulder workout is important to any well-rounded, upper body routine. Strengthening and sculpting the deltoid muscles can be beneficial for a variety of reasons. The shoulder muscle is used in all the major upper body workouts, but in the Christian's life, the shoulder has a much more crucial role to play. It is there for your brothers to lean on.

In prison, we face difficulties and problems all the time. One of the worst scenarios is bad news from home—a death in the family, financial dilemmas, or the kids getting into trouble. All of these become magnified because we cannot do anything about them. Unfortunately, we so often have to face these problems alone, and our lack of control over situations only intensifies the frustration and the guilt.

Paul exhorts the Philippians, and us as well, that if we have learned anything about the love of Christ, it is that we should count others more significant than ourselves. We must not only look to our own interests, but also to the interests of others (v. 4). So the next time you see your brother "going through it," offer to listen to his troubles; comfort him in love. You don't have to find a way to fix his problems, just be there for him and give him a shoulder to lean on. Put those delts to use, and let the love of Christ work through you. –Blevins

Morning: 1 Sam 17; Rom 15 — *Evening:* Lam 2; Ps 33

OLD WAYS

*"Let the thief no longer steal, but rather let him labor,
doing honest work with his own hands, so that he may
have something to share with anyone in need."*
Ephesians 4:28

The first time I read the passage for today, I set my Bible down and thought about my life. No matter how you stacked the deck, the cards always lined up the same: I was a thief. From the first time I stole candy as a child to my numerous arrests for armed robbery, my life has been defined by taking things that did not belong to me. And in every instance, except for my current conviction, I didn't feel much guilt when I committed the offense. Being a thief was something I learned at a very young age, just like many of us in prison did.

As Paul expresses to the believers in Ephesus, we are no longer to walk in the corrupt ways of our pasts. For those of us who were once thieves, we must steal no longer, but rather, work to help others in need. What Paul is conveying here is profound. We are not simply to abandon our former way of life; we are to transform completely our entire behavior. Instead of taking from others out of selfishness, we are to give out of love from our own labor. Giving, instead of taking, reflects our new self, who we now are in Christ—the total opposite of who we once were.

By walking in the newness of life that Christ has given us, our actions will tell the world that we are no longer who we used to be. Instead, we are people whose lives have been transformed by the gospel of Jesus Christ. –Solley

Morning: 1 Sam 18; Rom 16 — *Evening:* Lam 3; Ps 34

BE ABOUT IT

*"What good is it, my brothers, if someone says he has faith
but does not have works? Can that faith save him?"*
JAMES 2:14

C ontroversy abounds over James' position concerning faith and
works. Some consider James to be contrary to Paul's assertions,
while others see both James and Paul as asserting the same thing but
with different emphasis. The latter view seems to be the most plau-
sible, and when we think about it in contemporary terms, it becomes
more clear.

The population of every prison has one thing in common: they
maintain a sense of respect for authenticity. All prisoners respect people who are *real*—even when they are real about the wrong things.
As long as a person is not fake or displaying signs of hypocrisy, they
earn a certain level of respect for their authenticity. There is almost
an admiration for those who are not just talking about it, but who are
being about it. The same principle applies to Christianity. Christians
in prison are in a position to be respected if those around them recognize they are for real. This is the emphasis James is fleshing out here.
Where Paul is more theologically driven, James focuses on the more
practical side of things. Paul has worked out the theology; James wants
us to understand how to be about it.

Think about it: those around you who just talk about it don't get
much respect; it is those who are being about it that gain respect and
admiration. Ask the Lord to help you to be authentic, and begin to live
out the legitimacy of what Christ has already accomplished. Be about
what you profess and live out faith James talks about here. –Karch

Morning: 1 Sam 19; 1 Cor 1 — *Evening:* Lam 4; Ps 35

CROSS CONTAMINATION

*"Brothers, if anyone is caught in any transgression, you
who are spiritual should restore him in a spirit of gentleness.
Keep watch on yourself, lest you too be tempted."*
GALATIANS 6:1

O ne of the many things I learned while working in restaurants
was that food safety was vitally important to a restaurant's success. You must follow many different procedures when preparing food
in a commercial establishment. Standards for cooking temperatures,
storage methods, and food handling are all set with a customer's well-
being in mind. With all the various strains of bacteria out there, if you
are not careful, cross contamination of bacteria from one surface or
ingredient to another may occur. That is why most food preparation
instructions will warn you against using equipment for multiple tasks
like cutting up chicken and then slicing tomatoes. You must be very
careful and pay close attention to what you are doing.

Likewise, when you are ministering to other believers who are deal-
ing with sin in their lives, you must be on guard. Sin is not something
to be taken lightly. Even though you may have overcome a particular
temptation, it is not hard to fall back into old habits. Paul urges the
brethren to hold each other accountable and restore each other in a
spirit of gentleness. Yet, he warns us not to be careless or ignorant of
our own condition lest we get pulled back down, too.

Brothers, we must bear each other's burdens, and we do need to hold
each other accountable. But remember when doing so, we must use safe
sin-handling procedures and avoid any cross contamination. –Blevins

Morning: 1 Sam 20; 1 Cor 2 — *Evening:* Lam 5; Ps 36

TIRED OF WAITING

". . . Sarai, Abram's wife, took Hagar the Egyptian, her
servant, and gave her to Abram her husband as a wife.
And he went in to Hagar and she conceived."
GENESIS 16:3–4A

God promised that He would make Abram's descendants as numerous as the stars in the sky (Gen 15:5). For years, Abram faithfully waited for God's promise to be fulfilled. Year after year, God's promised descendants never came. Eventually, Abram became discouraged and grew tired of waiting. Rather than trusting in God, Abram took matters into his own hands. In his own attempt to fulfill God's promise, Abram took Hagar as his wife and she conceived. However, when God's promise was fulfilled by the birth of Isaac, Abram, now called "Abraham," had to clean up the mess he made in his attempt to play God. He was forced to cast out his eldest son, Ishmael (Gen 21:8–20).

Like Abraham, many of us have become tired of waiting on God. We have prayed and trusted in God for things in our lives, and when they did not come through as soon as desired, or exactly as planned, we took matters into our own hands. We played God by trying to do what only He can do in our lives. We basically told God that we really do not trust Him, and we can do a much better and quicker job than He can. And, just as Abraham learned, had we continued to wait on God, we would not have made such a mess of things.

Have you been waiting on God for a long time? If so, don't grow weary; don't give up. Continue to trust that God is not slack in His promises. He will come through when you least expect it. God will fulfill the promises He has given to us. –Solley

Morning: 1 Sam 21, 22; 1 Cor 3 — *Evening*: Ezek 1; Ps 37

THE RIDE

*"But now that you have been set free from sin and
have become slaves of God, the fruit you get leads
to sanctification and its end, eternal life."*
ROMANS 6:22

T hroughout Paul's letters, the concept of being slaves to God, or
to Christ, is a central focus. Yet, somehow we still read over the
fact that we are slaves and attempt to live as if we were completely free
in respect to God.

For the body of Christ inside prison, this tends to work itself out
in a way where we see ourselves as free to pursue a self-justifying righteousness of our own. We are often far too quick to point out that
brother or sister so-in-so is not displaying an agreeable level of the fruit
of the Spirit. Through overlooking our own slavery, we seek out our
own fruitfulness instead of seeing the Spirit produce His fruit in us. We
want to say that we are bearing fruit for God. Yet, Paul is clear that, as
slaves of God, we get fruit from Him; we are the vessel through which
He produces fruit. There is nothing of ourselves we can lay claim to;
we are merely along for the ride.

As Christians, we have been set free from sin and are now slaves to
God. Understand that it is His work—He works in you. The more you
submit, the more fruit He will produce in you. The work is entirely of
God. We are simply along for the ride, the end of which is eternal life.
Relax; trust Him to get you there, and enjoy the ride. –Karch

Morning: 1 Sam 23; 1 Cor 4 — *Evening:* Ezek 2; Ps 38

WHAT'S HOLDING YOU BACK?

*"'You lack one thing: go, sell all that you have and give to
the poor . . . and come follow me.' Disheartened by the saying,
he went away sorrowful, for he had great possessions."*
MARK 10:21B–22

Mark 10 tells of Jesus' encounter with a rich young man who
asked Jesus a question with eternal consequences: "What must I
do to inherit eternal life?" Jesus' response was simple, "go, sell all that
you have and give to the poor." At hearing Jesus' words, the rich young
man departed sorrowful. Though he had kept all the commandments
of God since his youth, something in his life kept him from following
Christ. His money was more important to him than his relationship
with Jesus.

Like the rich young man, some of us have that *something* we do
not want to give up, something we are holding on to so tight it is pre-
venting us from following Christ. For some, it may be the pursuit of
material gain, for others, an unhealthy relationship or gang affiliation.
Perhaps a particular stronghold such as drug addiction, pride, anger,
lust, promiscuity, gambling, or racism keeps you in bondage. Whatever
it may be, you are not willing to give it up for the sake of being a follower of Christ. That which holds you captive prevents you from inher-
iting eternal life, and that is a very serious matter.

Today, ask the Lord to search your heart and reveal to you anything
that you desire more than Him. If something is revealed to you, pray
that God gives you the courage and desire to forsake whatever prevents you from following Christ. Even if you do not think you have the
strength to give it up, with God, all things are possible (v. 27). –Solley

Morning: 1 Sam 24; 1 Cor 5 — *Evening:* Ezek 3; Ps 39

AHEAD OF THE GAME

"Before they call I will answer; while they are yet speaking I will hear."
ISAIAH 65:24

L ife is a lot like a game of chess. While chess is one of the most intensive and complex games in history, life possesses more variables and certainly much higher stakes. The best chess players are those who have the ability to think several moves ahead of their opponent. In the same way, the most successful people in life are those who can anticipate what life will throw at them next and calculate how to counter each situation. However, this type of anticipation is much easier said than done.

Experience teaches us that nature and circumstance are much better chess players than we are. There are simply too many variables to anticipate to counter all the situations we face on a day-to-day basis. Because of this, life seems uncertain and overwhelming at times, particularly when we get hemmed up without a way out of a situation. In today's text, the Lord comforts those who know Him by affirming that He is the ultimate chess player—He is always ahead of the game. Even before we consider calling on Him for help and direction and even before we get our request fully thought out or spoken, the Lord has heard and will act.

As we try to anticipate what life will throw at us next and when the situations we face seem to leave no way out, we can have comfort in knowing the Lord is always ahead of the game. He knows and understands all the variables. In calling on Him, we can be confident He has already heard. –Karch

Morning: 1 Sam 25; 1 Cor 6 — *Evening:* Ezek 4; Ps 40, 41

BLESS YOUR CHILDREN

*". . . Let the children come to Me; do not hinder them,
for to such belongs the kingdom of God.'"*
MARK 10:14

As incarcerated parents we often get too busy with day-to-day issues to focus on the important things in life. We overlook the relationships with our family and often take the people closest to us for granted. Yet, our relationship with our children is so vital that it must not be treated like just another task or chore. It is a big mistake to think that sending them another illustration board with their favorite cartoon character will make up for our absence. The time we've lost cannot be made up for by any amount of material things. However, there is one thing we can do that will benefit our children forever: share the gospel with them!

The crowds around Judea recognized the importance of sharing Jesus with their children. They brought them to Jesus to be blessed by Him. However, Jesus' disciples tried to stop them. Seeing this, Jesus quickly rebuked them and commanded them to allow the children to come and be blessed.

Can you imagine anything greater you could do for your children than lead them to Christ? No amount of decorated handkerchiefs or belated birthday cards can compare to the fountain of living water you can introduce to your children (Jer 2:13; John 4:14, 7:38). Your time away from your kids never truly can be made up; however, you can bring them to the feet of Jesus Christ by sharing the gospel. So take time out and bless your children by writing or speaking with them about Jesus today. –Blevins

Morning: 1 Sam 26; 1 Cor 7 — *Evening:* Ezek 5; Ps 42, 43

WHEN GOD WHISPERS

*"And after the earthquake, a fire, but the LORD was not
in the fire. And after the fire the sound of a low whisper.
And when Elijah heard it, he . . . went out."*
1 KINGS 19:12–13A

Not long ago, I attended *Kairos* where we received twelve dozen cookies, some to keep for ourselves and some to give away. I intended to keep two dozen. After giving all but *my* two dozen cookies away to *my* friends, I stood waiting to walk into my cell. Then I saw this rough looking character standing at the back of the stairs by himself. He was the "psych" patient no one talked to. A brief thought flashed through my mind—*give him some cookies*—which I ignored. I looked at my cookies, already tasting them, and suddenly, inside, I heard that whisper, "Give him some cookies." I started to walk away and heard it again.

When I walked over and handed the man some cookies, tears filled his eyes. He thanked me and told me everyone was giving cookies to *their* friends, but he had no friends. Out of all the cookies I gave away, those meant the most because they impacted someone's life. Yet, I almost missed it; I almost blew the opportunity God placed before me because I was not listening. In fact, God had to tell me three times before I received it. Had God spoken to me in some amazing way, I would have instantly responded.

So many times we expect God to show up and speak to us in a big way, with flashes of light and rolls of thunder. But as God showed Elijah, He is not in the mighty wind, or the earthquake, or the fire; but He is in the silence, where He speaks to us in whispers. If we are not careful, we can miss the gentle, urging voice of the Holy Spirit. –Solley

Morning: 1 Sam 27; 1 Cor 8 — *Evening:* Ezek 6; Ps 44

JEALOUS?

*"But Moses said to him, 'Are you jealous for my sake?
Would that all the LORD's people were prophets, that
the LORD would put his Spirit on them!'"*
NUMBERS 11:29

Moses bore a great burden while leading the Israelites through the wilderness to the Promised Land. The day-to-day responsibility of getting the people from one place to the next was almost too much for him. At the suggestion of Moses' father-in-law, seventy men were selected to help him. As the men were gathered around the tent, the Spirit of the Lord fell on them and they prophesied. Yet, there were two men, not among those gathered at the tent, who began to prophesy back at the camp. When someone ran and told those at the tent, Joshua told Moses to go and make them stop. As we find ourselves serving in various ways, we too can look on others with suspicion or become victims of others who want to stop us from serving. In view of that, we can become jealous for our own sakes or suffer the jealousy of others.

Moses is not surprised that the men were prophesying. He is, however, surprised at Joshua's jealousy. Moses informs Joshua that he would rather all of the Lord's people be prophets. Today, the Spirit of God indwells each Christian. Also, in a New Testament sense, prophecy is more in tune with proclamation, and all Christians are commissioned to proclaim the gospel.

We should never be resentful or envious of the service of others and never become jealous for our own sakes in our service to the Lord. So, let us rejoice when we see others proclaiming the gospel and design only to work alongside them praying the Lord would continue to bring others into His service as well. –Karch

Morning: 1 Sam 28; 1 Cor 9 — *Evening:* Ezek 7; Ps 45

FINISHED STRONG

*"And I am sure of this, that he who began a good work in
you will bring it to completion at the day of Jesus Christ."*
PHILIPPIANS 1:6

My life has mostly been chronicled by a list of failures. For some reason or another, I had an extremely persistent problem of beginning something and never finishing it. Whether it was drum lessons or home building projects, I typically lost interest in things rather swiftly and soon made excuses to quit. This was also typified by my incessant habit of changing majors in college. It even affected my relationships with other people. Hence, others often classified me as "flaky."

My faith, however, doesn't work like that. My sinful affliction hasn't affected my miraculous perseverance in the Lord. For some strange reason, my faith persists. Though there are times when I feel weak, inadequate, or dare I say doubtful, I persevere. I don't look back, and I keep "fighting the good fight" (2 Tim 4:7).

This is exactly what Paul was so confident about in his letter to the Philippians. Although he was thankful for the Philippians' continuance in the gospel, Paul was sure to note that there was a Higher Power sustaining it. God, Himself, the very giver of their faith, is the one who will bring their faith to completion. What greater news is there, especially for those of us who have difficulty seeing anything through to the end? In other words, thank God for being the author and finisher of our faith (Heb 12:2). Thank God because He promises to have you finish strong! –Blevins

Morning: 1 Sam 29, 30; 1 Cor 10 — *Evening:* Ezek 8; Ps 46, 47

WHAT DOES IT REALLY MEAN?

*"For if while we were enemies we were reconciled to
God by the death of his Son, much more, now that we
are reconciled, shall we be saved by his life."*
ROMANS 5:10

We have heard the phrase, "Christ died for your sins," so many
times that we are sometimes spiritually numb or calloused to
the reality of the cross and what the crucifixion of Christ really means
for us. It has become cliché, something that is often said or preached
without any true passion or heart behind it. This is the reason I think
some of us really miss it. God did not send Christ to die on the cross
so that we simply can be forgiven and live by-and-by in the sky, happily
ever after. God sent His Son to the cross to reconcile us to Himself because He loved us and desired intimate fellowship with us. God desires
the intimacy of walking with us and talking with us—like He did with
Adam in the Garden of Eden.

Because of God's holiness, sin separated us from Him. The result
of this was spiritual death: eternal separation from God. However, in
His love, God sent Christ to die so we could live, so that we could once
again have fellowship with him. Christ's death on the cross is the only
thing that makes this possible. His blood destroyed the insurmountable wall of sin making it possible for us to once again have fellowship
with our God, our Creator, the King of all Kings. That is what the cross
really means.

When we understand what the crucifixion of Christ really means
for us, we will never grow spiritually numb or calloused to the truth of
the cross. –Solley

Morning: 1 Sam 31; 1 Cor 11 — *Evening*: Ezek 9; Ps 48

IMITATORS

*"Brothers, join in imitating me, and keep your eyes on those
who walk according to the example you have in us."*
PHILIPPIANS 3:17

We have all known Christian inmates who seem to have it all to-gether. Yet, they get out of prison, and within a few weeks, they begin to slip away from what they so diligently professed while in pris-on. Inasmuch as it is discouraging to those of us left inside, it doesn't have to be the case. To stop the trend of professing Christians getting out of prison and coming back to prison, we must begin to take the call of Christ on our lives seriously and encourage others to take it seri-ously as well. Even so, it takes more than talk, and it begins by example. One way to combat the trend is accountability groups.

I am with brothers who have accountability groups that meet once a week for an hour or so to discuss what is going on in our lives. With a mind for the things of Christ, coupled with a desire to grow together in His grace and knowledge, we hold one another accountable, maintain-ing the truth in love. I encourage you to do the same where you are. Find brothers who are of like mind and begin to be a body; bear one another's burdens even when there are days and weeks when someone may not particularly be feeling it. As the importance of this type of support and accountability begins to become a living reality, it will be a given to find the same support and accountability within a body of believers once you are released.

It might be a little too optimistic to say that doing so will safeguard anyone from coming back to prison. All the same, my confidence in the gospel of Jesus Christ and the safeguard of His body as a commu-nity of believers naturally facilitates that optimism. Test it! –Karch

Morning: 2 Sam 1; 1 Cor 12 — *Evening:* Ezek 10; Ps 49

ERUPTION OF PRAISE

"My soul magnifies the Lord, and my spirit
rejoices in God my Savior,"
LUKE 1:46–47

Bursting with praise, Mary sang to the Lord, displaying her jubilant attitude at being chosen by God and blessed beyond measure. She was to become the mother of Jesus, son of God. After the initial consternation of being so blessed, Mary responded faithfully to the news and could no longer contain her joy. She erupted in praise.

Many times I have found myself awestruck by the wonderful knowledge of being blessed by the Almighty God. There is nothing that comes close to the joy of knowing I have been given the gift of eternal life. God's greatest gift to mankind is not the earthly blessings we experience daily but the eternal promise of being forever in His presence. If that just does not make you want to jump up and shout, "Hallelujah," I do not know what will!

God's precious gift of salvation should elicit feelings of gratitude; praise is one way of showing that gratitude. In the Bible, you can find many examples of people praising God for a variety of reasons, most often vocally. So the next time you're meditating on God's blessings, take a cue from Mary, and lift your voice in an eruption of praise! –Blevins

Morning: 2 Sam 2; 1 Cor 13 — *Evening:* Ezek 11; Ps 50

SEPTEMBER 9

I WILL NEVER LEAVE YOU

". . . for he has said, "I will never leave you nor forsake you."
HEBREWS 13:5

Almost everyone who has done any length of time knows that being locked up can be a very lonely experience. Over time, friends, acquaintances, and family abandon us. We are left alone to fend for ourselves year after year. Even those we think love us unconditionally and would never leave us or forsake us, often do. This usually occurs when we least expect it and are least prepared. Because we have no choice when this happens, we paint false smiles on our faces and keep on trucking. But loneliness resonates within us.

However, as lonely as we feel, we are not alone. We have a God who is right here with us and who has promised repeatedly in His Word that He will never leave us or forsake us. When the lights go out and we lie in our bunks, alone, He is here with us. When we wake up in the morning and do not know if we can make it another day, He is here with us. When we are sitting in a loud, crowded dayroom or chow hall and it feels like we are the only one on the face of the earth, He is here with us. In the midst of all the chaos in our lives due to our incarceration, He is here with us. For He has promised, "I will never leave you or forsake you."

Those we love the most may walk away, but we can rest assured that our God will always be here. He will never leave us nor forsake us. –Solley

Morning: 2 Sam 3; 1 Cor 14 — *Evening:* Ezek 12; Ps 51

SEALING THE DEAL

"I signed the deed, sealed it, got witnesses,
and weighed the money on scales."
JEREMIAH 32:10

During the siege of Jerusalem by the Babylonians, Jeremiah the prophet buys a field. In practical terms, this seems foolish because once Babylon takes the city, ownership of the field will be meaningless. Likewise, when we are apprehended by the gospel and the deal is sealed for us as followers of Christ, others see us as foolish. We seem particularly foolish when we are denied for parole or suffer on one level or another. Others see no immediate benefit to what has taken place for us as our relationship to God is restored.

For the unbeliever, sealing the deal for the reception of the forgiveness of sins in Christ may appear to be no big deal because it doesn't seem to change much of anything at all. It seems as foolish as buying a field in a city that is about to fall and be occupied by a foreign army. However, we see the benefits of buying the field in Jerusalem as Jeremiah's prophecy progresses. We read that houses, vineyards, and fields will again be purchased in the city and the Lord will bring back His people to the land to experience peace and a renewed relationship with Him. Thus, Jeremiah was not so foolish after all.

As believers, we are like Jeremiah's field; we have been bought for a price. Christ sealed the deal for us. The entire span of history is a witness to what He has done for humanity as He was weighed in the balance on the cross. May we rejoice in the hope we have in Him today. We have been bought with a price, and because of that, we know we have the assurance of a peaceful, right relationship with the Lord. –Karch

Morning: 2 Sam 4, 5; 1 Cor 15 — *Evening:* Ezek 13; Ps 52, 53, 54

THE LOST SHEEP

"Rejoice with me, for I have found my sheep that was lost."
LUKE 15:6B

Luke 15:1–7 contains a poignant illustration of Christ's love for the lost sheep of the world. In this parable, Jesus presents a picture of the heart of a shepherd who loves and cares for his sheep. Every sheep is of value to him, and he will go to the extreme to ensure the safety of his flock, even to the extent of leaving the ninety-nine behind to find the one that is lost (v. 4). When he finds his lost sheep, he does not chastise it or berate it. Rather, the loving shepherd, picks up the trembling, dirty sheep, lays it on his shoulders, and carries it home (v. 5). Then he calls all of his friends together and rejoices (v. 6). Jesus emphasizes His point by declaring that in the same way there was rejoicing over the lost sheep that was found, there will be more joy in heaven over one sinner who comes to repentance than over ninety-nine righteous who need no repentance (v. 7).

Like a helpless sheep bleating for its shepherd, many around us are lost and cannot find their way. Without the love of a shepherd who will risk everything to save them, they are headed for eternal destruction. The good shepherd, Jesus Christ has already laid His life down for His sheep (John 10:11), and it is the duty of every Christian to share this message with the lost sheep confined inside these walls. We must seek out the lost sheep of the world, pick them up, lay them on our shoulders, and carry them home to the foot of the cross.

That being the case, the question remains: Will we? –Solley

Morning: 2 Sam 6; 1 Cor 16 — *Evening:* Ezek 14; Ps 55

SUPREME COURT

*"I will bear the indignation of the LORD because I have sinned
against him, until he pleads my cause and executes judgment for me.
He will bring me out to the light; I shall look upon his vindication."*
MICAH 7:9

If asked, the majority of prisoners would readily accept a pardon or acquittal on their conviction. Likewise, the prophet Micah desired pardon for his people. The difference is those of us in prison tend to look to, or hope in, a judicial system that finds its effectiveness in efficiency. Micah, however, looked to a judge who established justice on mercy and the sufficiency of His own sovereign grace.

Ultimately, each of us has sinned against God, our supreme judge. In spite of that, our main concern tends to rest within the context of our earthly crimes. In relation to those crimes, we often wonder when atonement or vindication will come. The good news is that all of our cases have been pled by the blood of Jesus. On the cross, justice and judgment were executed on our behalf. God's own righteousness is revealed on the cross and is now being revealed in those of us who have been redeemed.

Christ's sacrifice applies to all cases across the board. By this we can be confident, even while we still experience some form of consequence for our past crimes, the Lord will also bring us "out to the light." Thank Him for this, and watch with expectation for Him to act in a mighty way—all while longing, in an ultimate sense, to "look upon his vindication." –Karch

Morning: 2 Sam 7; 2 Cor 1 — *Evening:* Ezek 15; Ps 56, 57

CASE CLOSED

"There is therefore now no condemnation for
those who are in Christ Jesus."
ROMANS 8:1

"Not guilty!" These are the words every prisoner wishes he or she would've heard in the court room. A verdict rendered in our favor and a wash of relief enveloping us as we realized how close we actually came. Unfortunately, if you're reading this, you've probably heard the exact opposite, and that wash of relief was actually a sigh of anguish as you were pronounced, "Guilty!" Feelings of regret, remorse, shame, and guilt began to roll in like an ocean tide, churning your stomach in knots.

These emotions are common among those found guilty of criminal acts, but according to the Word of God, we are all guilty. There is no one righteous (Rom 3:10). We are all sinners who deserve the death penalty. Nevertheless, the Word also tells us that Jesus Christ paid the penalty for our sins once and for all. Don't think, however, that your case was dismissed; somebody paid for your crimes in full. The punishment that we all deserve was reserved for another, and you have been redeemed on the basis of His perfect substitutionary sacrifice. Praise God!

So keep this act of compassion and mercy on the forefront of your mind as you go through your day. And when those old debilitating feelings of shame and guilt begin ebbing back into your life, remember, for those who are in Christ Jesus—the case is closed. –Blevins

Morning: 2 Sam 8, 9; 2 Cor 2 — *Evening:* Ezek 16; Ps 58, 59

DON'T WASTE IT

*". . . God of all comfort, who comforts us in our affliction, so that
we may be able to comfort those who are in any affliction, with
the comfort with which we ourselves are comforted by God."*

2 CORINTHIANS 1:3–4

I often find myself going through difficulties in life that I simply do not understand—major difficulties. Things that make me want to throw my hands in the air and say, "All right, God, I give up. I cannot take this anymore." Yet, it is when I am at my lowest point and when I feel like giving up, that God reaches down into the mess I have created and comforts me in my affliction. And often, it is not long before I run into someone battling the same demons of affliction God has recently helped me overcome, and I am able to help comfort them as God comforted me. This is only because I have been through it, too!

No matter who you are, especially if you are in prison, you have been through some difficulty in life. You have a story and testimony about what God has brought you through that can be used to help comfort others and draw them closer to Christ. As Paul tells us, God comforts us so that we may be able to comfort others. When you fail to use the story of your life and the comfort God has given you during your times of intense struggle to help others, you waste it. You allow your struggle to be all for nothing.

When the opportunity arises, use the story of your life and the comfort God has given you to comfort someone else in need. Do not allow it to be all for nothing. Do not waste it! –Solley

Morning: 2 Sam 10; 2 Cor 3 — *Evening:* Ezek 17; Ps 60, 61

YES AND AMEN

"For the Son of God, Jesus Christ, whom we proclaimed among you, Silvanius and Timothy and I, was not Yes and No, but in Him it is always Yes. For all the promises of God find their Yes in him."

2 CORINTHIANS 1:19–20A

P aul has no qualification or equivocation when it comes to what Christ accomplished for those who have faith in Him. He was not sure of his redemption one day, only to doubt it the next. He simply trusted in the *Yes* of Christ. This sureness comes because God's promise to those who believe in Jesus is not worked out through a *Yes* here and a *No* there, but rather, it is always an affirming *Yes*.

One of the most frustrating experiences of prison is having an official or another prisoner tell you one thing one minute, and in the next instant, say the exact opposite. In effect, telling you, "Yes" and then, "No." This breeds a level of distrust toward officials and other prisoners alike. In doing so, it is also very easy to allow this same distrust to spill over into our faith. When it comes to trusting Christ implicitly, there is no room for this type of dissonance as Paul makes perfectly clear. In spite of the trust issues we may have within an environment that promotes distrust, we can trust Jesus. We can say, as the *New King James Version* does, all the promises of God in Jesus are "Yes" and "Amen."

If there is any doubt as to the scope of all of God's promises being applicable to us, know that all of those promises are *Yes* and *Amen* in Jesus. There is nothing warranting our trust more than what Jesus has done for us. He is the great affirming *Yes*. –Karch

Morning: 2 Sam 11; 2 Cor 4 — *Evening:* Ezek 18; Ps 62, 63

SEPTEMBER 16

RULE NUMBER ONE

*"He has told you, O man, what is good; and what does
the LORD require of you but to do justice, and to love
kindness, and to walk humbly with your God?"*
MICAH 6:8

When I realized I was coming to the penitentiary for the first
time, I knew I was in for a huge culture shock. Having never
been incarcerated before, I was open to any and all advice from the
guys in the county jail who had done big time. One of the older guys
in the tank who had been down two or three times came and told me,
"Rule number one: when you hit the farm, *mind your own business."* I
could tell by all the affirmative nods that this was probably the consen-
sus of everyone who had any kind of experience doing time.

However, while I have found it is not hard to look the other way
when something is going down, it grates against something inside of
me. Ignoring people who need help goes against everything Jesus
taught. One of the problems with "minding my own business" is that
I am created in the glorious image of God, and as such, I have a sense
of justice that conflicts with those worldly words of wisdom. So, when I
see the strong preying on the weak or any other number of wicked and
detestable things, it bothers me. And, as a born-again child of God, it
should.

Maybe, just maybe, rule number one shouldn't be a rule at all.
Maybe instead of prison being a culture shock, it is time for us to
shock the culture of prison. Maybe, as men of God, our rule *numero
uno* should be: do justice, love kindness, and walk humbly with our
God. –Blevins

Morning: 2 Sam 12; 2 Cor 5 — *Evening:* Ezek 19; Ps 64, 65

GOD IS WATCHING

*"For my eyes are on all their ways. They are not hidden
from me, nor is their iniquity concealed from my eyes."*
JEREMIAH 16:17

Yeah, we got away with it. In and out, no witnesses, smooth as molasses—nothing but smiles and spending money. How many times have we had that feeling? We were ecstatic because we just got away with something. We pulled it off, and there was no way anyone was going to find out. Whether it was something as petty as stealing twenty-five cents out of our momma's purse when we were kids or a much greater offense committed as adults, we all have had that type of experience.

In Jeremiah's time, the Israelites convinced themselves that no one saw the evil they did. We have the tendency to do likewise. We fooled ourselves into thinking no one saw the evil things we did. However, God saw everything. No matter how much we tried to hide the things we did or how slick we thought we were, God was always watching. Nothing was hidden from Him, nor was any of our iniquity concealed from His eyes. He saw every act we committed, every thought we had, and every deep, dark secret we kept. Amazingly, even knowing all of that—how dirty and rotten we were inside—God still sent His son to die for our sins so that we could be cleansed from our iniquity and reconciled unto Him (Rom 5:8). That ought to make you think deeply about how much your heavenly Father loves you.

Because of God's love for us, we no longer have to be concerned with Him watching us as a judge; He watches over us as His children. –Solley

Morning: 2 Sam 13; 2 Cor 6 — *Evening:* Ezek 20; Ps 66, 67

WAITING FOR WAITING

*"Therefore the LORD waits to be gracious to you, and therefore
he exalts himself to show mercy to you. For the LORD is a
God of justice; blessed are all those who wait for him."*
ISAIAH 30:18

In the midst of his warnings against Judah, Isaiah makes the declaration that God "waits to be gracious" to them. In the contemporary Christian context, particularly for those in prison, we are often confronted with the concept of waiting. The majority of the time we are encouraged or admonished to wait for the Lord to act in some way on our behalf for any number of reasons: to bring a spouse back, restore relationships, or release us. We seldom, however, hear anything about the Lord waiting on us.

When we think about the Lord waiting on us, the question naturally emerges: What is he waiting for? Isaiah tells us the Lord waits to be gracious to us, and the reception of His graciousness comes directly from our waiting for Him. It seems like a strange paradox doesn't it? The Lord waits for us to wait for him. There is something gracious about waiting, in and of itself. The grace of God meets us in our waiting. Too many times we easily get caught up in the idea that the Lord responds and meets us when we move or act in some way. We are told that when we act in faith, then the Lord moves. Isaiah challenges this in a profound way.

If you find yourself struggling and worn out by doing all you can do to earn the Lord's grace, mercy, and favor, understand that he is waiting for you to wait for him. As you wait, sense the peace that comes from Him in the midst of the waiting and know that "blessed are all those who wait for him." –Karch

Morning: 2 Sam 14; 2 Cor 7 — *Evening:* Ezek 21; Ps 68

POISON CONTROL

*"Flee from sexual immorality. Every other sin a
person commits is outside the body, but the sexually
immoral person sins against his own body."*
1 CORINTHIANS 6:18

With the overload of indecent photos, half-nude magazines, racy radio songs, and scandalous novels, the average inmate is inundated with numerous enticements to engage in sexually impure thoughts and actions. All of these poison the mind and draw one away from God. Paul tells the Corinthians, who were known for being sexually deviant, that this particular sin is not only against God, but also against one's own body. Committing this type of sin was akin to poisoning yourself because it spreads throughout the body, from the mind to the members, and destroys one from the inside out.

The body is the temple of the Holy Spirit, so no wonder it feels so despicable when you commit sexually immoral acts or think sexually immoral thoughts. That's the poison control center letting you know what you are doing is wrong and detrimental to your health. The Holy Spirit is trying to get you to purge the poison from your body by making you aware of His presence and His effects. Yet, in the limited space and restricted freedom in prison, how is one to flee from sexual sin? One way is by avoiding things that cause us to stumble. Whether it is photos, TV programs, or magazines, we can guard our eyes more closely and avoid conversations that invoke our imagination to wander in the wrong direction.

If you've been poisoned by this debilitating condition, call the poison control center immediately, and let the Holy Spirit lead you to clear the toxin from your mind and heart. Pray right now and ask the Holy Spirit to reveal areas in your life where sexual sin is rampant; then ask Him to help you take measures to purge it from your life. –Blevins

Morning: 2 Sam 15; 2 Cor 8 — *Evening:* Ezek 22; Ps 69

THE DISGRACE OF YOUTH

*"For after I had turned away, I relented, and after I was
instructed, I struck my thigh; I was ashamed, and I was
confounded, because I bore the disgrace of my youth."*
JEREMIAH 31:19

J eremiah describes a process of faith for those who know and serve
God. Through the convicting power of the Spirit of God we become
aware of our sinfulness. Once our sinfulness is realized, we become
ashamed and confounded. When the gospel message is appropriated
to our lives and we are saved by the grace of the Lord Jesus Christ, we
are turned away from those sins toward God. We have turned away,
relented, and become instructed in the faith. This is the necessary process of the Christian faith.

Often times, in coming to understand our sinfulness, even after
knowing Christ, we remain sick with shame. For those of us who are
in prison, this sense of shame is particularly heavy simply because we
are not here for being little angels. The disgrace of our youth can be
overwhelming. We continue to bear that disgrace through those subtle
everyday reminders: we wear that disgrace in our uniforms and bear it
every time we have to repeat our identification number. To one degree
or another, we continue to be ashamed because of the sins of the past.

May we be encouraged today knowing that the Lord remembers us
and continues to have mercy on us for Christ's sake. In Him we have
our forgiveness of sin, redemption, and reconciliation. No matter what
our pasts were, in Him we need not be ashamed. He has borne the
disgrace of our youth for us so that we may become the righteousness
of God in Him (2 Cor 5:21). –Karch

Morning: 2 Sam 16; 2 Cor 9 — *Evening:* Ezek 23; Ps 70, 71

OTHERS ARE LISTENING

*"About midnight Paul and Silas were praying and singing
hymns to God, and the prisoners were listening to them."*
ACTS 16:25

P aul and Silas were arrested for "disturbing the peace." After being stripped and beaten, they were thrown into jail and chained to the walls, as was customary in first century prisons (vv. 22–23). Paul and Silas passed the long, painful night praying and singing hymns to God, and the other prisoners were listening.

Can you imagine the impression Paul and Silas' actions had on their fellow prisoners? In the midst of horrific circumstances, these two men still praised God. Beaten, bloody, and chained to prison walls, they prayed and sang hymns all night. Even when the earth quaked, the doors opened, and their bonds were unfastened, no one escaped! When the jailer went to kill himself, Paul cried out, ". . . we are all here" (v. 28).

How Paul and Silas did their time greatly affected those around them. To someone like me, who has spent two decades in prison, the miracle that night was not merely the earthquake, the doors opening, or the bonds breaking, but that even when they had the perfect opportunity to, not *one* prisoner escaped. When Luke penned this passage, he left the reader with the impression that no one escaping was a direct result of having listened to Paul and Silas pray and sing to God. Something more powerful and compelling than a shot at freedom was happening in their lives.

What about you? Are you praising God in the midst of horrific circumstances? Can others around you see the powerful and compelling work of God in your life? What do others come away with when they listen to you? –Solley

Morning: 2 Sam 17; 2 Cor 10 — *Evening:* Ezek 24; Ps 72

PATH-BREAKER

*"looking to Jesus, the founder and perfecter of our faith, who for
the joy that was set before him endured the cross, despising the
shame, and is seated at the right hand of the throne of God."*
HEBREWS 12:2

A s a fan of history, I have always been fascinated by the many stories of men and women who made a way for others where there
was no way. Those people throughout history who have accomplished
these feats are generally labeled as innovators, trailblazers, or path-
breakers. They do what seems impossible and go where no other has
gone or could go. In doing so, they open up the way for others. In
many ways, these are the people who have carried us through history
from one epoch to the next.

In today's text, the words *founder and perfecter* are translated from a
single Greek word that has no translatable one-for-one English equivalent. The connotation of the word, however, carries the idea of an
innovator, trailblazer, or path-breaker. With this word, the author of
Hebrews attempts to capture the scope of what Christ accomplished
for otherwise hopeless sinners like you and me. Jesus blazed a trail and
broke a path into eternal glory so that the human race, which had no
other way to salvation, now has a means of being reconciled to God.
Jesus opened a path reconciling us with God so we could spend eternity with Him.

As a true innovator, Jesus blazed the trail for us in the most unexpected way—He traversed the oddest path and endured the horror of
the cross. He laid down the way that leads us into eternity so we will
one day stand before Him at the throne of God. With the same enthusiasm as the author of Hebrews, we should joyfully look to Jesus—our
path-breaker. –Karch

Morning: 2 Sam 18; 2 Cor 11 — *Evening:* Ezek 25; Ps 73

SLAYING YOUR GIANTS

". . . For the battle is the LORD's, . . ."
1 SAMUEL 17:47

We all love the story of David and Goliath. It is the ultimate story of the underdog triumphing over all odds to become the victor. Goliath seemed fierce and invincible to the Israelites. In their minds, there was no way anyone could defeat this nine-foot-tall behemoth who mocked and tormented them every day. Yet, along came this little shepherd boy named David who trusted in the Lord and refused to be intimidated by Goliath. With a mere sling and a stone, David took out Goliath! You see, David recognized something vital. He knew the battle was not his. He did not try to defeat Goliath in his own strength, but relied solely on God for victory. He boldly proclaimed, "The battle is the Lord's."

How many of us rely on our own strength to slay the nine-foot giants in our lives? We become so encumbered by our circumstances and situations that we lose sight of the fact that, as Christians, we have a mighty and awesome God who has delivered us from the hand of the enemy time and time again. As David understood as a young boy, the battle is not ours; it is the Lord's. It is only by His strength that we shall overcome and slay the giants in our lives.

What kind of spiritual giants are you facing today? Is it a temptation you cannot overcome: lust, pride, anger, unforgiveness, guilt, shame, regret? Maybe it is a loved one's salvation you have been praying for or a broken relationship you long to have restored. Whatever the case may be, always remember the battle is not yours: it belongs to the Lord. To Him, for Him, and through Him is victory! –Solley

Morning: 2 Sam 19; 2 Cor 12 — *Evening:* Ezek 26; Ps 74

SILENCE IS GOLDEN

*"Whoever guards his mouth preserves his life; he
who opens wide his lips comes to ruin."*
PROVERBS 13:3

T ime after time I see guys in prison who can't help themselves
from speaking about anything and everything. From the greatest running back ever to play the game of football to the weather in
Pakistan, these guys always have something to say. The topic could be
the price of beans in Guatemala, and these fellas will argue you down
to your socks. Sometimes, I wonder if it's just because they like hearing the sound of their own voice. However you look at it though, they
do not know the meaning of holding their tongue. Whether it's with
officers or inmates, they feel obligated to open their mouths even if it
gets them into trouble.

While rigorous and superfluous debate is a popular hobby in any
dayroom or dormitory, the Bible encourages us to mind our words. It
says there is "a time to keep silence, and a time to speak" (Ecc 3:7).
It tells us, "the tongue is a fire, a world of unrighteousness . . . setting
on fire the entire course of life" (Jas 3:6). Opening our mouths and
sputtering out the first words that cross our minds is never a good idea.
Stopping to think about what we're about to say before we speak is
wisdom that we would all do well to remember.

There will undoubtedly be a never-ending supply of arguments to
take part in, but knowing when to open your mouth and when to keep
it closed will take wisdom and discernment. The temptation to spew
unwholesome and unedifying banter will never abate, but we can be
on guard against such dangerous prattle by remembering that silence
is golden! –Blevins

Morning: 2 Sam 20; 2 Cor 13 — *Evening:* Ezek 27; Ps 75, 76

IT ISN'T EASY

*"For the gate is narrow and the way is hard that
leads to life, and those who find it are few."*
MATTHEW 7:14

Being a criminal, con-artist, gangster, hustler, or a dope fiend is easy. We have all been there, and if we are honest with ourselves, we could easily go there again. It would not take much to give in to the enticement to take the easy road in life and return to the wide path of destruction that is well traveled (v. 13). In fact, many would be there with open arms to welcome us, glad that we had returned.

However, being a Christian is not easy, especially in prison. When you commit your life to the Lord, and are serious about following Him, things can quickly become very difficult. Many of your so-called friends will turn their backs on you; others will take your newfound faith as weakness, and some will want to test your commitment to Christ, hoping you fall. Then there is the spiritual enemy who will do everything possible to kill, steal, and destroy your faith. He will make you doubt, hit you where you are weakest, and tempt you like he never has before.

We should not be surprised though, for we have been warned. Christ told us that the way that leads to eternal life is hard, and few find it. If we expected the Christian life to be easy, then we were greatly mistaken. Being a Christian is probably the hardest thing you will ever do, but it all pays off in the long run. God has promised us a crown of life if we remain steadfast (Jas 1:12).

Therefore, when—not if—the Christian life gets hard, don't give up. Stay strong and hang in there because it isn't easy. –Solley

Morning: 2 Sam 21; Gal 1 — *Evening:* Ezek 28; Ps 77

SET TRIPPIN'

*"And the LORD said to him, 'Pass through the city, through
Jerusalem, and put a mark on the foreheads of the men who sigh
and groan over all the abominations that are committed in it.'"*
EZEKIEL 9:4

I n Ezekiel's vision, the Lord tells a man clothed in linen to place a
mark on the foreheads of those in Jerusalem who grieved the sins
committed in the city. Those who were given this mark represented the
Lord as His faithful remnant. The six executioners sent by the Lord
into Jerusalem to destroy the sinful people there, would not kill—indeed they would not even touch—anyone who bore the mark (v. 1-6).

Many of us have utilized a number of symbols, marks, and signs
representing gangs, sets, or hoods that conveyed an entire mentality
and defined who we were. Accordingly, we understood what it meant
when somebody started throwing up signs and were "set-trippin'." It
usually meant trouble. In the same way, when the Lord sees signs, symbols, marks, and colors that represent something other than Him, He
takes offense and trouble is coming. Many of us in prison have a tendency to waffle back and forth between what we are representing—we
go back and forth between the old mentality and the new way the Lord
has shown us.

If the Lord were to return today, what would He find you representing? Do we really bear His mark and represent Him in a way pleasing to Him? Do we sigh and groan over those bad things that happen
around us? We should desire to represent Him in a way that stands
apart from the world. Even if those around us consider it a form of set-trippin', we shouldn't hesitate to represent Him in that way because
the stakes in this game are far too high—they are eternal. –Karch

Morning: 2 Sam 22; Gal 2 — *Evening:* Ezek 29; Ps 78:1–37

VINDICATION

*"For the day of the LORD is near upon all the
nations. As you have done, it shall be done to you;
your deeds shall return on your own head."*
 OBADIAH 15

The book of Obadiah is one of the shortest books in the entire Bible. It's probably one of the least read as well. I would certainly believe that most people reading through its short twenty-one verses don't find too much to cling to during their daily devotional time. However, I would implore you to take a closer look at God's Word as spoken through the prophet Obadiah.

The entire book concerns God's judgment against the nation of Edom. The Edomites have an interesting story behind them dating back to the patriarchal period (c.2000–1500 B.C.) and their progenitor, Esau (Gen 25:27–34). The storied conflict between the Israelites and Edomites spanned many centuries (Num 20:14–21), and the enmity between the two people groups was well documented. Even Paul, quoting from the prophet Malachi, alludes to the sovereign choosing of Jacob over Esau to illustrate God's eternal election and gracious calling (Rom 9:10–13).

As Christians who have been redeemed by the precious blood of our Lord and Savior Jesus Christ, we don't need to fear the conflict that arises from society's rejection of us. Our past mistakes have been forgiven, regardless of how others may continue to treat us. So then, what possible comfort can we find in a book about God's judgment upon a nation that continually fought against His people, who refused His people help in their time of need, and who kicked His people when they were at their lowest point? One word—vindication. –Blevins

Morning: 2 Sam 23; Gal 3 — *Evening:* Ezek 30; Ps 78:38–72

THE GIFT OF WAITING

*"Wait for the LORD; be strong, and let your
heart take courage; wait for the LORD."*
PSALM 27:14

Whether we realize it or not, as prisoners, we wait for just about everything. We wait for simple things like chow, commissary, showers, and recreation. We wait for more important things like letters, phone calls, and visits. And we even wait for the most important things like parole hearings, parole answers, and release dates. But no matter how much waiting we do, we always get tired of waiting; we grow weary.

Waiting is very difficult to do, especially when we pray and pray, and it seems our prayers are not being heard or answered. Yet, little do we know, it is during these times when we grow in our faith the most. What seems like God's silence is His gift to us. Through the waiting process, God is teaching us to trust and depend on Him, and not on ourselves. Making us wait is God's way of stripping us of all of our self-reliance, independence, impatience, and personal agendas. The added beauty of waiting is that, when our prayers are answered or we realize that what we were waiting on was not as important as we thought, we can look back and tell God, "Now I see. Now I understand." It is then that we can thank Him for the gift of waiting.

When God seems silent and the wait goes on, do not get discouraged. Stand strong, and let your heart take courage. Learn what God is trying to teach you, and thank Him for the gift of waiting. –Solley

Morning: 2 Sam 24; Gal 4 — *Evening:* Ezek 31; Ps 79

THE GENTRY

*"But you are a chosen race, a royal priesthood, a holy nation, a
people for his own possession, that you may proclaim the excellencies
of him who called you out of darkness into his marvelous light."*

1 PETER 2:9

Peter, who was by no means born into the upper echelons of first
century Roman society, knew fully what it was like to be despised.
First, he was Jewish living under Roman occupation and domination.
Further, as a Jewish fisherman, he was part of the lower class of his own
people. Finally, as a Christian, he was despised by both Romans and
Jews alike, and whatever status he did have within society was forfeited.

We can easily relate to Peter's situation. The majority of the prison
population comes from the lower class of society. We did not grow up
with money or power that comes with social prestige. Also, coming to
prison, we understand what it is like to have lost what little social status
we did have. Furthermore, we now know what it is like to be despised
by society as we are viewed as its urchins. However, neither the Romans
nor the Jews were the determiner of Peter's real social status, just as
contemporary society does not determine ours. Having been chosen
by God, we have become a new gentry—a new social elite. Peter says we
are a royal priesthood and a holy nation. Social stratification reaches
its zenith with us: the people of God.

No matter what our social position seems to be, like Peter, we
should see ourselves for who we are in Christ. The Lord calls us into
this particular status to proclaim the excellency of what He has done
for us and to encourage others to respond to the same call to be part
of the gentry. –Karch

Morning: 1 Kgs 1; Gal 5 — *Evening:* Ezek 32; Ps 80

THE WRONG DIRECTION

"Come to me, all who labor and are heavy
laden, and I will give you rest."
MATTHEW 11:28

I have a family member who has experienced many difficult things in her life. She has a precious heart and many gifts that God has given her. Yet, the heartaches and pains she has been through have been more than she has been able to bear. In her search for relief from her pain, she has taken refuge in drugs and found her solace in the highs and lows that come from a drug induced haze.

How often do we find ourselves turning toward the things of the world to seek temporary relief from the harsh realities of life? We have often sought comfort in drugs, alcohol, sex, music, and even violence to alleviate the internal burdens we bear. Yet, these things can never cure what ails our hearts and souls. They can never give us true comfort and rest but are only temporary respites that mask our eternal problem. However, true rest can be found in Christ. He has called all who are weary and heavy laden to come to Him, assuring us that He will give us rest for our souls.

When you have felt weary and heavy laden, have you been running toward the things of the world that only can give you a temporal comfort and a false sense of security? If so, turn around! You are headed in the wrong direction. It is only in Christ that you will find true rest and comfort. Run to Him! –Solley

Morning: 1 Kgs 2; Gal 6 — *Evening:* Ezek 33; Ps 81, 82

WIPED OUT

"Thus Jehu wiped out Baal from Israel."
2 KINGS 10:28

After years of tumultuous wilderness wanderings, the nation of Israel is finally able to cross the Jordan River into the Promised Land. As soon as they do, however, they began to run into problems. One of the main obstacles they faced again and again was the idolatry associated with the pseudo-god, Baal. Various people groups throughout the land of Canaan were religiously oriented to this false deity.

After King Ahab paid for defying the Lord, the new king, Jehu, began a campaign to eradicate from the land all vestiges of Baal worship.

For the Christian, before we come to know Christ, we are more or less oblivious to the idols in our lives. Once we are converted, just as the Israelites entering into the Promised Land, we begin to face opposition from the former idols in our lives, as well as those that previously never really tempted us. We are confronted with a number of idol-like Baals: anger, lust, envy, and the like. As a result, many times we react the way Ahab did by taking on a defiant attitude toward the things of God. However, we need to recognize the Baals for what they are, react like Jehu did, and wipe them out of our lives.

In reading the historical accounts of Israel's kings, we see how easy it is to slip into various forms of idolatry. This is particularly the case when we look at the life of Ahab. Inasmuch as Jehu did a good thing, he too eventually fell into destructive sin (v. 31). We must daily take stock of the influence of idols in our lives. What are the Baals that tempt us away from the Lord? Find them; and through the power of the Holy Spirit, wipe them out of your life. –Karch

Morning: 1 Kg 3; Eph 1 — *Evening:* Ezek 34; Ps 83, 84

SIN *AD NAUSEAM*

"as it is written: 'None is righteous, no, not one;'"
ROMANS 3:10

P rison has a powerful way of forcing us to take a long look at ourselves. The time spent in solitude and reflection compels us to examine our true selves—the people we really are. All the bad decisions we've made and all the right decisions we should've made are laid bare. When we're confined to five-by-nine foot cells, we can no longer run from our mistakes. We suddenly stand face to face with our true identity—sinners.

When writing to the first century Roman church, which was made up of both Jews and Gentiles, Paul laid out the fundamentals of the gospel. The problem was that the Jewish believers thought they had a leg up on the Gentiles because they possessed the Law. Consequently, they assumed they were somehow innately better than their non-religious counterparts. The truth of the matter is that they, too, were hopelessly apart from the saving grace of Jesus Christ. One of Paul's first tasks was to eliminate the self-righteous barriers erected in the minds of his audience.

The interesting lesson learned from Paul's systematic distribution of the gospel in Romans is that, as a minister of the gospel, sometimes one must unashamedly help people take a good look in the mirror. While today's culture is quick to deride the sins of others, God's word points the finger squarely back at the self-righteous. In order for one to accept the Good News, one first needs to be told the bad news. The human condition is universal and utterly devoid of any good of its own. Paul's condemnation of all of humanity sheds light on the sorry state humanity finds itself and allows us all to humbly come before the Creator and cry out like the psalmist, "Oh, that salvation for Israel would come out of Zion!" (Ps 14:7a). –Blevins

Morning: 1 Kgs 4, 5; Eph 2 — *Evening:* Ezek 35; Ps 85

A GUILT YOU CAN'T WISH AWAY

"Wash me thoroughly from my iniquity, and cleanse me from my sin!"
PSALM 51:2

I recently heard a sermon titled, "A Guilt You Can't Wish Away," which seemed to speak right to my heart. You see, like a lot of prisoners, I have lived for many years consumed with the guilt of hurting my wife and leaving her to raise our daughter alone. It seemed like every time I thought I was finally starting to come to terms with what I had done, the guilt inside would rear up and kick my feet out from under me all over again. It seemed like the more I tried to wish the guilt away, the more intense it became.

I have realized over time that in order to be free from the guilt of past sins, we must fully understand that guilt has no place in a believer's life. When we were born again, all of our sins were forgiven. Not just some of them, but all of them, including the ones that we often regret the most—the ones that fill us with that unbearable and overwhelming sense of guilt. To continue to hold on to the guilt from sins we already have been forgiven for is basically our way of telling God, "I know I am forgiven, but . . ." As the preacher so rightly said, "Our guilt can't be wished away; it must be washed away by the blood of Christ."

Have you been consumed by guilt lately? Has it kicked your feet out from under you, *again?* If so, choose to accept the finished work of the cross. Stop trying to wish away your guilt and let the precious blood of Christ wash it away. –Solley

Morning: 1 Kgs 6; Eph 3 — *Evening:* Ezek 36; Ps 86

IF, THEN

"And Elijah came near to all the people and said, 'How long will you go limping between two different opinions? If the LORD is God, follow him; but if Baal, then follow him.'"
1 KINGS 18:21

H ave you ever pondered your allegiances? To whom or what are you loyal? If we really think about it, due to life's complexity, we easily find our loyalties spread thin. I can say I am loyal to my family, friends, country, company. Ultimately, however, I can say that my loyalties reside with God. When we boil things down to a bare allegiance, we are faced with a choice—either our loyalties are with God, or against Him.

Toward the end of Elijah's ministry, the Scriptures describe the show-down between him and the four hundred fifty prophets of Baal. Against what seemed to be insurmountable odds, Elijah displayed a cool, calm, and collected confidence in God. His loyalties were with God alone. Elijah expected to see the same loyalty from the people of God. He challenged those gathered on the mountain and told them to choose: either follow the Lord or Baal. The challenge implied they were not loyal to the Lord. There is no real limping between two different opinions. They either served the Lord or Baal.

When we consider our allegiances, we can convince ourselves that we can be a little bit loyal to the Lord and a little bit loyal to something or somebody else. In reality, we are not left with that option. Either we are following God or not. Each day is a conscious effort to express our singular loyalty to our God over and against the numerous other things that vie for our allegiance. If the LORD is God, then follow Him. –Karch

Morning: 1 Kgs 7; Eph 4 — *Evening:* Ezek 37; Ps 87, 88

DEVOTED

*"And they devoted themselves to the apostles' teaching and
the fellowship, to the breaking of bread and the prayers."*
ACTS 2:42

I n prison we have so much time on our hands that it's easy to get
lost sitting around doing absolutely nothing. We might have a few
items on the daily agenda—shower, work, class, chow; but for the most
part, we have lots of unproductive time. Even when we desire to do
something better with our time (i.e. college, vocation, and craft shop),
there are obstacles in our way. When I first came down, having delu-
sions of grandeur, I thought I would slip right into college, get a good
Officer's Dining Room job, and keep busy until I went home. Yet, it
took over six years to get into school, and they told me I couldn't have
a decent job for at least a decade.

However, I found that I could do something better with my time
than just sit around and watch TV or play dominoes. I began reading
my Bible and discovered a new passion for God's Word. I discovered
that I didn't need a school counselor or job assignment to study the
eternal truths of Scripture. Pretty soon, I found others who were interested in learning God's Word, too. It's funny how God will open just
the right doors at just the right time.

After preaching the first Christian sermon, Peter witnessed around
3,000 souls added to the church. These new Spirit-filled converts realized that the previous manner in which they spent their time would
have to change. So what did those newly baptized believers begin doing? They devoted themselves to learning from the apostles, fellowshipping with each other, breaking bread, and praying—all excellent
ways to spend time in first century Israel as well as in a twenty-first century prison. So with all the empty hours passing you by, what are you
going to devote yourself to? –Blevins

Morning: 1 Kgs 8; Eph 5 — *Evening*: Ezek 38; Ps 89

SPIRITUAL BASEBALL

*"For you did not receive the spirit of slavery to fall back
into fear, but you have received the Spirit of adoption
as sons, by whom we cry, 'Abba! Father!'"*
ROMANS 8:15

N ot long ago, I wanted to do something specific for God. I had
things all planned out and ready. I stepped up to the plate, ready
to hit a spiritual home run, and struck out. I did not even make it off
home plate. For the next few days, I felt like I had let God down, and
He was disappointed in me—until Jason Karch told me a story. His dad
coached his little league baseball team for several years. During that
time, his team did not win one single game. They struck out, overthrew
first base, and missed fly balls. Yet, no matter how much they messed
up, after each losing game, Jason's dad would slap him on the back
and say with a smile, "We'll get them next time!"

Jason's dad was not disappointed that his son's team did not win
any baseball games, nor did Jason cower in fear every time they lost,
thinking he had disappointed his father. Their father-son relationship
was not based on performance, but on love. Likewise, our relationship
with our Heavenly Father is not based on our performance but on His
love. When we attempt things for God and fail or just plain fail in our
everyday Christian lives, we need not fear that we have failed God or
let Him down in some way. We can take confidence in the fact that we
have received the spirit of adoption as sons by whom we cry, "Abba,
Father!"

When you try to hit those spiritual home runs but can never seem
to make it off first base, don't worry; we'll get 'em next time! –Solley

Morning: 1 Kgs 9; Eph 6 — *Evening:* Ezek 39; Ps 90

THE CRUCIBLE

*"In this you rejoice, though now for a little while, if necessary,
you have been grieved by various trials, so that the tested
genuineness of your faith—more precious than gold that perishes
though it is tested by fire—may be found to result in praise
and glory and honor at the revelation of Jesus Christ."*
1 PETER 1:6–7

The mature Peter makes some relevant observations to those he is writing. Understanding the persecution these believers are experiencing, he opens his letter encouraging those who are in the crucible of testing and trials. Even though they are in the thick of it, not only do they have a concrete hope of something better in the future, but in the midst of the trials they have something more precious than refined gold: their faith in Christ. This faith, when tested, will "result in praise and glory and honor."

Living in prison, we often witness the lives of those who allow their entire existence to be defined by some future parole date. Their vision for and expectation of that date almost numbs them to the present. We also know the majority of those who live in such a way end up returning once they do get out. Peter encourages believers to take our present trials as an opportunity to rejoice because this crucible refines our faith. As we begin to recognize the genuineness of that faith, we grow stronger; and hope for the future is solidified.

As difficult as times can be, Christians cannot afford to ignore the here and now. In enduring the pressures of trials and testing, our faith emerges as more precious than refined gold. That kind of faith is more valuable than any parole or release date. –Karch

Morning: 1 Kgs 10; Phil 1 — *Evening:* Ezek 40; Ps 91

HEAVENLY REWARD

". . . And your Father who sees in secret will reward you. "
MATTHEW 6:4

T he Sermon on the Mount found in Matthew 5–7 is one of Jesus' most profound discourses. It covers a variety of topics, but in Matthew 6, Jesus specifically warns against performing with ulterior motives certain deeds such as giving to the poor, praying, and fasting. Jesus is conveying that God desires for us to be sincere about what we do and that we do it from a heart of love and obedience, not for the accolades of men.

When we do good deeds, we always have to keep our motives in check. If we do these things for a reward, we are doing them for the wrong reasons. Likewise, when our actions are done for the sake of the approval of others or out of desire for reward from them, we act with the wrong intentions; we act from an impure heart. Sure, we may earn momentary reward or approval from others, but these things hold no eternal value. They are merely temporal treasures that moths and rust destroy (v. 19). Our focus then, should not be on the acts themselves, but on doing the will of God. It is only when we act out of obedience to God and love for others that we will be eternally rewarded.

It is not who sees you give or where you pray, but why you are doing those things that matters. Jesus is concerned about a man's heart, not his outward appearance. If our actions stem from love and obedience to Christ, we can take solace in knowing that our Father who sees in secret will give us reward of eternal value. –Solley

Morning: 1 Kgs 11; Phil 2 — *Evening:* Ezek 41; Ps 92, 93

INDIFFERENCE

"At that time I will search Jerusalem with lamps, and I will
punish the men who are complacent, those who say in their
hearts, 'The LORD will not do good, nor will he do ill.'"
ZEPHANIAH 1:12

I remember flipping through a small book of famous quotes. Among the quotes was one by Eleanor Roosevelt that I have never forgotten. The former First Lady once said, "There is only one thing worse than hatred, and that is indifference." When I first read the quote, I thought it was wrong. Hatred is an intense emotion *against* someone or something while indifference is emotionless and neither for nor against. As I thought about it a little more, however, Mrs. Roosevelt was right. Something about indifference is more extreme than hatred. Hatred, at least, has emotion. If a person hates, he cares. Indifference doesn't care one way or the other.

The prophecy of Zephaniah begins with a series of judgments. The first of which is against Judah. The people of God in the Southern Kingdom had begun to view God as indifferent toward them. In doing so, they had also become indifferent. How could a people so blessed by the Lord become indifferent to Him? How could they adopt an attitude toward their God that was worse than hatred? Simply put, they had become complacent in their service to and worship of the Lord.

In our own moments of complacency, when we neglect to offer the Lord reverence, service, and worship honoring to Him, we are a step away from indifference. Whether we think so or not, our actions demonstrate that we don't care one way or the other about God. Express your love to Him today, and be careful against indifference. –Karch

Morning: 1 Kgs 12; Phil 3 — *Evening:* Ezek 42; Ps 94

THE CHRISTIAN SWAGGER

"Now this I say and testify in the Lord, that you must no longer walk as the Gentiles do, in the futility of their minds."
EPHESIANS 4:17

Making a change in your life can be extremely difficult, especially when it is a dramatic change. In prison it can be even harder because switching your style up is often associated with uncertainty and weakness. However, when you come to a genuine saving relationship with Jesus Christ, that's exactly what you must do. We can no longer be satisfied or content living the way we used to live. Immediately people will want to test the sincerity of your convictions, but you must "walk in a manner worthy of the calling to which you have been called" (Eph 4:1).

Paul exhorts us and the Ephesians to lay aside the old self and embrace the new life, a life that is full of righteousness and holiness of truth and contrary to the world; one renewed in the spirit of your mind. Obviously, going with the flow and entertaining old habits are not part of God's plan for your new life. It won't be easy, but then again, swimming against the current never is.

Your changed life is the external evidence of the Holy Spirit's sanctifying work within you. We must now, "let [our] manner of life be worthy of the gospel of Christ" (Phil 1:27). No matter what others may say or think in the futility of their mind, you just keep on walking. –Blevins

Morning: 1 Kgs 13; Phil 4 — *Evening:* Ezek 43; Ps 95, 96

THE WORD OF TRUTH

"Do your best to present yourself to God as one approved, a worker who has no need to be ashamed, rightly handling the word of truth."
2 TIMOTHY 2:15

As most of us who have done time know, many people in prison build destructive ideologies based upon *their* understanding of certain passages of Scripture. They use God's Word as a weapon to defend their racial beliefs or religious superiority and to justify their sinful lifestyles. Instead of reading Scripture, they read *into* Scripture. To their detriment, their faulty handling of the Word of God has led to a faulty understanding of who they are in relation to God and to others.

A proper understanding of Scripture plays a vital role in how we understand who God is, who we are, and what Christ has done for us. Outside of the revealed Word of God, it is impossible to understand these things. Many have tried and just as many have failed. As Christians, Scripture is the foundation we stand on and the ultimate authority that guides our lives. Unfortunately, our understanding of Scripture is often flawed by our own presuppositions concerning God. The daily study of Scripture is vital to our spiritual health and understanding. Through our study of Scripture, God illuminates His truth to us and increases our understanding of who He is, who we are, and how we are to relate to others.

With this in mind, let's heed Paul's words to a young man named Timothy. Let us study the Scriptures daily so that we are able to present ourselves to God as workers who need not be ashamed. For it is in the study of Scripture, through the power of the Holy Spirit alone, that we rightly divide the Word of truth. –Solley

Morning: 1 Kgs 14; Col 1 — *Evening:* Ezek 44; Ps 97, 98

REQUIEM

"But if there is no resurrection of the dead, then not even
Christ has been raised. And if Christ has not been raised,
then our preaching is in vain and your faith is in vain."
1 CORINTHIANS 15:13–14

Have you ever realized you have been had? Have you ever been the butt of a terrible joke? Even if this is not something we have personally experienced, we certainly know somebody who has been on the wrong end of a bad scam or joke. Things like that are never fun for the one on the receiving end. Yet, what if the stakes were of an eternal sort? What if the result of the scam or joke turned out to have led a person to misrepresent God and ended with eternal judgment by Him?

Because Paul played out the hypotheticals in his mind, he understood these stakes. In relation to some who were saying there was no literal resurrection, Paul pushed the claim to its logical conclusion. If there were no resurrection, then Christ has not really been raised from the dead. Following this a step further, if Christ is not risen from the dead, then our entire lives are an exercise in futility—even our faith is in vain. We stand under the judgment of God for misrepresenting Him. The only thing left for us is the requiem, an act or token of remembrance often a song. As a service for the dead, somebody needs to sing our dirge as we lament our fate.

Fortunately, just as the requiem for Christ's own death was beginning to fade, He was raised from the dead. Because of His resurrection, our faith in Him and hope for resurrection is vindicated. Because He was raised, so we will be also. Because of His resurrection, our faith is not in vain. Because of His resurrection, the final enemy—death—has been defeated, and there will never be a need for anybody to sing our requiem. –Karch

Morning: 1 Kgs 15; Col 2 — *Evening:* Ezek 45; Ps 99, 100, 101

A REAL MAN OF GOD

"Then the king commanded, and Daniel was brought and
cast into the den of lions. The king declared to Daniel, 'May
your God, whom you serve continually, deliver you!'"
DANIEL 6:16

H ave you ever asked yourself what a real man of God looks like? If you had to describe a true follower of Christ, what would that description include? What characteristics or features of a godly man's life stick out the most? Do you know anyone like that? Could you describe yourself in that way?

Daniel was an educated man carried into Babylonian captivity. Deprived of his freedom and homeland, Daniel had every opportunity to forsake the God Most High. However, throughout his captivity, Daniel was repeatedly tested by the foreign authorities, yet was found without fault. Even when he was unjustly accused, convicted, and thrown into a lions' den, his faith and commitment to God endured. In fact, his godly character was so obvious that even the foreign rulers who worshipped other gods, recognized the hand of the Almighty God in Daniel's life.

What about you? Are you living for God in such a way that those around you take notice? Can people who don't know God catch a glimpse of Him by looking at your life? During your stay in prison, there are going to be many opportunities for you to show others who you truly are. So what are people going to find? Will they see God working in and through you? Will they find one like Daniel—a real man of God? –Blevins

Morning: 1 Kgs 16; Col 3 — *Evening*: Ezek 46; Ps 102

CRY OUT TO JESUS

"And when he heard that it was Jesus of Nazareth, he began to cry out and say, 'Jesus, Son of David, have mercy on me!'"
MARK 10:47

In Mark 10, as Jesus was leaving the city of Jericho, a blind man named Bartimaeus was sitting by the roadside begging. When Jesus' entourage approached, Bartimaeus cried out, "Jesus . . . have mercy on me!" Not wanting a blind beggar to bother Jesus, many in the crowd rebuked Bartimaeus and tried to silence him. Yet, undeterred, he cried out even louder, "Son of David, have mercy on me!" Hearing him, Jesus instructed His disciples to call him over. When they had done so, Jesus healed him. No matter his condition as a blind man, or his position as a beggar on the side of the road, Bartimaeus was not going to allow anyone to stand in his way of receiving what Christ had for him.

Like those who attempted to silence Bartimaeus, there will be people who will attempt to silence us because of our position as inmates and our depraved condition as sinners. Whether out of spite or self-righteousness, there will be those who feel we do not deserve anything other than what the State has given us—a whole lot of time to do. They will try to stand in the way of our receiving what Christ has for us no matter how loud we cry out or how much we beg for God's mercy. It is during these times that our only recourse is to cry louder, because as Christ demonstrated with Bartimaeus, He is listening.

If there are those, no matter who they are, who are trying to stand between you and what Christ has to offer, learn from a blind beggar—scream louder! Do not allow anyone to stand between you and Jesus. –Solley

Morning: 1 Kgs 17; Col 4 — *Evening:* Ezek 47; Ps 103

HOT PURSUIT

"Surely goodness and mercy shall follow me all the days of my life, and I shall dwell in the house of the LORD forever."
PSALM 23:6

Most people in America can recite at least some part of Psalm 23. No matter what a person's religious convictions, Psalm 23 has become part of American culture. On the one hand, this is a good thing. On the other hand, the danger is we tend to become numb to the rich meaning that has made it such a beloved psalm. Even when we retain some sense of the psalm's meaning, it tends only to be a feature of the verses which talk about the valley of the shadow of death or the preparation of a table in the presence of our enemies.

However, the final verse is where the culmination of all that has gone before merges. The *Holman Christian Standard Bible* reads, "Only goodness and mercy shall pursue me all the days of my life." This is amazing! We need not be anxious over pursuing goodness or mercy, those things pursue us. Even when things seem bad or trying, we can know surely that goodness and mercy shall follow us, in hot pursuit, all the days of our lives. Now we know why David can say everything else in the psalm. We know why he can walk through the valley of death and fear no evil. We know how a table is prepared for him in the presence of his enemies.

So, when the days feel as though we are walking through the valley of the shadow of death, think about the pursuit of the goodness and mercy of the Lord who is our shepherd. We can know the Lord's plans for us are only good; and when we are at our weakest and cannot pursue His goodness and mercy, those things follow and pursue us. –Karch

Morning: 1 Kgs 18; 1 Thess 1 — *Evening:* Ezek 48; Ps 104

THE PEACE OF GOD

"And the peace of God, which surpasses all understanding,
will guard your hearts and your minds in Christ Jesus."
PHILIPPIANS 4:7

Dietrich Bonhoeffer, one of eight children of a famous psychologist, lived in Germany during the tumultuous days of World War II. Unlike many influential German Christians, Bonhoeffer stood firmly against the Nazi Party and resisted their efforts to oust Jewish Christians from the Church. Eventually, Bonhoeffer was arrested and imprisoned for his suspected involvement in a plot to assassinate Adolf Hitler. Bonhoeffer was sentenced to death and spent the last two years of his life in prison. As the world raged around him and death crept closer, Bonhoeffer remained at peace. In *Bonhoeffer: Pastor, Martyr, Prophet, Spy,* biographer Eric Metaxas references the prison doctor's description of Bonhoeffer's death, "In almost fifty years that I worked as a doctor, I have hardly ever seen a man die so entirely submissive to the will of God."

Prison is a place where peace is extremely elusive. So, what made Bonhoeffer so different? How could he have had such peace in prison, especially on death row? The key is that Bonhoeffer understood that no matter what happened to him, whether prison or death, God was ultimately in control. His confidence in God, and not his circumstances, allowed him to have a peace which surpassed all understanding that baffled everyone who came into contact with him.

Like Bonhoeffer, we do not have to allow our incarceration to rob us of our peace. We can have the same peace Bonhoeffer had as he walked to the gallows if we, too, come to fully realize that no matter what happens, God is in control. In the midst of chaos and confusion, concrete and razor wire, God will give us a peace that surpasses all human understanding. We simply have to trust Him. –Solley

Morning: 1 Kgs 19; 1 Thess 2 — *Evening:* Dan 1; Ps 105

THE PAYBACK

"Do not repay evil for evil or reviling for reviling, but on the contrary, bless, for to this you were called, that you may obtain a blessing."
1 PETER 3:9

There they were, standing in the garden of Gethsemane surrounded by a crowd of enemies, soldiers, chief priests, Pharisees, and of course, Judas. This crowd came to arrest Jesus, the Son of God. Peter had spent the last three years of his life devoted to Him and left everything to follow Him. When the servant of the high priest, Malchus, reached out to seize Jesus, Peter couldn't stand it anymore. He'd come to his wits end. Drawing his sword, he sliced Malchus' ear clean off his head (John 18:1–11).

After roughly three decades, one notices a vastly different Peter. He is now exhorting early Christians, who are facing some serious persecution, not to retaliate. He doesn't tell them to draw their swords and fight back like he once did, but to bless those who revile them. What a transformation Peter underwent: from brazenly defiant to tender-hearted and humble!

Could this change in Peter be an indication of a similar change which occurs in all of God's children? My personal experience with retribution and seeking my own type of justice only landed me a life sentence. Now, however, I find myself, by God's grace, able to avoid needing to have the last word or repaying people back for the wrongs they've done to me.

Thank you Lord that Your eyes are on the righteous, and Your ears are open to their prayers. But Your face is against those who do evil, and it is You who will deliver the final payback. –Blevins

Morning: 1 Kgs 20; 1 Thess 3 — *Evening:* Dan 2; Ps 106

KEEP YOUR HEART

*"Keep your heart with all vigilance, for
from it flow the springs of life."*
PROVERBS 4:23

Proverbs 4 depicts the instruction of a father to his son. Most people in prison cannot reflect on any substantively wise counsel from their earthly fathers. Although my father tried to do right by me, he never really expressed the words of life pointed to in Proverbs 4. Because of this, I had nobody who instilled those concepts into my heart. Without the words, I was unable to keep my heart with all vigilance.

The world goes to great lengths to provide this excuse. I could easily blame my father for not teaching me the words of life, for not teaching me to guard my heart. The heavenly Father, however, has always had an available avenue through which I could have learned His Words of life. I could have pursued any one of them had I wanted to. I didn't want to guard my heart, and any time I came into contact with God's Word, I would close up my heart and refuse to hear it. The same can be said for many of us. While we can blame any number of people, including our earthly fathers, the blame ultimately resides with us. When it came time for us to receive the Word of God into our hearts, we would reject Him.

The tendency to close our hearts against hearing and receiving the Word of God is still with us as believers. Resist closing your heart to the Word of God. Allow the Words of life to flow through your heart freely, keep it there, and hear what the Lord is saying to you through His Word. When He speaks to your heart, let it flow and don't reject Him. –Karch

Morning: 1 Kgs 21; 1 Thess 4 — *Evening:* Dan 3; Ps 107

IN PICTURES

". . . and the glory of children is their fathers."
PROVERBS 17:6

One of the most difficult things about being an incarcerated parent is watching your children grow up in pictures. We are captivated by our children's pictures—by the joy on their faces and the light in their eyes. We are proud parents. However, beneath this pride, sadness resonates within us. Though we live from picture to picture, we miss all of the in-betweens. We miss their lives and regret not being there.

I have struggled with this as a parent because I know that not only am I missing being part of my daughter's life, she is also missing being part of mine. She will be affected greatly by having to grow up with her father in prison. I stare at her pictures and want so much to change her circumstances, to bring her daddy home to her, but deep inside I know I cannot. I want to do something, but I feel helpless.

One day I poured my heart out to God. I told Him how helpless I felt, how ashamed I was for leaving my daughter to grow up without her father. I asked God to show me what I could do for my daughter to make life a little easier for her and to let her know that her daddy loves her dearly. Through my prayers, I came to understand that, as a parent, the most effective thing I can do for my child is to pray for her, to trust her Heavenly Father with her life and with her heart.

What about you? Are you praying for your children? Do you trust their Heavenly Father with the in-betweens? If not, today is a good day to start! –Solley

Morning: 1 Kgs 22; 1 Thess 5 — *Evening*: Dan 4; Ps 108, 109

BY THIS

*"By this all people will know that you are my
disciples, if you have love for one another."*
JOHN 13:35

J esus, foretelling His imminent departure, began to comfort His disciples in an upper room somewhere in Jerusalem. Before He left, He gave them a few more instructions. After teaching His disciples many things over the course of His three-year ministry, Jesus gave them one more commandment. While the commandment to love one another was not explicitly stated, Jesus taught this by example from the beginning. In a few hours' time, the greatest display of that love would occur on the cross.

As Christians, we have to start realizing that people are watching us closely. Even when we don't think we're under observation, somebody is watching. This is especially true for incarcerated Christians. Somebody is looking at you 24 hours a day, 365 days a year. You can't escape the microscope of thousands of pairs of eyes. However, that burden can also be a blessing.

So many people in prison are looking for genuine and authentic men of God. They are so used to seeing the bickering, the fussing, and the divisiveness among Christians that they have no desire to be a part of something so hypocritical. We stand up and preach love for one another, yet, as soon as we turn around, our hands are at each other's throats. I bet Satan gets a kick out of that. Starting today, meditate on Jesus' example. Think about how He displayed love for His disciples. How can you show the same love for your brothers? Knowing that *by this* all people will know that we are His. –Blevins

Morning: 2 Kgs 1; 2 Thess 1 — *Evening:* Dan 5; Ps 110, 111

NOW I LAY ME DOWN TO SLEEP

*"In peace I will both lie down and sleep; for you
alone, O LORD, make me dwell in safety."*
PSALM 4:8

At times, prison life can get very violent, very quick. I am talking about those moments when the dayroom or chow hall goes deathly quiet and all the hair on the back of your neck rises. You know something is about to happen, and it is not going to be good. Like everyone around you, your head swivels, heart racing, as you look for the source of the change in the atmosphere, hoping you are not the victim. We have all witnessed violent situations in prison that leave you lying in your bunk at night unable to sleep, thankful that it was not you.

As a warrior whose life was characterized by one violent episode after another, King David experienced those times, too—moments when death lurked around the corner waiting to strike unexpectedly. I am sure that like us, King David experienced times of uneasiness and fear. Yet David understood he belonged to the Lord, and God would protect him. No matter what was going on around him in the chaos, the turmoil, and the battle, David could lie down at night in peace, and sleep, because he knew it was the Lord who allowed him to dwell in safety.

Even in the midst of a violent prison environment, as children of God, we can experience the same peace David had. When we understand that we belong to the Lord and He will protect us, our hearts will not fear, and we will be able to lie down and sleep in peace. –Solley

Morning. 2 Kgs 2; 2 Thess 2 — *Evening.* Dan 6; Ps 112, 113

MERCENARIES OR SOLDIERS?

"Share in suffering as a good soldier of Christ Jesus."
2 TIMOTHY 2:3

The sixteenth century Italian political philosopher, Niccolo Machiavelli, was introduced to a new generation in the 1990s through the music of Tupac. As an entire culture was shaped by Tupac's music, it was through his rhymes that gangsters became introduced to Machiavelli. Even though Machiavelli's name is now familiar, most people know nothing about the man, nor do they understand that the gangster lifestyle itself is a direct reflection of one of the things Machiavelli warned against in his book, *The Prince.* He warns his ideal prince against employing mercenaries who fight for and are loyal only to money. Thus, for Machiavelli, one good soldier is worth far more than a dozen mercenaries.

Those of us who have been involved in or exposed to the gangster lifestyle know that the overarching principle is to make money. The single loyalty in the game is to stack paper. Likewise, Machiavelli says the same principle is the single loyalty of the mercenary. In his mind, mercenaries are basically worthless for the preservation of anything really important. While Machiavelli was certainly not a Christian, he understood the importance of good soldiers who were loyal to a prince or king. In the same way, Paul encourages Timothy to be a good soldier of the Prince of Peace and King of kings, Jesus Christ (Isa 9:6, 1 Tim 6:15).

The gangsters know Machiavelli's name but do not realize that Machiavelli would have viewed them as mercenaries and warned princes against having anything to do with them. As Christians, however, we know Jesus Christ and He knows us. The mercenary mindset is no longer our driving principle because of what Jesus has accomplished for us as our King; so let us be good soldiers for Him. –Karch

Morning: 2 Kgs 3; 2 Thess 3 — *Evening:* Dan 7; Ps 114, 115

JUDGMENT AND MERCY

*"and I will sow her for myself in the land. And I will have
mercy on No Mercy, and I will say to Not My People, 'You
are my people'; and he shall say, 'You are my God.'"*
HOSEA 2:23

The life of an Old Testament prophet was often illustrative of
God's relationship with Israel. In the case of Hosea, God commanded him to marry a whore in order to symbolize the unfaithfulness of Israel. Even Hosea and Gomer's three children had names that
represented an aspect of that tumultuous relationship—*Jezreel* ("God
sows"), *Lo-ruhama* ("No Mercy"), and *Lo-ammi* ("Not My People").

The predominant theme running through most of the Old
Testament prophets is one of judgment. God, fed up with Israel's re-
belliousness, sent forth His Word, declaring His righteous justice on
Israel's abominable acts. However, for those who would turn from
their wickedness and idolatry, God offered His mercy and forgiveness. His loving-kindness was never far from those who were wise and
discerning.

We too should understand that God's just punishment of the
wicked is not a result of a bipolar God. His righteousness, justice, and
holiness are not separate from His love, mercy, and kindness. He is
the same yesterday, today, and forevermore (Heb 13:8). He still demands the faithfulness of His people and still punishes transgressors.
But, we can be thankful that His steadfast love "is from everlasting to
everlasting on those who fear him, and his righteousness to children's
children, to those who keep his covenant and remember to do his
commandments" (Ps 103:17–18). Thank you Lord for being a God of
both judgment and mercy. –Blevins

Morning: 2 Kgs 4; 1 Tim 1 — *Evening*: Dan 8; Ps 116

WHAT ABOUT ME?

"Are not two sparrows sold for a penny? And not one of them
will fall to the ground apart from your Father . . . Fear not,
therefore; you are of more value than many sparrows."
MATTHEW 10:29–31

H ave you ever wondered if God cares about you personally? I know
I have. Intellectually, I never doubt that God loves us collectively
and that He demonstrated that love toward us by sending Christ to die
on the cross so that we may be reconciled to Him (John 3:16).

Yet, emotionally, the circumstances of life often leave me wondering, "What about me? Does God really care about me, personally?" I
mean, if He did, why would life be so difficult? Why would it seem like
all of my prayers fall on deaf ears? As honest as my emotions are when
they cry out, "What about me?" they are simply emotions. Emotions
are not always based on truth but rather, how we perceive things.

The truth is that Christ assures us that God does care about each
and every one of us as individuals. In His discourse with His disciples
shortly before He sent them out to spread the good news in Matthew
10:29–31, Christ gave an illustration in language so simple, yet so profound: "Are not two sparrows sold for a penny? And not one of them
will fall to the ground apart from your Father...Fear not, therefore;
you are of more value than many sparrows." Just stop and think about
that. If God cares about birds so much that not one of them falls to the
ground without His knowledge, imagine how much more He cares for
you and for me.

As God's children, we can be assured that we are much more valuable than many sparrows when our emotions cry out, "What about
me?" Our Father does care about each and every one of us. –Solley

Morning: 2 Kgs 5; 1 Tim 2 — *Evening:* Dan 9; Ps 117, 118

MYSTERY

*"the mystery hidden for ages and generations but now
revealed to his saints. To them God chose to make known
how great among the Gentiles are the riches of the glory of
this mystery, which is Christ in you, the hope of glory."*
COLOSSIANS 1:26–27

E veryone enjoys a good mystery. The excitement in reading a good
mystery is trying to think through all of the variables and figure
out what rests at the bottom of it all. As the story develops, the desire
to understand how everything fits together grows. In prison, it is almost therapeutic to settle down during a lock-down and read a good
mystery novel or to kick back on a Saturday evening and catch a good
mystery movie. Something about a mystery is altogether appealing and
is nothing new.

Even in the first century, people could appreciate a good mystery.
However, there was one mystery that had intrigued people for centuries—particularly the Jewish people. It was one mystery nobody could
quite figure out. In time though, God Himself chose to reveal it—to
the Jew first, and then to the Gentile (Rom 1:16). This particular mystery involved discovering a treasure with riches beyond measure. It is
the mystery of Christ in us which is our hope of glory. The surpassing
riches of Christ dwelling in us supply us with the hope for our future
glory.

Those of us in prison are in a position to understand the worth
of possessing a treasure in the midst of deprivation. We understand
the eternal value of *hope* and how hope for a better future sustains us
from one day to the next. As the ancient mystery of the hope of glory
unfolds in our own lives, may our hope grow as we desire to see how all
things come together in the end. –Karch

Morning: 2 Kgs 6; 1 Tim 3 — *Evening:* Dan 10; Ps 119:1–24

THE NEXT MAN

*"But it displeased Jonah exceedingly, and he was angry . . . 'for
I knew that you are a gracious God and merciful, slow to anger
and abounding in steadfast love, and relenting from disaster.'"*
JONAH 4:1–2

When God calls us out of darkness, a wonderful thing happens. A miracle actually occurs when God turns our stoney, stubborn, and rebellious hearts into caring, loving hearts of flesh (Ezek 36:26). We are spiritually reborn and adopted into the family of God. We are given a new nature as the old is put to death. But as with most newborns, it takes some time learning how to walk in this new self.

One of the most common traps we fall into as young Christians is trying to dictate or determine on whom God should have mercy. This newfound aversion to sin causes us to hate the things associated with our old lifestyle. Occasionally, that hatred will lead us to making some decisions that contradict what God commands us to do—share the gospel with those who are still lost in their sin. Jonah had a similar issue when God called on him to go and preach the gospel to Nineveh, an Assyrian city full of idol worshippers. After a harrowing encounter with one extremely large fish, Jonah conceded to go to Nineveh, thus allowing the Assyrians an opportunity to repent and believe in the one true God.

Sometimes, we want to share God's good news with others, but usually aim for those who we think will respond. We deliberately avoid those we think are too far lost, or who will never want to hear about Jesus Christ. We must remember that God is the One who affects salvation, not us. Furthermore, our God is not a respecter of persons. We should remember where we've come from, and if God can pull us out of our mess, He can do it for the next man. –Blevins

Morning: 2 Kgs 7; 1 Tim 4 — *Evening:* Dan 11; Ps 119:25–48

FIRE BLIND

"He said, 'Do not be afraid, for those who are with
us are more than those who are with them.'"
2 KINGS 6:16

I'd venture to say none of us have ever watched a man of God raise a boy from the dead, direct a man to be cleansed of leprosy, or make an axe-head float. Elisha's servant, Gehazi was privy to all these things. In each instance, his perspective was driven by cynicism. While it is easy to judge Gehazi, we often act in the same cynicism. We see what is going on around us quite clearly but fail to see the power and influence of God behind everything around us—we are *fire blind*.

The king of Syria had gained intelligence that Elisha was helping the king of Israel preempt his military advances. Naturally, the Syrian king wanted Elisha dead. The Syrian army tracked Elisha and Gehazi to Dothan and surrounded the city. This was a significant show of force for just one man. Gehazi knew they had no chance of evading the army, much less defeating it. On the verge of panic, Gehazi looked to Elisha for direction. Elisha calmly replied, "Do not be afraid, for those who are with us are more than those who are with them." Elisha saw a vast army with numerous horses and chariots of fire. Consequently, Elisha knew the Syrians didn't stand a chance. Even so, Gehazi saw only the Syrians.

We will inevitably find ourselves opposed by insurmountable odds, in the midst of situations we cannot overcome on our own, or merely needing strength to face another day. These things are part and parcel of the Christian life, particularly inside prison. Yet, we do not have to be in the company of an Elisha to see the power of God as our support. All we have to do is open our eyes and stop being fire blind. –Karch

Morning: 2 Kgs 8; 1 Tim 5 — *Evening:* Dan 12; Ps 119:49–72

THINK

"Finally, brothers, whatever is true, whatever is honorable,
whatever is just, whatever is pure, whatever is lovely,
whatever is commendable, if there is any excellence, if there
is anything worthy of praise, think about these things."
PHILIPPIANS 4:8

I used to dread rack time. It was the one time of day I was truly left alone with just my thoughts and me. My mind roamed over all of my mistakes in life, the people I hurt, the ones I disappointed—my wife, my daughter. So many thoughts consumed me that I would lie there lost in the past, regretting so much and wishing I could turn back time and do things all over again. Lost in my thoughts, unable to sleep, the night would drag on. I would eventually drift off to sleep, but it always seemed that as soon as I woke up the next morning, those thoughts were right there tapping me on the shoulder, reminding me that they would be right there waiting on me at the next rack time.

We have all been there. Whether it is thinking of past regrets or simply worrying about something we cannot change, we have all let our thoughts consume us. We have spent hours upon hours meditating on things that hold no real value. Yet, it is when our thoughts run wild that we ought to turn them to more important matters. As Paul encouraged the Philippians, we ought to meditate on things that hold eternal value; that which is true, that which is honorable, that which is lovely, that which is just . . . It is by doing so that we focus our attention on the things of God and not on the things of this world.

The next time your thoughts take off, rein them in. If there is *anything* worthy of praise, think about these things. –Solley

Morning: 2 Kgs 9; 1 Tim 6 — *Evening:* Hosea 1; Ps 119:73–96

STRANGE

"For I would have you know, brothers, that the gospel
that was preached by me is not man's gospel."
GALATIANS 1:11

G. K. Chesterton once wrote that truth is stranger than fiction. Think about that for a minute. We see it every day to one degree or another. On the news, the harmless neighbor seemed like the nicest guy, always polite and willing to help anybody. Then the bombshell drops and everybody is exposed to the truth that, all the while, he was another Jeffery Dahmer. The truth is he has always been a sociopath, and the fiction was him being a nice guy. In this particular case, the truth is definitely stranger than the fiction.

Likewise, we tend to believe that we are good people. We convince ourselves that God is willing to set aside His justice and accept us for the good people we are. That is pure fiction. The truth is slightly stranger: it is altogether alien for us to believe that we are inherently sinful and God's wrath is levied against us. Stranger still, is God's coming in the flesh to appease His own wrath, satisfy His own justice, and make atonement for our sins. In this particular case, the truth is stranger than fiction.

Long before Chesterton ever penned his epigram, Paul understood man's difficulty of accepting the strangeness of the truth. Paul could scarcely believe it himself. As educated as he was, the gospel was alien to him. Yet, the gospel of Jesus Christ is no fiction. In fact, it is stranger than any of man's fabrications. This is why Paul makes it a point to say he received the gospel from Jesus and not man. So, when you find it strange that the God of the universe would include you in His plan of rescuing mankind from sin, the sentiment is strange for a reason. It is strange because it is the truth. –Karch

Morning: 2 Kgs 10; 2 Tim 1 — *Evening:* Hosea 2; Ps 119:97–120

ON HIM

". . . For we were so utterly burdened beyond our strength
that we despaired of life itself . . . But that was to
make us rely not on ourselves but on God . . ."
2 CORINTHIANS 1:8–9

T here was a time in my life when it seemed like everything was fall-ing apart, as if life as I knew it was coming to a sudden end. I had reached a point where I was burdened beyond my strength. I felt like I could not go on, nor did I did want to at times. When I tried to grasp at straws in hopes of pulling things back together, of making some sense out of the mess that had become my life, I only made matters worse.

My feelings of utter despair are not unique. Almost everyone incar-cerated feels burdened beyond their strength at one point or another. However, how often do we rely solely on ourselves—our own strength and capabilities—to accomplish what we know we cannot. No matter how hard we try or how bad we want to, we cannot change our circum-stances or fix some things in our lives that are broken. We must realize, as Paul articulated, it is when we are burdened beyond our strength that we are being taught not to rely on ourselves but on God. At times, our circumstances put us in the position where we have no choice but to look to God and rely on Him for the strength we so desperately need.

When life seems to overwhelm us, when we are burdened beyond our strength, let us not despair. Rather, let us rely on God—the author and finisher of our faith (Heb 12:2). –Solley

Morning: 2 Kgs 11, 12; 2 Tim 2 — *Evening:* Hosea 3, 4; Ps 119:121–144

EIN' FESTE BURG

"God is our refuge and strength, a very present help in trouble."
PSALM 46:1

The most famous hymn born out of the Protestant Reformation is Martin Luther's, "A Mighty Fortress is Our God (*Ein' feste burg ist unser Gött*)." The words of the hymn are derived from Psalm 46. After Luther's death, those who continued his work would often gather together when they were on the verge of despair. As their burdens seemed too much to bear, they would rally their spirits as they sang the Forty-Sixth. In the same spirit as Luther, these men understood, in the face of insurmountable opposition, that the God of Jacob was their stronghold—their mighty fortress (v. 11).

How deeply do we understand and believe that God is indeed our refuge and strength—our mighty fortress? The word *trouble* in this verse can also be translated, "tight places." For those of us in prison, our lives are walled in by tight places within tight places. Yet, does it dawn on us that God is an ever present help even in the tight places of prison?

Luther wrote in the words of the hymn, "That word above all earthly powers, no thanks to them, abideth; the Spirit and the gifts are ours through him who with us sideth." If you belong to Christ, then God is your refuge and strength, and all that God has offered in Christ is yours. Reflect on this today. And, if not out loud, at least in your heart, sing the Forty-Sixth—knowing beyond a doubt that the Lord of Hosts is with you. –Karch

Morning: 2 Kgs 13; 2 Tim 3 — *Evening:* Hosea 5, 6; Ps 119:145–176

WHEN WE LEAST EXPECT IT

*"And he lay down and slept under a broom tree. And behold,
an angel touched him and said to him, 'Arise and eat.'"*
1 KINGS 19:5

Man, can we get caught up in our circumstances. With so many things going wrong in our lives, it is easy to feel like nobody cares. When everything bad seems to happen at the same time, it is not hard to take on an attitude of despair. Even when we remember we are children of God, adopted into His heavenly family, our situation or emotions can cloud the realization of that eternal blessing. The day-to-day rigors of serving time in prison pull even the most joyful of us down sometimes.

Yet, it is precisely during those times when the Lord is there by your side. Just like the Lord provided for the prophet Elijah when he thought he was all alone and no one cared, He is there providing for you when you don't even realize it. God is protecting you from things of which you are completely unaware. He has promised never to leave you nor forsake you. Even when the times get tough and you think you just can't take it anymore, the Lord is providing for and guarding His precious possession—you.

You are not some disposable pawn in the grand scheme of God's eternal plan. You are a special creation, loved and cared about, made in His image. You never have to feel like your circumstances are too big for you to handle, you're under the watchful eye of the Creator of the universe. Sure, things may seem bad, but we're apt to look at things through human eyes. God has an all-encompassing perspective. So, let's keep our heads up a little higher with the assurance that He is there when we least expect it. –Blevins

Morning: 2 Kgs 14; 2 Tim 4 — *Evening:* Hosea 7; Ps 120, 121, 122

NEVER PROMISED A TOMORROW

"Behold, now is the favorable time; behold,
now is the day of salvation."
2 CORINTHIANS 6:2B

I n the summer of 1997, Bill Glass Ministries came to our unit for a three-day revival. Two homeboys—Bobby and David—and I were sitting on the rec yard listening to Murph the Surf give his testimony. All three of us were caught up in sinful lifestyles and running from God. While Murph the Surf gave an altar call, David sat next to me with his head down, lost deep in thought. David had been feeling sick for a couple of weeks and was also going through a lot of stressful issues. I knew that he was struggling inside. Silently, I watched him for a moment before leaning over and telling him, "Bro, if you want to go up there, go." For reasons very personal to him, David looked at me with sorrow in his eyes and said, "I can't, bro." David died the next morning.

David's death affected Bobby and me greatly and eventually helped to lead both of us back to Christ. However, all of these years later, I still mourn that David did not give his life to Christ, that I know of, when he had the opportunity. I would love to say with confidence that I knew my friend was in heaven, but as much as it pains me, I cannot. God called my friend that day, yet, he did not accept the call.

David's death is a stark reminder of the eternal risk you take when you ignore the call of God. If you have heard the call of God, yet you have hesitated, remember that now is the favorable time, today is the day of salvation because, like David, you are never promised a tomorrow. –Solley

Morning: 2 Kgs 15; Titus 1 — *Evening:* Hosea 8; Ps 123, 124, 125

GOOD FOR IT

"The LORD is good, a stronghold in the day of trouble;
he knows those who take refuge in him."
NAHUM 1:7

The goodness of God is a given for the Christian. We accept and acknowledge God's goodness for a number of reasons, and in doing so, find ourselves reflecting on the goodness of God as an attribute of God. Yet, we seldom pause to reflect on the specifics relating for what exactly is God good. In times of trouble, we quickly ask where God is or what He is up to in the midst of our troubles. But, do we reflect on His goodness? Do we consider if He is good for it even in our times of trouble and distress? Will He make right what seems all wrong?

Nahum is one of the more obscure minor prophets and generates little attention and study. He does, however, give us one specific example of for what God is good. The Hebrew construction is somewhat difficult to translate into English, but the idea conveyed by the prophet is that God is good for protection, aid, or refuge in the day of trouble or distress. And being good for this protection, He therefore looks out for those who trust in Him.

Being in prison qualifies as a time of trouble and distress. So, for those of us who are doing time, take what you already know about God's goodness and consider Nahum's declaration of what God is good for. Know that God is good, not just in an abstract attributive way, but He is good for *you*. He is good for help, aid and support—He is good for it all. –Karch

Morning: 2 Kgs 16; Titus 2 — *Evening:* Hosea 9; Ps 126, 127, 128

STAND TALL

*"I am the LORD your God, who brought you out of the land
of Egypt, that you should not be their slaves. And I have
broken the bars of your yoke and made you walk erect."*
LEVITICUS 26:13

As incarcerated individuals, we experience a myriad of emotions. On a daily basis, we run the gamut of emotions. From joyful to despondent, sometimes it's hard to say what the day will bring. Other people's unpredictable mood swings also impact our emotional state. Furthermore, our bad days are frequently a result of our own inner turmoil. Our countenance may have fallen due to overwhelming feelings of regret, shame, or guilt that has built up or perhaps as a result of refusing to let go of anger, resentment, or bitterness. But, thank God it doesn't have to be that way.

Throughout the Old Testament God constantly reaffirms His covenant with His people, especially when they seem to be on an emotional high or low. God never lets them forget the wonderful blessings they have in Him if they just trust and obey Him. He reminds them of past blessings He's bestowed upon them as well as the future blessings promised long ago. Constantly declaring that He is their God and they are His people, God's steadfast love is on full display page after page.

These aren't just ancient narratives with no meaningful application for us today. We are His people, joined with Him in a new covenant— one fulfilled and mediated by Jesus Christ through whom all blessings flow (Heb 12:24). God continues to have a relationship with His own, whether they're behind prison walls or living in the free-world. Our yokes have been broken; we are no longer slaves to sin (Rom 6:17). We have been made to walk upright; so stop letting unstable emotions control you. Remember what He has done for you and start standing tall. –Blevins

Morning: 2 Kgs 17; Titus 3 — *Evening:* Hosea 10; Ps 129, 130, 131

IT'S YOUR CHOICE

"My son, if sinners entice you, do not consent . . . my son, do not walk in the way with them; hold back your foot from their paths,"
PROVERBS 1:10–15

In prison, there will always be many opportunities to become involved in things that Christians should not. Furthermore, there will always be those people tempting us to partake in their lifestyles. Gang members want you to be gang members, hustlers want you to be hustlers, thieves want you to be thieves, and perverts want you to be perverts. That is simply part of doing time—misery loves company.

The immediate payoffs gained by walking in the way of sinners may seem enticing, but the eventual consequences are grave. Solomon, in all of his wisdom, warns us about these types of people. They lie in wait for blood, ambush the innocent (Prov 1:11). They fill their houses with plunder, and their feet run to evil (Prov 1:13, 16). Yet, as the rest of Proverbs 1 tells us, the end of the road for them is not pretty. The blood they lie in wait for is their own. They ambush their own lives, and their lives are taken away (Prov 1:18–19). Eventually, they pay the ultimate consequences for their actions.

There will come a time when you are enticed by others to walk down a path that leads to destruction. It's not a question of if, but of when. However, the choice is yours to make. Only you can consent to follow in the ways of the sinner. Only you can choose to walk down the roads of destruction. When that time comes, you have to decide for yourself what path in life you want to take. So choose wisely—your life depends on it! –Solley

Morning: 2 Kgs 18; Phlm 1— *Evening:* Hosea 11; Ps 132, 133, 134

APPROVAL RATING

"For am I now seeking the approval of man, or of God?
Or am I trying to please man? If I were still trying to
please man, I would not be a servant of Christ."
GALATIANS 1:10

Have you ever watched the various toothpaste commercials that boast their product is approved by four out of five dentists? Approval ratings can be applied to almost anything in today's society. Elected officials, television shows, even Bible translations have ratings. In each case, companies want their products to have the highest rate of approval. Likewise, as humans, we have an inherent desire to have other people approve of us; we want the highest approval ratings for ourselves.

God created us as social beings, so it is natural to want to associate with other people. Even so, throughout Paul's writings, he disassociates himself with the notion that he has to have the highest approval ratings. In fact, he takes the opposite approach and expresses that he does not seek the approval of men. He doesn't desire to please people but only seeks the approval and pleasure of God. There is a sense in which, when we seek the approval of people, we are not pleasing to God. Thus, Paul says outright that if he were seeking the approval and pleasure of men, he would not be a Christian.

A lot of times, particularly in prison, we understand that a strong stance for the gospel will not win us the approval of others. Nevertheless, a strong stance for the gospel is approved by God. For Christians, the highest approval rating we can ever have is the approval of God. Therefore, don't worry about the approval of men. Continue to stand in what you have received in Christ, and know you are pleasing to and approved of by God. –Karch

Morning: 2 Kgs 19; Heb 1 — *Evening:* Hosea 12; Ps 135, 136

HOW ARE YOU KNOWN?

*"For no good tree bears bad fruit, nor again does a bad tree
bear good fruit, for each tree is known by its own fruit."*
LUKE 6:43–44A

Prior to making Jesus Lord over my life, I would go to the chapel to kick it with my homeboys. We would sit in the back and watch everyone: the active homosexual in the choir, the sexual predator lifting his hands praising Jesus, the gamblers in the front row with their Bibles in their hands and their socks full of parley tickets, the chaplain's assistant who, for just the right price, could get you anything you want. I would sit there in disgust! These guys could fool the chaplain and all of the volunteers, but they could not fool me and my friends. Why? Because we lived with them; we saw the fruit of their lives—and it was bad.

In the Sermon on the Mount, Jesus tells us that each tree is known by its fruit, no good tree bears bad fruit and no bad tree bears good fruit. This is very simple when applied to our Christian walk. If our lives are continuously bearing bad fruit, then our tree is bad. We have major problems, and we probably need to get saved! On the other hand, if our lives are bearing good fruit, then we can be assured that our tree is good. To make it plain, like those I used to sit in church and watch, we will be known by the fruit our lives bear.

While we are never in a position to judge the state of someone's salvation, we are always in the position to be fruit inspectors. So, how are you known? Does your tree bear good fruit? –Solley

Morning: 2 Kgs 20; Heb 2 — *Evening:* Hosea 13; Ps 137, 138

EVERYTHING

*"His divine power has granted to us all things that
pertain to life and godliness, through the knowledge of
him who called us to his own glory and excellence,"*
2 PETER 1:3

For several weeks, I had been encouraging a man who desired a change in his life. During our many conversations, he would often convey his desire to serve the Lord and grow in his faith only to qualify these things by saying that he knew he was not yet a "full blown" Christian. Finally, I asked him to tell me his definition of a Christian. He quickly responded with a list of prohibitions: a Christian does not lie, steal, curse, and so on. In a general way, this is how many of us tend to view Christianity.

Peter explains, that by God's own power, He has granted to us everything pertaining to life and godliness. Biblical expressions of life and godliness are not things to which we have to force ourselves to conform—there is no way we could measure up to God in that respect anyway—because God grants them to us. Through knowing Christ in a saving way, God gives to us these things for His own glory and excellence.

Realizing exactly what we have been granted by God through what Jesus has done for us helps us to get beyond the idea of Christianity being defined by a series of prohibitions—*thou shalt not's.* We are better equipped to see Christianity as a series of affirmations: God has accomplished our salvation, declared our righteousness, and granted us those things which pertain to life and godliness—He has done everything. Be encouraged that the change you seek and your desire to serve God are themselves affirmation of what the Lord has accomplished for you. Be thankful and encourage someone else today. –Karch

Morning: 2 Kgs 21; Heb 3 — *Evening:* Hosea 14; Ps 139

KNIT TOGETHER

*"As soon as he had finished speaking to Saul, the
soul of Jonathan was knit to the soul of David,
and Jonathan loved him as his own soul."*
1 SAMUEL 18:1

Friendship is a word with lost meaning in the penitentiary. It is
casually thrown around in various forms but is ultimately devoid
of any real significance. We use words like "homeboy," "my boy," "ace,"
"cuz," "dawg," or any other word we can think of to mean friend, but
they are all really just empty words. Prison is full of superficial relationships that have no real meaning or value, most of which center around
some benefit or selfish gain.

Jonathan, King Saul's son, knew what true friendship meant. He
and David had a relationship that went beyond the typical surface-
deep friendships most of us experience today. The friendship between
David and Jonathan sometimes meant sacrifice, as in the case when
Jonathan risked his father's ire by helping David escape (1 Sam 20).
It also meant seeking the good for one another, sometimes at the ex-
pense of their own personal gain. For instance, Jonathan gave up his
claim to the throne to ensure the safety of the future king of Israel.
Jonathan loved David as he loved his own soul.

Building meaningful friendships in prison is difficult, sometimes
downright impossible. With the constant moves and turnover from one
day to the next, our ability to build bridges into people's lives is limited,
but it doesn't mean you stop trying. Being a true friend is going to entail
taking the ups along with the downs. It's going to mean breaking through
the masks and pretentious walls to the heart of a person. As Christians, we
are commanded to love our brothers (John13:34), our neighbors (Matt
22:39), and our enemies (Matt 5:44), which doesn't leave us any excuses.
So examine your relationships today. Are they the garden variety—pseu-
do-friendships? Or are they the type that knits souls together? –Blevins

Morning: 2 Kgs 22; Heb 4 — *Evening:* Joel 1; Ps 140, 141

A HERITAGE FROM THE LORD

*"Behold, children are a heritage from the LORD,
the fruit of the womb a reward."*
PSALM 127:3

S he flew across the gym and leaped into my arms. Her tiny legs wrapped around my waist, and she squeezed my neck tight, holding on for dear life. As I carried her to the side of the gym to let the next man behind me embrace his child, she whispered into my ear, "Daddy, I love you." My heart melted. It was my first Day with Dad event, and the first time I had seen my seven-year-old daughter in a year. It was such a relief to hold my little girl in my arms and to know that she was okay and that she loved her daddy.

Being an incarcerated parent is not easy. We miss our children and worry about them constantly. We lie on our bunks at night wondering how their day went, if they are okay, if they miss us as much as we miss them, if they love us, if they think about us. Then there are the endless emotions we struggle with for not being there. The psalmist, however, tells us our children are a heritage from the Lord. They are God's gift to us. In understanding this, we can see that not only do we have a vested interest in our children's lives, God does, too. How can He not? He gave them to us. This being the case, we can trust God to watch over and protect our children.

When you find yourself thinking about your children, take the time to thank God for each and every one of them. Thank Him for watching over and protecting them and for the heritage He has given you in them. –Solley

Morning: 2 Kgs 23; Heb 5 — *Evening:* Joel 2; Ps 142

TELLIN' IT

*"Whoever goes about slandering reveals secrets, but he
who is trustworthy in spirit keeps a thing covered."*
PROVERBS 11:13

C rime is typically a tight-lipped enterprise. All prisons are full of
criminals. So, one would think that prisons are highly secretive
places. However, those of us who have spent any time inside prison
know that the opposite is true. There are hardly any secrets and everyone knows each other's business. For some reason, as long as nobody
is telling the officers anything, it is perfectly acceptable to tell anybody
and everybody else. While this may be the way prisons are, it is not the
way Christians ought to operate.

Whether it is the nature of the prison environment or something
else, we tend to forget the seemingly insignificant sins like gossip. We
have the attitude that so long as we are not committing the real bad
sins, it is alright for us to talk about the guy who is. Sometimes, we
even broadcast the other person's sins after he has come to us for help.
Proverbs isn't the only place in the Scriptures that condemns this type
of behavior. Yet, it does provide us a clear picture of what it means
to behave in such a way. The implication is that the person who tells
things about others in a slanderous manner is not trustworthy in spirit.

All prisons have at least some Christians. Christianity is a non-slan-
derous enterprise. In that sense, it is altogether tight-lipped. Whatever
the nature of prison may be in respect to telling everybody's business,
for the Christian we must seek to be upright with the secrets of our
brother's or sister's hearts. Let us always be sensitive about what we
reveal and what we cover concerning those we serve with and to whom
we minister. Always be trustworthy in spirit, and don't be one of those
who go around tellin' it. –Karch

Morning: 2 Kgs 24; Heb 6 — *Evening:* Joel 3; Ps 143

CHOOSE FOR YOURSELF!

"See, I have set before you today life and good, death and evil."
DEUTERONOMY 30:15

God couldn't have spelled it out any clearer to the ancient Israelites. Moses just finished laying out the covenant between God and His people along with the blessings and curses which were promised for their obedience and disobedience. The ball was now in their court. They could follow God's precepts and walk in His ways, or they could choose to worship other gods. They could receive the blessings of God or His just punishment. Seems like a no brainier, right?

Jesus proclaimed a new and better covenant, one proclaimed (*kerygma*, "preached") from the mouths of redeemed sinners and written on our hearts through faith in Him (Jer 31:31-34; Heb 7:22, 8:6, 12:24). However, we have a much similar choice before us. We can choose to follow our Lord and Savior, or we can choose to follow other gods. Our gods might not resemble the wood, stone, silver, or gold idols that caused the Israelites to stumble, but the penitentiary is packed with idols nonetheless. Every day, choices present themselves to us, and decisions need to be made. Don't think for one second that professing faith in Christ will make these choices easy. On the contrary, you have now declared yourself to be an enemy of sin, and your life should reflect that.

God is faithful, and His promises are still true. Life is still offered for a faithful response to difficult choices, as is death to those who turn from God. The Israelites found this out the hard way. Don't make the same mistake. Choose life! –Blevins

Morning: 2 Kgs 25; Heb 7 — *Evening:* Amos 1; Ps 144

DO NOT FEAR

"When I am afraid, I put my trust in you."
PSALM 56:3

A friend of mine spoke the other day about something that touched me deeply. When he was incarcerated, he lost contact with one of his daughters. He thought about her every day, and his heart longed for his little girl. But out of fear of her rejecting him because he was incarcerated, he never contacted her. One day he received a letter from his daughter wanting to know why he didn't love her or want her in his life. Little did she know, he had loved her every minute of every day they were apart. When he explained this to his daughter, instead of being angry or ashamed of him, she forgave him and loved him. All she cared about was having her daddy in her life. In a few weeks, he will see his daughter for the first time in sixteen years.

Like my friend, we are sometimes so ashamed of where we are and what we have done that we allow our shame to hold us in bondage to fear. Our fear of rejection often prevents us from reaching out to those we love and care about so we run from the risk of more hurt and pain. Yet, many times, the individuals we are hesitant to reach out to long to hear from us and feel as if we have rejected them—especially our children. The truth is, as parents, we owe it to our children to face our fears and reach out to them.

If there is someone you have been hesitant to reach out to because you fear rejection, trust in God, and do not be afraid—mail that letter or make that phone call. You will be surprised what He will do when you trust in Him for the restoration of broken relationships. –Solley

Morning: 1 Chr 1, 2; Heb 8 — *Evening:* Amos 2; Ps 145

I AM WHAT I AM

*"But by the grace of God I am what I am, and
his grace toward me was not in vain. "*
1 CORINTHIANS 15:10A

For many of us, there are things in our pasts that haunt us. In most
cases, our journeys to prison weren't born out of an instant. Most
of the time, we started slowly down a path, and through a series of
events, eventually ended up on the wrong side of the fence. The culmination of all the things that got us to where we are sticks around in
our consciences and haunts us.

This was no different for Paul. Throughout his writings, we get the
sense of his shame over what happened with Stephen (Acts 8). In the
context of our Scripture today, Paul considered himself unworthy to
be called an apostle because of his attitude toward, and persecution
of, the Church of Jesus Christ. Even so, he qualifies his position before
God and attributes who he is to the grace of God alone. He is what he
is—an apostle—not because he has special talents or because he out-
worked all other apostles (although he did), but because of the grace
of God. Paul understands that everything he is stems directly from
God's grace.

So it is with us. No matter what our backgrounds or what haunts
our pasts, we are what we are today because of the grace of God. We
must attribute who we are to nothing other than the grace of God. We
may compare our work against that of fellow brothers or sisters, but
even ours is a result of God's grace. Accordingly, God has extended His
grace to us in a way that lifts us beyond our pasts. This grace of God
toward us is not in vain, therefore, let us always be thankful for that
grace. –Karch

Morning: 1 Chr 3, 4; Heb 9 — *Evening:* Amos 3; Ps 146, 147

NOVEMBER 15

FLAVOR ENHANCER

"You are the salt of the earth, but if salt has lost its taste, how
shall its saltiness be restored? It is no longer good for anything
except to be thrown out and trampled under people's feet."
MATTHEW 5:13

A quick glance around the chow hall is all you'd need to figure
out that salt is an integral part of prison fare. Without it, I doubt
most of us could stomach the hastily prepared, often unidentified mystery dishes staring back at us every day. For some reason, salt adds such
a measure of flavor that a pork noodle casserole ends up tasting like a
New York strip steak—well maybe not that good, but you get my point.
Now imagine if salt had no flavor at all. What good would it do?

Jesus tells His disciples that they have been called for a special
purpose. They would be embarking on a mission that would be difficult and possibly fatal but one which carried the promise of eternal
rewards. Their objective was to take all that Jesus taught them and
spread it out into the world. In order to fulfill this task, they couldn't
be scared or fearful but had to allow their light to shine forth so that
the entire world could see.

In a prison context, this mission is still in effect for followers of
Christ. Our culture is one that has been marred by violence and filth
far too long. The seeds of darkness and oppression have been allowed
to grow behind these walls unchecked for decades. It's time to start
living up to your purpose. It's time to start taking what God has given
you back into the very pits from which He's pulled you. It's time to enhance the flavor of the world around you: a world that is still struggling
with the bad taste of sin. So go forth and be salty! –Blevins

Morning: 1 Chr 5, 6; Heb 10 — *Evening:* Amos 4; Ps 148, 149, 150

A LIVING HOPE

*". . . According to his great mercy, he has caused
us to be born again to a living hope through the
resurrection of Jesus Christ from the dead,"*
1 PETER 1:3

I n *Shawshank Redemption,* Andy Dufresne is convicted of a crime he didn't commit and sentenced to life in prison. There, he strikes up a friendship with another convict named Red. Years later, Andy escapes, but shortly before he does, he tells Red that if he is ever released from prison to go to a specific town, find a specific tree in a specific cornfield, lift up a specific rock, and use the money there to travel to Mexico to meet him. Red is eventually paroled and does exactly what Andy told him to do. He discovers a tin can full of money and a note from Andy.

The note says, "Red, never forget. Hope is a good thing, maybe the best of things, and no good thing ever dies."

This is a great truth. Because we are incarcerated, we live with the hope of someday going home to our families, of someday tasting freedom again. This hope keeps us strong. However, this is a greater truth when viewed from a Christian perspective. In Christ, we have been born again to a living hope through His resurrection from the dead. We have been given an inheritance kept in heaven that is imperishable, undefiled, and unfading (v. 4). This heavenly hope far surpasses any earthly hope we can have. Though earthly hope will sustain us for a while, it cannot be compared to the real hope we have in Christ.

When you have days where it seems like all hope is gone, do not despair; simply remember that you have a living hope already stored in heaven. –Solley

Morning: 1 Chr 7, 8; Heb 11 — *Evening:* Amos 5; Luke 1:1–38

THE WONDERFUL WAS, IS, AND IS TO COME

*"John to the seven churches that are in Asia: Grace to you
and peace from him who is and who was and who is to come,
and from the seven spirits who are before his throne,"*
REVELATION 1:4

O ne of the most compelling things about the New Testament for inmates is that a large portion of it was written from prison. The book of Revelation is among those. John was writing as an exile on the island of Patmos which served as a penal colony for first century Rome. His initial greeting here is that those he is addressing may have grace and peace *from him who is and who was and who is to come.*

Think of the times you have written letters to loved ones and friends in which the initial greeting is standard. Many of us, over the years, have crafted a way of introducing letters that say the same thing in a standard way. There is nothing wrong with that. In fact, it was no different in the first century. However, it is clear from John's introduction that his central focus is the Lord. He has a firm understanding of where his grace and peace comes from and desires to depart those same things to his readers. Throughout the letter, as he writes to those who are suffering persecution, John maintains his focus on the wonderful *Was, Is,* and *Is To Come.*

Do our letters focus on complaining, sadness, or blame? If so, we should think deeply about the grace and peace we have in the Lord. As you are encouraged by that, use your standard introduction in your letters as an opportunity to convey the same grace and peace you have today to those who receive your letters. –Karch

Morning: 1 Chr 9, 10; Heb 12 — *Evening:* Amos 6; Luke 1:39–80

SHACKLED BY THE PAST

"Brothers, I do not consider that I have made it my
own. But one thing I do: forgetting what lies behind
and straining forward to what lies ahead,"
PHILIPPIANS 3:13

I t is easy for those of us incarcerated to allow our pasts to hold us in bondage. Many of us have lived very destructive lifestyles. We have not only harmed our fellow members of society, but we have also hurt those who love us the most. So, we live our lives tormented by all of the regrets—the what-ifs and could-have-beens. We become so focused on the failures of the past that we become blind to what God has ahead of us.

Imagine you are driving a car on a busy highway. Rather than looking through the windshield at what is in front of you, you decide only to look in the rearview mirror at what is behind you. How far do you think you would get before you crashed? Probably not far at all. That is how life is. If we are constantly looking back over our shoulder at all of the mistakes we have made, consumed by all the what-ifs and could-have-beens, we won't get far before we crash and burn. As difficult as it may be to do, we must follow in the apostle Paul's footsteps and forget what lies behind us and reach to what lies ahead: "the upward call of God in Christ Jesus" (v.14). Only then can we truly see what God has in store for us.

If you have been shackled by your past, maybe it is time to let it go. Maybe it is time to get your eyes off the rearview mirror and put them on the road ahead of you. –Solley

Morning: 1 Chr 11, 12; Heb 13 — *Evening:* Amos 7; Luke 2

ESCAPISM

"But in Mount Zion there shall be those who escape, and it shall be holy, and the house of Jacob shall possess their own possessions."
OBADIAH 17

J. R. R. Tolkien, the author of *The Hobbit* and *The Lord of the Rings*, was once accused of promoting escapism through his books. Tolkien responded that our understanding of escapism depends on what a person is trying to escape from. People have very different views of the deserter who escapes from duty and the prisoner who escapes from jail. Tolkien asks, "Why should a man be scorned if, finding himself in prison, he tries to get out and go home?"

The small prophecy of Obadiah is often overlooked by Christians. In the grand scheme of things, its relevance for those redeemed by Christ seems obscure. Yet, because of the experiences of Christians inside prison, Obadiah has the ability to speak to us in a special way. As we have been stripped of our worldly possessions and locked away from all things dear to us, there resides in our hearts a longing for home, for what is familiar. Some would say our daydreams for a better time are a form of escapism. But, long before Tolkien, Obadiah knew better. He knew the hearts of Israel longed for better times. The promise the Lord placed on the lips of Obadiah is one Israel found great comfort in—it gave them something to daydream about.

Likewise, this same promise gives Christians a great deal to daydream about. We know that no matter how long our sentences may be, there is a day of escape. No matter how much we have lost due to our past mistakes, the Lord has new possessions for us in His kingdom. For all of us, there is a day when we will get out and go home. –Karch

Morning: 1 Chr 13, 14; Jas 1 — *Evening:* Amos 8; Luke 3

CERTIFIED

"In him you also, when you heard the word of truth,
the gospel of your salvation, and believed in him,
were sealed with the promised Holy Spirit,"
EPHESIANS 1:13

C attle drives were a regular occurrence in the Wild West. Ranchers would send a large number, sometimes up to 2,500 head of cattle, to meat auctions hundreds of miles away. In preparation for this, cowboys would round up the herds in the autumn and brand the cattle headed for the markets in the spring. Because ranchers and cowboys needed to know which steers belonged to which ranch, they branded them with identifying marks. These brands were seared into the backsides of the cattle and were permanent marks which certified the cattle as belonging to a certain owner.

Similarly, when we arrive at saving faith in Jesus Christ after listening to the message of truth, God puts His own special brand on us. He stamps us as His own and identifies us as inheritors of a promise. We are His precious possession, and no one will snatch us out of His hand. The seal of God is none other than the third person of the Trinity, the Holy Spirit, who indwells every regenerated, born again child of God. This seal is what Paul calls a guarantee of our inheritance and what Jesus calls the Spirit of Truth (Eph 1:14, John 14:17).

When you're facing trials and times of testing, keep in mind that you're not alone. You've been marked with more than just something to identify you; you've been sealed with the third person of the Godhead who will teach you all things and bring to remembrance all that Jesus has said (John 14:26). Isn't it a comfort to know we have a Heavenly Father who will never leave us nor forsake us, who has actually put His very own mark on us? Praise God, we have been certified. –Blevins

Morning: 1 Chr 15; Jas 2 — *Evening*: Amos 9; Luke 4

HIS BANNER OVER ME IS LOVE

*"He brought me to the banqueting house,
and his banner over me was love."*
SONG OF SOLOMON 2:4

When I was six years old, my father was arrested in Lafayette, Louisiana, for armed robbery. My mother had six kids, no money, and nowhere to go. We ended up in The Faith House, a local Christian women and children's shelter. Several times a week, a volunteer Christian couple would come to The Faith House to sing and share the message of the gospel. Part of the lyrics to a song they sang mesmerized me so much that they still resonate within my soul over 30 years later: "His banner over me is love." It was the first time in my life I ever heard about Christ and His love for me.

It was not until many years later that I would discover the lyrics that touched me so deeply as a child originated from the Song of Solomon. The Song of Solomon is the love story of all love stories. It demonstrates the intimate, joyous relationship between a man and his bride, but it also can be understood to reflect the love of Christ for His bride—the Church. Woven into the eight chapters of this book is a picture of Christ's love for us. Not only does Christ love us, He delights in us, longs to be with us, and cherishes us as His beloved. His love completely covers us. Or, better said, "His banner over *us* is love!"

Meditate today on Christ's love for you. His banner over *you* is love! Let these words resonate within your soul. –Solley

Morning: 1 Chr 16; Jas 3 — *Evening:* Obad 1; Luke 5

ON OUR SIDE

"if it had not been the LORD who was on our side when people rose up against us, then they would have swallowed us up alive, . . ."
PSALM 124:2–3

A s soon as we begin to run afoul of the law, the odds are stacked against us. Think of the way the case is read in each court hearing: "The State of _____, versus _____." How can a single man or woman measure against those odds? How does a single person stand against an entire state? Even those in a position of wealth and power can feel the weight of what he or she is up against.

David understood what it was like to have the odds against him as he penned Psalm 124. He knew there was no way he could stand against his enemies by himself. Nevertheless, he came through unscathed. David realized he and his men would have been swallowed had it not been for the fact that the Lord was on his side. In the same way, we too, find ourselves up against things in our lives we cannot overcome alone. We easily recognize, in hindsight, we would have been swallowed up many times had the Lord not been for us.

Let us think of those things we have faced where we would have been swallowed up had the Lord not been on our side. As a result of how the Lord has dealt with us when the odds were stacked against us, we can have confidence He will continue to be on our side. In any situation, and against all odds, we can put our hope in Him no matter what we face. He is always on our side. –Karch

Morning: 1 Chr 17; Jas 4 — *Evening:* Jonah 1; Luke 6

IF THEY HAD ONLY KNOWN!

*"They came up to him, saying, 'Hail, King of the
Jews!' and struck him with their hands."*

JOHN 19:3

Beaten, cursed, and despised, the last hours of Jesus' life on earth were truly deplorable. The chief priests and Pharisees hated Him. The Roman officers disrespected Him. The soldiers abused Him, and Pilate crucified Him. As we look back on that day nearly 2,000 years ago we can only imagine what it must have felt like to have gone through so much pain and suffering. We wonder how they could have treated Jesus so badly.

Of course, it is easy for us to glance back through history and place ourselves among the multitudes knowing what we know now. God's glorious plan of redemption occurred just as He planned it, but we can always wonder if those men and women who conspired and carried out the crucifixion of our Lord and Savior would have done so if they had known who He truly was. Would they have done all that they did to Jesus if they had known He was the Son of God?

Today it is no different. Dayrooms are full of guys cursing the name of God. Recreation yards are crowded with "Jesus haters." Would those same people curse and hate Jesus if they knew He was the Son of God? As a Christian, you have a chance today to find out the answer to that age-old question. Sharing the gospel with the people who need to hear it most alleviates the excuse, "If I had only known!" –Blevins

Morning: 1 Chr 18; Jas 5 — *Evening:* Jonah 2; Luke 7

FOOLISH PRIDE

"Pride goes before destruction, and a haughty spirit before a fall."
PROVERBS 16:18

Like many, I was young and prideful when I entered the criminal justice system at eighteen. Before I even left the county jail, I had gained a reputation for meeting any perceived disrespect with violence. I was pretty good with my hands and had a chip on my shoulder as big as the world, so there was no way you were going to disrespect me and get away with it. I carried that mentality with me to prison and earned a type of respect for it, which only fed my ego more. I walked around with my head held high and my chest puffed out with foolish pride.

Yet, as the proverb asserts, my misguided pride would be my downfall. I ended up spending more than eight years in administrative segregation because my pride caught me up in things in which I should not have been involved. It was not until I understood the state of my depravity that I discovered I had no reason to be proud of the sinful man I was. Only then did I see my actions for what they truly were: arrogant and haughty disobedience to God. And there is absolutely no pride in that. Yet, because I was hardheaded, it required me falling flat on my face for my eyes to be opened.

It is easy to become full of pride in prison. Yet, it is important to understand that pride is offensive to God. Pride deceives us into believing we can do it on our own; we have what it takes so we do not need God. That is why, as Christians, we must always fight the temptation to become caught up in the prideful mentality which runs rampant among prisoners. If we don't, we shall surely fall. –Solley

Morning: 1 Chr 19, 20; 1 Pet 1 — *Evening:* Jonah 3; Luke 8

NAVIGATOR

*"Trust in the LORD with all your heart, and do not lean
on your own understanding. In all your ways acknowledge
him, and he will make straight your paths."*
PROVERBS 3:5–6

For centuries, shipping was the main means of transporting commodities long distance. For ships to get from one port to another, the captain had to trust his navigator. Whatever the captain's own experience and understanding, it was ultimately the navigator's job to plot their course and guide them to their destination. The navigator's skill was acknowledged by virtue of him being the ship's sailing master.

From his proverbs, we see Solomon was wise enough to know that life is a lot like sailing from one port to the next. Since we have command of the vessel of our life, we need a navigator. Whatever our experience and understanding may be, we need somebody who has mapped our course and who will guide us to our desired destination. There is a great deal of comfort knowing that we have the Lord as our navigator. We can trust Him to guide us to where we need to be although we do not understand where He is leading us. We can trust Him to steer our course through the dangers of the rocks and reefs of life. We can acknowledge His mastery and ability to steer us away from, or safely through, the storms of life.

Being sent to prison can be thought of as a shipwreck, but it doesn't have to be so. If the Lord is your navigator, He can steer you safely through even the dark and difficult time of prison. Trust that He will guide you back to your loved ones. Even when storms come, trust He will see to it your journey is blessed. Most of all, trust Him to guide you into His kingdom. –Karch

Morning: 1 Chr 21; 1 Pet 2 — *Evening:* Jonah 4; Luke 9

NEVER AGAIN

*"You shall know that I am in the midst of Israel, and
that I am the LORD your God and there is none else.
And my people shall never again be put to shame."*

JOEL 2:27

When I think about all the stupid things I've done in my life, I can't help but wonder how many could have been avoided. If only I would've listened to the advice of the people who loved me, I could have caused myself and others a lot less pain. I definitely wouldn't have suffered as much guilt concerning my actions or shame from their consequences. When I close my eyes at night, I can almost hear all those "I-told-ya-sos."

After the split of the kingdom of Israel, God's people had a serious decision to make. They could either follow after God or after the gods of the foreign nations surrounding them. I think we all know which direction they chose. Likewise, browse through any of the books of the prophets and you'll come to the conclusion that God continually called His people back to repentance. When that didn't happen, the children of Israel faced God's just punishment. Sometimes that came in the form of being humbled and put to shame by other ungodly nations. Yet, after judgment came mercy and the promise of restoration.

As Christians who have been pulled from the mire, we no longer need to feel guilty or ashamed. We have turned from our wicked ways by the gracious hand of our loving Lord. Our pasts are our pasts. Although those poor choices aren't something to be proud of, we need to understand that God has dealt wondrously with us, and never again will we be put to shame. –Blevins

Morning: 1 Chr 22; 1 Pet 3 — *Evening:* Mic 1; Luke 10

DON'T BE A FLUNKY

"Examine yourselves, to see whether you are in the faith. Test
yourselves. Or do you not realize this about yourselves, that Jesus
Christ is in you?—unless indeed you fail to meet the test!"
2 CORINTHIANS 13:5

Ask the average person incarcerated if he or she is a Christian, and the answer will more than likely be yes. Yet, the lifestyles of the majority of people in prison prove this to be false. Though many profess to be Christians, their actions do not conform to what they claim to be. Their actions leave no doubt that Jesus Christ is not in them. Upon examination, they have failed the test. All we have to do is sit back in the dayroom, or dare I say even the chapel, and watch the "professed" Christians around us to see that many claim to be something they are not.

As Christians, we are commanded to examine ourselves to see whether we are in the faith. We must take a close look at our lives to determine what our actions are saying about what we believe. Do our lifestyles represent the faith that we profess? Do our behaviors consistently show others that Christ lives in us? Or, like the many who profess Christ, yet live lifestyles far from the faith, are we, too, claiming to be something while our actions prove otherwise. If so, we must stop and listen to our actions because they often speak much louder than our words.

It is important that we stop and examine our lives to see if what we profess is being lived out in what we do. Our actions are a good indicator of whether or not we are in the faith. Ultimately, this is one test where you do not want to be a flunky. –Solley

Morning: 1 Chr 23; 1 Pet 4 — *Evening:* Mic 2; Luke 11

OLD AND GRAY

*"Do not cast me off in the time of old age; forsake
me not when my strength is spent."*
PSALM 71:9

Books have been written about the American idolization of youth. Subsequently, inside prison, youth is often thought of as a necessity. In many ways, "old timers" in prison are respected because they have spent years cultivating and earning reputations. The youngster, on the other hand, feels he is forced to prove something. In general, prisons continue to perpetuate the idolization of youth to some degree on every compound.

In prison, there is a tendency for us to feel a need to be young, to have the strength, energy, and health to be considered a threat to potential predators. With this comes dismay toward getting old, particularly for those of us with lengthy sentences. In the context of Psalm 71, David—a warrior who understands the importance of strength and vigor—prays for both strength and deliverance. There seems to be a tension between which of the two is the most pressing. Those of us in prison, who face long sentences where the potential for getting old within the walls of prison is an ever present reality, are in a position to appreciate this tension as well. What do we need most? The strength to make it from one day to the next, or do our hearts express a deeper need for deliverance from our present bonds?

Even if deliverance from prison were the most pressing of the two, the necessity of strength and sustenance in the free-world is just as pressing. Therefore, it essentially boils down to strength for the day. We continually ask the Lord for the strength to make it from one day to the next. We understand that when our strength is spent physically, mentally, and spiritually, He will not forsake us. –Karch

Morning: 1 Chr 24, 25; 1 Pet 5 — *Evening:* Mic 3; Luke 12

NEVERTHELESS

"And going a little farther he fell on his face and prayed, saying, 'My Father, if it be possible, let this cup pass from me; nevertheless, not as I will, but as you will.'"
MATTHEW 26:39

M atthew 26 contains the story of Jesus in the Garden of Gethsemane. Knowing that His death was looming troubled His soul, so Jesus sought a quiet place to be alone. Falling on His face, Jesus prayed, "My father, if it be possible, let this cup pass from me." Jesus understood what awaited Him, and if there was any way possible, He did not want to experience the agony of the cross. Yet, no matter how much He wanted to avoid His coming crucifixion, He prayed, "[N]evertheless, not as I will, but as you will." For the joy that was before Him, Christ endured the cross (Heb 12:2).

In our Christian walk, there are many situations we do not want to experience—things that will ultimately bring glory to God, but will be frustrating, painful, and even heartbreaking to go through. When those times come, our natural inclination will be to fall on our faces and beg God to remove us out of these situations or to rescue and deliver us from the circumstances in which we find ourselves. We will more often desire our will to be done instead of God's. Yet, sometimes, we need more "nevertheless" in our lives. We need God's will to be done, not ours.

As Christ did when faced with the cross, we must be willing to pray, "Nevertheless, not as I will, but as you will."

When we go through the trying times of our Christian faith, and we feel burdened beyond what we can bear, let our hearts cry be, "Nevertheless." –Solley

Morning: 1 Chr 26, 27; 2 Pet 1 — *Evening:* Mic 4; Luke 13

NOVEMBER 30

PLAY IT AGAIN

"Then the word of the LORD came to Jonah the second time, saying, 'Arise, go to Nineveh, that great city, and call out against it the message that I tell you.'"
JONAH 3:1–2

Everybody runs from God. Even those who do not acknowledge God's existence, by the nature of their denials, run from God. More poignant, however, is the admission that believers sometimes run from Him. The prophet Jonah was reluctant to go to Nineveh for many reasons. Chief among his reasons was that the Assyrians were the most brutal and feared people on earth at the time. Jonah's reluctance manifested itself when he ran.

In the same way, we are often reluctant to follow where God wants us to go; or even more, we express reluctance to let go of some of the things or people we know God is calling us to let go. Like Jonah, when the places the Lord wants us to go or those things He wants us to leave behind don't quite fit our plans, we run from Him and His will. The good news is demonstrated when, even though Jonah ran, the Lord spoke to him a second time. The Lord did not count Jonah out, nor does He count us out when we don't get things right the first time. He reaches out to us again, just as with Jonah. If we don't get it right, we can be encouraged because the Lord will play it again. Of course, we may not experience the radical way in which He got Jonah's attention, but God will get our attention nonetheless.

As we think about Jonah, we are moved to think about how we, too, have run from the Lord and to question if we may still be running. If so, listen for the way the word of the Lord may be coming the second time. Listen for how He may be playing it again. –Karch

Morning: 1 Chr 28; 2 Pet 2 — *Evening:* Mic 5; Luke 14

THE RIGHT RESPONSE

"A soft answer turns away wrath, but a harsh word stirs up anger."
PROVERBS 15:1

Judging by his facial expressions, I could tell he was mad. The volume, tone, and choice of vocabulary made me feel about an inch tall, but the worst part was it was all for no apparent reason. I'd been making Johnnies one minute and the next thing I knew the kitchen captain was cursing me. The looks on my coworkers' faces were of astonishment and disbelief. I could tell they were all expecting me to retaliate or at least verbalize my anger at being unjustly targeted.

Have you ever been in a situation like that, where heated words have been directed toward you, and every last fiber of your being wants to lash out in response? I know if you've been incarcerated for any length of time, this type of encounter is all too familiar. Whether by another inmate or an officer, you've been provoked to anger by another's actions or words.

Our response, as Christian men, should always be given in accordance with our faith. The writer of Proverbs tells us that a gentle answer is the correct retort while harsh words will lead to trouble. This is most clearly displayed by Jesus when he was being degraded by the chief priests and Roman leaders; not once did He respond in anger.

The next time you are provoked by another and your flesh wants to rise up and unload, think about the faith you profess to have. Think about Jesus' response to His antagonists, and then think about the right response you can give. –Blevins

Morning: 1 Chr 29; 2 Pet 3 — *Evening:* Mic 6; Luke 15

GOD WILLING

"Instead you ought to say, 'If the Lord wills,
we will live and do this or that.'"
JAMES 4:15

We often sit in our cells for hours at a time planning our futures in our minds, envisioning all of our tomorrows. We already know what we are going to do the first day we are out: what we are going to eat, what we are going to wear, who we are going to see, what we are going to say to those who we feel gave up on us and left us by the wayside. We have so many plans, so many people to see and places to go, and so much lost time to regain. Over the years, we daydream about these things, and as time goes by, our dreams change—but not much.

Yet, it is not that simple. As most of us who have done time know, life happens while we are busy dreaming, and most of our dreams do not come true. Why is that? It is because we do not hold the future in the palm of our hands, nor do we control the circumstances that surround our lives. Only God does. James hit the nail on the head when he warned the twelve tribes in the Dispersion not to boast about what they were going to do in the future. The future did not belong to them: it belonged to God—so does yours, so does mine.

With that in mind, do not boast about all of the tomorrows; rather, leave all the tomorrows in God's hands. Do as James commands and say, "If the Lord wills, we will live and do this or that." –Solley

Morning: 2 Chr 1; 1 John 1 — *Evening*: Mic 7; Luke 16

CAPTIVES

*"See to it that no one takes you captive by philosophy and
empty deceit, according to human tradition, according to the
elemental spirits of the world, and not according to Christ."*
COLOSSIANS 2:8

P rison has philosophy. While that may seem contradictory, prisons
tend to function based on a particular philosophy. For instance,
consider the prison concept of *respect*. Prisons have an entire philosophy surrounding a pseudo-ideal of respect. The same can be said in relation to the interaction of different ethnic groups, the guards, or any
other of the myriad of sub-sets behind the wire. The point is, prison
has philosophy. Not only does prison have philosophy, but the philosophy that tends to permeate prisons is entirely opposed to Christianity.

Paul warns the Colossians not to be taken captive by various systems of thought. Some translations render this "vain philosophy." If
prison philosophy is anything, it is certainly vain. Yet, even after we
become redeemed believers, in Christ, we still cling to the prison philosophy that is so pervasive among the population. We continue to be
held captive to a wrong mindset, a backward way of thinking about everything. This mindset is empty, based on corrupt traditions, and not
at all in accord with the things of Christ.

What vestiges of prison philosophy are still holding you captive?
What part of the prison way of thinking is still so deeply ingrained in
you that you are refusing freedom? What do you see about the prison
way of thinking that is not in accord with the things of Christ? Consider
Paul's warning to the Colossians, and consider how it applies to us today, particularly to those of us who attempt to live for Christ inside a
place like prison. See to it that you are not taken captive by the deceitful thinking of prison philosophy. –Karch

Morning: 2 Chr 2; 1 John 2 — *Evening*: Nah 1; Luke 17

FOR THE LORD'S SAKE

"Be subject for the Lord's sake to every human institution . . .
For this is the will of God, that by doing good you should
put to silence the ignorance of foolish people."
1 PETER 2:13–15

I cannot count the times I have been told to do something by the prison administration that made absolutely no sense. During my younger years, I usually responded in a very negative fashion which usually resulted in very negative consequences. And to be honest, at times I still do, but not to the extreme I once did. My attitude is still not always one of humble submission, but rather, often one of defiant concession. Moreover, I am quite sure that you are just like me.

Admit it—we have always been hardheads. This is why it is so difficult for us to submit to authority. Had we done so, we would not be where we are. Yet, the Bible commands us to submit to the authority of those God has placed over us, and as much as we do not like it at times, that includes the prison administration. They are the ones God has placed in authority over us while we are here. Scripture clearly indicates that we submit not for our sake, but for the Lord's sake, so that by doing right we may silence the ignorance of foolish men. That is a heavy responsibility; nevertheless, one we must fulfill.

Whether they are right or wrong, the prison administrators are in authority over us. As hard as it is at times, we must obey them; not for our own sake, but for the sake of our Lord Jesus. Therefore, the next time we are given an order that does not seem to make sense—let us honor the Lord. –Solley

Morning: 2 Chr 3, 4; 1 John 3 — *Evening:* Nah 2; Luke 18

COGNITIVE INTERVENTION

*"to put off your old self, which belongs to your former manner of
life and is corrupt through deceitful desires, and to be renewed
in the spirit of your minds, and to put on the new self, created
after the likeness of God in true righteousness and holiness."*
EPHESIANS 4:22–24

When I began the arduous process of getting out of administrative segregation, the program requirements included an extended version of the popular Cognitive Intervention class. In prisons all over the United States, CI classes are utilized to help rehabilitate prisoners. As the name implies, CI classes are designed to help people engage their own thinking. Integral to the process is learning to identify and overcome "thinking errors." These thinking errors are thought to be derived from any number of sources and influences. However, they are never attributed to self. There is no real sense of responsibility for the deceitful desires that lurk in the background of an ever erroneous way of thinking.

Interestingly enough, Christianity refuses to allow its adherents to escape responsibility. Part of being a Christian is recognizing that the basic problems of humanity stem from self. The key to overcoming the errors of self is not to try and fix what is irreparable, but to get a new self altogether. The book of Ephesians instructs us to "put off" our former manner of life and "put on" an entire new self. We don't "engage" our thinking: we ask God to renew it. We need something far greater than a mere intervention: we have to have our minds created anew.

The main thinking error of mankind is thinking he can somehow fix or change himself. To engage that kind of thinking leads further into deception. Acknowledging our inability to intervene in our own cognitive processes, however, is the initial step toward real rehabilitation. It helps us to turn to the only one who can renew our minds for us: Jesus Christ. –Karch

Morning: 2 Chr 5, 6:1–11; 1 John 4 — *Evening:* Nah 3; Luke 19

GETTING BACK UP

*"Create in me a clean heart, O God, and
renew a right spirit within me."*
PSALM 51:10

O ften when Christians find themselves falling back into old patterns of behavior, the first thing they think about is completely giving up. They question the commitment they have made to follow Christ and struggle against the sin that is constantly crouching at their door. The temptations of the world are a lure back into the easy-life, and they attempt to ensnare us when we least expect it. However, when the Holy Spirit shines His searing light of conviction on our hearts and reveals the sin within us, the feelings of guilt and shame follow.

David was not unfamiliar with sin. During his time as king, he not only committed adultery with Bathsheba, but also had her husband Uriah killed. Like all of us, when it comes to committing sin, David was at a crossroads in his life. He could easily take the path of his predecessor Saul and disgrace the kingdom, or he could heed the words of Nathan the prophet and turn back to the Lord.

David's response to conviction of sin was one of contrition and repentance, as our response should be, too. When the Holy Spirit shines His searing light of conviction on you, revealing your sinfulness, call on the Lord to purify your heart and to renew a steadfast spirit within you. And remember, it's not about whether you fall, but whether you get back up. –Blevins

Morning: 2 Chr 6:12–42; 1 John 5 — *Evening:* Hab 1; Luke 20

NO APPOINTMENT NECESSARY

*"But he was pierced for our transgressions; he was crushed
for our iniquities; upon him was the chastisement that
brought us peace, and with his wounds we are healed."*
ISAIAH 53:5

We all have experienced the slow, agonizing wait to see the prison doctor. We are shuffled into crowded holding cells full of sick men coughing and sneezing everywhere, each of whom has a story to tell the man sitting next to him. One by one we're called out for vital signs and then packed back into our concrete cage to continue the tedious wait. Finally, our turn arrives, and we are escorted to the doctor's office only to be told by the nurse, "Sit right here, the doctor will be with you in a moment."

Thank God that when it comes to the ultimate physician, there are no long, boring waits in crowded and noisy holding cells full of people sniffling, sneezing, coughing, or shouting at the man sitting right next to them. In fact, no appointments are necessary. You don't have to wait one second longer to be eternally healed. Jesus Christ is only a prayer away. He will meet you right where you are and heal you of the inherent disease you have called sin. Jesus is like no other physician. He does not simply cure your diseases; He takes them upon Himself. In other words, He bears your disease so that you do not have to. It is by His stripes that you are healed and by His blood that you are reconciled to God (Rom 5:1).

Today, know that the Healer of all healers is waiting for you to call out to Him. You can do that right now; there are no appointments necessary. –Solley

Morning: 2 Chr 7; 2 John 1 — *Evening*: Hab 2; Luke 21

SET YOUR MIND ON IT

*"So we built the wall. And all the wall was joined together
to half its height, for the people had a mind to work. "*
NEHEMIAH 4:6

Do you ever feel like you are spinning your wheels? Ministering inside prison can easily generate those types of feelings. Just when things start to come together on some ministry front and you see the fruits of your labor, you get moved to another housing area, or the people you are working with get moved. Any number of similar setbacks can and often do occur. Obviously, there is little to be encouraged about when you are in the thick of things and your ministry work seems fruitless.

The Jewish exiles that came back to Jerusalem with Nehemiah could have easily been experiencing the same things. Sanballat and Tobiah were in direct opposition to the work the Jews were doing on the walls of Jerusalem. The opposition was discouraging. The strength of those working was beginning to fail, and the way forward didn't appear to be very promising. Yet, under the encouragement of Nehemiah they continued to build the wall, brick by brick, stone by stone. Nehemiah made sure the focus wasn't the wall, but the labor itself. *The people had a mind to work.*

The key to our labor in any ministry, particularly inside prison, is having our mind set to work. If our minds begin to drift to success or failure, setbacks or advances, then our focus becomes distorted and we lose sight of what the ministry truly is about. Where is your focus when you minister? Is your mind set to work? If so, don't be discouraged. Continue to labor for the Lord, serve Him even in the midst of the opposition and difficulties, and set your mind on the work. –Karch

Morning: 2 Chr 8; 3 John 1 — *Evening:* Hab 3; Luke 22

ALL YOUR MIND

*". . . You shall love the Lord your God with all your heart
and with all your soul and with all your mind.'"*
MATTHEW 22:37

S o many things in prison compete for our attention that it's hard to
stay focused. Whether it's televisions, radios, chess boards, dominoes, officers, or inmates, our attention is constantly being pulled in
a million different directions at one time. Sometimes it seems like the
only quiet time available is in Ad-Seg, but that's a place most of us really don't want to be. So what is a man supposed to do when he wants
to escape from all the ruckus of prison life?

Jesus said the greatest commandment was to love the Lord God
with all our heart, soul, and mind. Loving God with all my heart and
soul I understand, but what does loving God with my mind look like?
And how do I apply that in a place where my mind is never at rest?
One answer lies in the spiritual discipline of meditation. Spiritual dis-
ciplines are those internal and external habits we continually perform
that help cultivate godly character, and the discipline of meditation is
an internal discipline all Christians should attend regularly. The Bible
proclaims: "Oh, how I love your law! It is my meditation all the day" (Ps
119:97). The primary difference between transcendental new-age or
Eastern concepts of meditation and genuine godly meditation is that
instead of emptying our minds we actually fill them with the things of
God.

So, wherever you find yourself, start training your mind today.
Learn to block those unwanted distractions out, and like Paul, meditate on the true, honorable, just, pure, lovely, commendable, excellent, and things worthy of praise (Phil 4:8). In other words, love God
with all of your mind. –Blevins

Morning: 2 Chr 9; Jude 1 — *Evening:* Zeph 1; Luke 23

DON'T BE STUPID

*"Whoever loves discipline loves knowledge,
but he who hates reproof is stupid."*
PROVERBS 12:1

Not long ago, I almost had an altercation with a very young officer. Can you believe that this guy, who probably was in diapers when I started doing time, had the nerve to tell *me* to quit talking in the hallway. I thought to myself, "Who is this young punk, who can barely shave, telling me what to do!" As I looked at this freckle-faced kid glaring at me, my first instinct was to buck and put this youngster in his place. It would have been easy. I could have embarrassed him, challenged his authority, and probably won. However, it was only with great strength, and a little wisdom, that I simply nodded my head in obedience and kept on trucking—with my mouth shut! To do anything less would have been, well, stupid.

Solomon pulls no punches. He makes it very clear: those of us who hate reproof are stupid. Strong words, but biblical truth. Just look at us. Stop for one second, and look around you at the world we live in. It is full of stupid people, including us, who hated reproof. We would not listen to our parents, our spouses, our teachers, or our probation or parole officers. We had to have things our own way, when we wanted it, no matter the cost. And the cost we paid dearly. Now, how stupid is that?

It is at times when we're confronted with reproof from authority, even in the form of a freckle-faced kid, that we have a choice to make. We can be stupid and continue the behavior that has cost us so much, or we can simply obey. Though it may seem difficult, it is not a hard choice to make. So, don't be stupid. –Solley

Morning: 2 Chr 10; Rev 1 — *Evening:* Zeph 2; Luke 24

MY PLEASURE

". . . but just as we have been approved by God to be
entrusted with the gospel, so we speak, not to please
man, but to please God who tests our hearts."
1 THESSALONIANS 2:4

By the time I was nineteen, I had been all over the Eastern part of the world and was on my way to prison. Even at that age, I had quite a repertoire of war stories. For a long time I used stories of exploits in foreign countries, narrow escapes from the police, or great schemes and scams to my every advantage. I could see pleasure in the faces of those I entertained with my stories which created a desire in me to fuel that pleasure. Because I could tell a good story, people were pleased with me. Consequently, because they were pleased, I was pleased. Before long, I wasn't only telling stories, I was trying to please people.

Paul was encouraging the Thessalonians to speak in order to please God, not men. Paul understood how easy it is to fall into the habit of speaking in such a way to seek the pleasure of an audience. When doing so, there is a subtle shift where pleasing them results in pleasing ourselves. Our pleasure easily becomes pleasing others.

Since we have been entrusted with the gospel, we speak to please God, not men. The same subtle shift occurs when we speak in such a way that pleases God. We, too, become pleased when we begin to recognize God's pleasure at our speaking the gospel. Pleasing God with the way we speak becomes *our* pleasure. The next time you realize God's pleasure with your ministry efforts, prayerfully tell Him, "My pleasure." –Karch

Morning: 2 Chr 11, 12; Rev 2 — *Evening:* Zeph 3; John 1

HE LIGHTENS MY DARKNESS

*"For it is you who light my lamp; the LORD
my God lightens my darkness."*
PSALM 18:28

P salm 18 is a wonderful expression of King David's confidence in the Lord, his God, who repeatedly delivered him from the hands of his enemies. Throughout this chapter, he refers to God as his strength, his rock, his deliverer, his shield, his horn of salvation, and his support. In verse 28, King David declares that God lightens his darkness. He knew what it was like to be overwhelmed by darkness. However, he also knew what it felt for God to reach down and turn that darkness into light, to intervene in his life in a way that only God could.

In prison, we experience many dark times, times when it feels like all hope is gone. Appeals do not work. Parole is not granted. Letters and visits do not come, and prayers do not seem to be answered. Sometimes, this overwhelms us, and we reach the point where we feel hopeless and helpless—as if all the light in our lives is gone. Inside, our world has become one of darkness. Yet, as King David experienced, we have a God that turns all of our darkness into light, a God we can call our strength, our rock, our deliverer, and our shield—a God we can call upon in times of distress.

If your life seems like constant darkness and you feel as if you have no hope, turn to the God in heaven who will turn your darkness into light. –Solley

Morning: 2 Chr 13; Rev 3 — *Evening:* Hag 1; John 2

WHO CARES?

*"So the law is paralyzed, and justice never goes forth. For the
wicked surround the righteous; so justice goes forth perverted."*
HABAKKUK 1:4

Habakkuk is sometimes labeled as the philosopher prophet. In the first few verses of this short prophecy, he is addressing one of the most philosophically and theologically challenging questions of all time: Why do bad things happen to those who try so hard to do right? Not only does Habakkuk pose a similar question, he goes to the only one who can really answer it adequately; he goes straight to God.

Habakkuk was alive during the time of the Babylonian invasions, and had, to some degree, witnessed his people being taken away into captivity. He questions God as to how the lawless and evil Babylonians repeatedly get away with such injustices toward people who are crying out to Him and trying to do what is right in His eyes. Likewise, for those who have experienced the criminal justice system, it is common to have some of the same sentiments as Habakkuk. We often see or endure things that cause us to question where justice is. Those who represent power, at times, fall into the temptation to abuse it in unrighteous and unjust ways. In the face of such abuses, it is easy to begin to wonder if anybody really does care.

When we suffer injustice and unrighteousness and begin to have similar questions, we can know there are answers. The most comforting of answers comes from God as He tells Habakkuk that the injustices and evils of the Babylonians do not escape His notice. In the same way, as His people, what we endure and suffer as injustice and unrighteousness does not escape His attention. As we look at the prophet Habakkuk, we can know for sure that God cares. –Karch

Morning: 2 Chr 14, 15; Rev 4 — *Evening:* Hag 2; John 3

HUMBLE SUBMISSION

"Let every person be subject to the governing authorities."
ROMANS 13:1A

O ne of the first things I had to learn when I came to prison, was that I was no longer in control over many things in my life. This included when I ate or showered, what clothes I wore, or even when I woke up or went to sleep. It took a while to get used to having some-body constantly in authority over my most basic life choices. In the beginning of my sentence, I crashed into a few walls trying to gain dominance, but it always resulted in the same outcome—I lost, they won.

When I finally committed my life to the Lord, I understood com-pletely that He is the supreme ruler, the Creator of the universe, and in absolute control. God was an authority I recognized, but what about the earthly authorities? What about those in positions of power over me here and now? Paul explains in Romans 13 that there are no au-thorities that exist except those instituted by God. He has established those in governing positions; therefore resisting such authorities will incur God's judgment. God's command of obedience overflows not just to His holy precepts, but also to those who He's placed in charge here on earth. That principle applies to the men and women who work day in and day out to keep our environment safe. All the little rules are in place for reasons, sometimes beyond our immediate understand-ing, but nevertheless designed for our safety and theirs.

The next time an officer tells you to do something in accordance with the rules of the institution, don't let your pride drive you to rebel-lion. Try a new approach; try responding in a righteous way. Knowing fully who the ultimate authority belongs to and that He is in absolute control, try a little humble submission. –Blevins

Morning: 2 Chr 16; Rev 5 — *Evening*: Zech 1; John 4

NOT OUR HOME

*"In my Father's house are many rooms. If it were not so, would
I have told you that I go to prepare a place for you?"*
JOHN 14:2

Many of my friends are serving life sentences. Some of them will never go home. Unless God miraculously intervenes, they will spend the rest of their lives in prison and die here old men. It is a harsh reality, but it is true. As I was lying in my bunk thinking about this the other day, it greatly disturbed me. Inside, I began to get angry, and I thought to myself, *Lord, why?*

Then I thought of Jesus' words to His disciples in John 14. Here, Jesus comforts His disciples by telling them not to let their hearts be troubled (v. 1), that He was going ahead of them to prepare a place for them (v. 2). Jesus gives His disciples hope by informing them that though he was leaving, He would someday return for them (v. 3). The idea that this world is not our home and that Christ will return for His people is a universal theme throughout all of the New Testament. This has great ramifications for all believers, yet for all of us doing time, especially those who will never go home, this is our greatest hope. Though we may never go to our earthly homes, we will someday go to our eternal home in heaven.

If you are like many of my friends and you may never walk out of prison, take comfort in knowing that someday you will be home in heaven where Christ has gone ahead to prepare a place for *you*. –Solley

Morning: 2 Chr 17; Rev 6 — *Evening:* Zech 2; John 5

WOWSER

*". . . they shall do no injustice and speak no lies, nor shall
there be found in their mouth a deceitful tongue. For they shall
graze and lie down, and none shall make them afraid."*

ZEPHANIAH 3:13

WOWSER originated in Australia and was used as an acronym for the motto of Australian social reform, "We Only Want Social Evils Remedied." It naturally developed into slang and was used in association with the identification of or bold attempts to correct social ills. Sadly, the world we live in today is full of social evils. Even the most casual glance at the evening news elicits the use of the slang word, "Wowser!"

In Zephaniah's time, there were many wowser moments. Jerusalem and the surrounding nations had earned God's judgment. Wherever the prophet turned, there were social evils. Entire nations acted with systematic injustice, and no care or love for the truth existed.

In the midst of all the madness, the Lord spoke to Zephaniah. God also wanted social evils righted and was preparing to bring about real righteous judgment against those who had participated in them. Yet, from the judgment, the Lord promised to bring about something that almost defies imagination. Through judgment, the Lord would bring forth a humble and lowly people in a place where social evils would no longer exist.

Those of us in prison can relate to the Australian motto as well as Zephaniah's concerns. As Christians, we only want social evils righted. Consequently, it is far too easy to allow ourselves to focus only on those things—we are constantly overwhelmed by the wowser.

However, the promise the Lord offered to Zephaniah still stands for us. We have the assurance that the Lord will bring about a time where there will be no injustice, lies, indifference, or fear. There will be no more need for the word "wowser." –Karch

Morning: 2 Chr 18; Rev 7 — *Evening:* Zech 3; John 6

PERFECT TIMING

". . . And who knows whether you have not come
to the kingdom for such a time as this?"
Esther 4:14b

G od's providence is sometimes a hard concept to grasp. Most of the time we treat God like some far-distant being who only reacts to punish wrongdoers when they sin. We seldom think about His guiding hand which has driven and shaped the course of history since the beginning of time. We have difficulty wrapping our minds around a God who governs and sustains all things by the power of His might. Sure, we might see Him in the big events like creation or the flood, but what about smaller events like the flight of a sparrow or the hair that falls from your head?

We see a perfect example of God in the story of Esther. Granting her favor in the eyes of a foreign king, God positioned Esther in the right spot and at the right time to save her people from destruction at the hands of Haman. Had it not been for God's providential intervention, all of Israel would have been lost. Yet, once again, God displayed His providential care and used it to bring about His purpose.

The great thing about narratives like Esther's are that they remind us God is still at work in His creation. He has a purpose and plan for each of us, regardless of how clearly we might see it. If you're having a hard time seeing God's purpose for your life, especially in prison, pray for Him to reveal it to you. Who knows? You may have come here for just such a time as this. –Blevins

Morning: 2 Chr 19, 20; Rev 8 — *Evening:* Zech 4; John 7

A GOD OF RECONCILIATION

"And this is from God, who through Christ reconciled us
to himself and gave us the ministry of reconciliation;"
2 CORINTHIANS 5:18

My relationship with someone who is very dear to my heart has been broken for a number of years. She is the most important person in my life, someone I love deeply. Yet, my actions in the past made her feel like I did not love her and that she was not important to me. When I came back to prison, she felt abandoned, betrayed, and left alone. She felt I had broken every promise I had made to her. The truth is she has every right to feel the way she does. She is my wife, and I failed her as a husband.

I have asked for her forgiveness, prayed that God would heal our relationship, and done all I know to do to fix what I have broken. Yet, the circumstances of life over the years have strained our relationship even more. However, I have not given up. As hopeless as it may seem, I know God is a God of reconciliation. He demonstrated on the cross the extent He was willing to go to reconcile us to Himself through the blood of Christ. God does not only desire that we be reconciled to Him, but that we be reconciled to each other as well (Mt 5:24). That is something we can trust Him for—reconciliation of broken relationships.

Like me, maybe you have broken a relationship with someone who is dear to your heart, and no matter how much you have prayed, asked for forgiveness, and sought reconciliation, that relationship is still strained. Do not give up! Trust in the God of reconciliation to heal what you have broken; trust in the God who set the standard by reconciling us unto Himself through the blood of His son. –Solley

Morning: 2 Chr 21; Rev 9 — *Evening:* Zech 5; John 8

TRANSPARENCY

*"But we have renounced disgraceful, underhanded ways.
We refuse to practice cunning or to tamper with God's word,
but by the open statement of the truth we would commend
ourselves to everyone's conscience in the sight of God."*

2 CORINTHIANS 4:2

Since I was a kid I've analyzed the lyrics of songs. Even as a teenager, I knew the lyrics to the song, "Home Sweet Home," by Motley Crue implied vulnerability. Of course, vulnerability was a bad thing. This is particularly the case in prison. To allow anyone to know you are vulnerable is dangerous. One of the easiest ways to betray your own vulnerabilities is by being transparent, by allowing your heart to be "an open book for the whole world to read."

When it comes to being a Christian, however, there are some unavoidable vulnerabilities. The ministry we have been given demands transparency. Paul tells the Corinthian church, as ministers of the gospel, we are to commend ourselves to everyone's conscience in the sight of God. Thus, the same transparency we have before God—the same way our hearts are open to Him—ought to be the same transparency we display for others. The world should see our hearts and see through us to know we have really renounced disgraceful and underhanded ways. The truth of what Jesus Christ has accomplished for us should never be opaque.

I try to spend more time now thinking about Scripture than song lyrics. Obviously, transparency still implies vulnerability. Yet, Christianity turns vulnerability on its head. Fascinatingly enough, when we are transparent, others around us will begin to share pages from the open book of their hearts. –Karch

Morning: 2 Chr 22, 23; Rev 10 — *Evening:* Zech 6; John 9

LOST TREASURE

"Behold, children are a heritage from the LORD,
the fruit of the womb a reward."
PSALM 127:3

C oming to prison was hard. It was hard on my mom and my wife, but it was hardest on my daughter. The stupid things we do often affect more than just ourselves and our victims. The residual effects of our crimes have both direct and indirect victims. Sadly, statistics show that our actions are going to negatively impact our precious children for years to come, but there are things we can do even in prison to dampen those effects.

Our children are a blessing from God that many of us take for granted. We go through life focused on ourselves and never think how our selfishness is hurting our little ones. When that selfishness lands us in prison, we tend to cry, "Woe is me!" and continue with our me-focused living as we serve our sentence. I run into so many men who never think twice about the treasure they've left behind. For one reason or another they've given up on their relationship with their kids.

God doesn't give us the blessing of children so that we can give up on them. They are given to us for a purpose, and I can assure you that purpose doesn't include abandonment by their fathers. Those heavenly God-sends are valuable in His eyes and should be in ours, too. In fact, they should be so important to you that nothing should keep you and me from reaching out and trying to be a part of their lives— that includes long distances that separate us or non-responses to our many letters. Our children are a heritage from the Lord, a precious reward—now go out and recover your lost treasure. –Blevins

Morning: 2 Chr 24; Rev 11 — *Evening:* Zech 7; John 10

MY REFUGE AND FORTRESS

"I will say to the LORD, 'My refuge and my
fortress, my God, in whom I trust.'"
PSALM 91:2

From a young boy fighting Goliath to his many conflicts with the surrounding heathen nations, King David's life was characterized by one battle after another. David was a fearless warrior, yet he understood what it meant to be in the heat of battle, surrounded by an enemy so overwhelming that he had no other choice but to flee and take refuge inside the safety of a fortress. He knew the comfort and sense of security that came from slamming the fortress doors shut in the face of the enemy, knowing they could no longer harm him.

Throughout the Psalms, particularly Psalm 91, King David repeatedly used the analogy of a refuge and fortress as an illustration for God. In times of overwhelming personal and national conflict when he felt overwhelmed by physical and spiritual enemies, David knew that he could seek safety and security in God, his spiritual refuge and fortress, the God in whom he trusted. David proclaimed with a confidence that came from personal experience that though a thousand may fall at his right hand and ten thousand at his left hand, God would not allow any harm to come near him (v. 7).

How about you? When times and circumstances seem to overwhelm you, when you are at your wit's end and it feels like you are being run over by spiritual enemies, where do you run? Like King David, can you proclaim with confidence that the Lord is your refuge and fortress, your God in whom you trust? –Solley

Morning: 2 Chr 25; Rev 12 — *Evening:* Zech 8; John 11

DON'T CRAWFISH

"If this be so, our God whom we serve is able to deliver us from the burning fiery furnace, and he will deliver us out of your hand, O king. But if not, be it known to you, O king, that we will not serve your gods or worship the golden image that you have set up."
DANIEL 3:17–18

Where I grew up, the drainage ditches would fill with water when it rained. Afterward, it was always neat to find crawfish when the water went down. A crawfish can walk forward, but when one wants to move fast, it goes backward. Because of this fast backward walk, the word "crawfish" became a euphemism for retreating from something—generally from some form of danger. As Christians, far too often in the face of doing what we know to be right, we crawfish.

In Daniel's time, the Babylonians took captives from the southern kingdom of Judah in three waves. Daniel and his three friends were taken, along with the royal courts, in the first wave. As they lived among the Babylonians, it would have been easy to adapt to that culture and to pick up various tendencies of the Babylonians. In their minds, however, to do so would be a form of retreating away from what they knew of their God. For instance, they knew it was especially wrong for them to bow before any idols. Unlike Daniel's friends, we are not faced with golden statues of oppressive kings; we make idols of things like anger and lust. At the slightest provocation, we bow to them—we crawfish.

What are those things within our environment that are acceptable within the culture but are wrong nonetheless? Do we bow before those things instead of standing against them? Do we bow before those things that easily become idols in our lives? Either way, let us learn from Daniel's friends; stand for what is right and don't crawfish. –Karch

Morning: 2 Chr 26; Rev 13 — *Evening:* Zech 9; John 12

STEAMING

"Be angry and do not sin; do not let the sun go down on
your anger, and give no opportunity to the devil."
EPHESIANS 4:26–27

I stood expectantly at my cell door watching the officer come down the run passing out mail. It was the last day mail would run before Christmas, and I was certain that I would at least receive a Christmas card from my daughter. When the officer slowly passed my cell shuffling through letters in his hand, anger consumed me—I was furious! Once again I was stuck out on mail call. I could not believe that my wife had not at least bought a Christmas card for my daughter to send to me.

For hours I sat there on my bed, angry. I even started writing a letter to my wife to tell her just what I thought and how not receiving a Christmas card from my little girl made me feel.

Finally, getting a hold of myself, I prayed, "Lord, I don't want to feel this way. Please take this anger away from me before it turns into resentment." Though I may not have been wrong for being angry, I knew the danger of allowing my anger to fester.

Many times, our anger may be justified. However, we have to be very careful that we do not allow our anger to simmer and lead to other negative emotions, thoughts, or actions. When we do not control our anger, we give opportunity to the devil and allow him to creep in and have a field day with our minds. While we are busy steaming, he is busy laughing. The devil uses our uncontrolled anger to sidetrack us.

If you find yourself angry, deal with it then and there. Do not let the sun go down on your anger, and do not give the devil an opportunity to use your anger to cause you to do something you will regret later. –Solley

Morning: 2 Chr 27, 28; Rev 14 — *Evening:* Zech 10; John 13

BEFORE

"Before the mountains were brought forth, or ever you had formed the earth and the world, from everlasting to everlasting you are God."
PSALM 90:2

Do you ever wonder about words? It becomes sort of an interesting habit when you begin to wonder about what a specific word means, where it comes from, and what its implications are. This is particularly the case when it comes to wondering about various words we find in the Scriptures. For instance, think about the word *before*, a small, seemingly insignificant word that we use all of the time in everyday conversation. We talk about the time before we came to prison or before we got saved. In each instance there is always a time before the period we are referencing.

The word before comes from an old English word that, in a temporal sense, literally means to exist in front of—to precede in time. The Holy Spirit makes no mistake by inspiring Moses to use this word when he penned this psalm. The Hebrew word has the same connotative force as the English. God literally exists before the mountains were brought forth. He exists before He created the world. He is from everlasting to everlasting. The essence here is that there is nothing before God. Nothing exists in front of Him—nothing precedes Him in time.

When we think about God, the concept of before isn't a reality. This is what Moses is trying to convey; because of God's eternality, He existed before there was a before. On the one hand, there are instances where some deny this attribute, and in doing so they inadvertently deny God. On the other hand, understanding God as before affirms His sovereignty over all things. This affirmation provokes the same praise Moses offers in Psalm 90. It is a great thing to worship the God of before. –Karch

Morning: 2 Chr 29; Rev 15 — *Evening:* Zech 11; John 14

CHRISTMAS TIME

*"Fear not, for behold, I bring you good news of great
joy . . . For unto you is born this day in the city of
David a Savior, who is Christ the Lord."*
LUKE 2:10–11

Many of us remember Christmas time in the free-world—a time of gift giving, fancy decorations, and good eating. However, once we've spent our first Christmas in prison, those memories tend to hurt more than bring joy. We miss times spent with friends and family, sharing in the festivities and time honored traditions. Now, Christmas becomes just another day we have to do behind bars. Bah-humbug!

Yet, when we truly understand the meaning of Christmas, it doesn't have to be such a downer. Think about it. This is the day that the universal church, the entire body of believers, past and present, has chosen to celebrate the coming of our Lord and Savior. The advent of Christ was the inaugural event that began the ushering in of God's eternal kingdom. Jesus' birth fulfilled prophecies of ancient past and embodied God's promise to Adam and Eve in the Garden of Eden (Gen 3:15). How awesome is that?

If that isn't enough to be joyful about, think about how the forgiveness of your sins would not even be possible without propitiation, a perfect sacrifice. Jesus had to die on that cross for there to be a way for us to be reconciled back to God. He couldn't have died if He didn't first come.

This Christmas, when old memories of egg-nog, tinsel, and honey-glazed ham start to make you bitter, remember the real reason we celebrate Christmas. God chose a specific way to enact His purpose of redeeming mankind. He sent His son Jesus Christ, born of a virgin, in the likeness of man, to die for our sins. Hallelujah! –Blevins

Morning: 2 Chr 30; Rev 16 — *Evening:* Zech 12, 13:1; John 15

THE GOSPEL

"For God so loved the world, that he gave his only Son, that whoever believes in him should not perish but have eternal life."
JOHN 3:16

To many people, the gospel means a variety of things. Some believe that Jesus was simply a man or a great prophet sent by God to call humanity to repentance. Others believe that Jesus became the Son of God by His obedience to God's commandments and the righteous life that He lived. Then there are those who hold to the idea that Jesus is just one of many ways to heaven. However, a true study of the Scripture will show that the gospel is so much more.

The gospel teaches that man was lost in his sin, separated from God, and destined to spend an eternity in hell. Furthermore, Jesus (who was not simply some great man or great prophet but God in the flesh) came down from heaven and lived among man for the sole purpose of redeeming mankind from eternal damnation. The gospel is based on the premise that as inherently evil and vile beings, we deserve death as the wages for our sin (Rom 3:23). However, in His love, God (in the form of Jesus Christ) willingly paid that ultimate penalty for us by taking our sins upon Himself at the cross.

This good news, the gospel, is culminated in one of the most quoted Scriptures in the Bible: "For God so loved the world, that he gave his only Son, that whosoever believes in him should not perish but have eternal life." We were once sinners destined for eternal damnation, but Christ, in His love, died so that we may have life. That is the good news! That is the gospel. –Solley

Morning: 2 Chr 31; Rev 17 — *Evening:* Zech 13:2–9; John 16

GOIN' DOWN

*"But Jonah rose to flee to Tarshish from the presence f the LORD.
He went down to Joppa and found a ship going to Tarshish . . ."*
JONAH 1:3A

U pon receiving his commission from the Lord to go and preach to
Nineveh, Jonah fled. There isn't anything surprising about this
to those who have either heard or read the story of Jonah. We know
what happens at the end of the story: Jonah eventually gets it right and
answers the call of God. Yet, knowing these things has a tendency to
cause us to miss some of the nuance of Jonah's story. In many ways,
his story is our story. Those of us who, in one way or another, spent a
considerable number of years running from the Lord understand how
our running resulted in a series of downturns in life.

In today's text, we see when Jonah fled from the presence of the
Lord, he went *down* to Tarshish. A couple of verses later, Jonah went
down into the lower compartments of the ship. When he finally made
it as low as he could go, he lay *down* to rest (v. 5). Jonah went *down* into
the belly of a whale which, no doubt, took him *down* even farther (v.
17). Jonah's progression *down* is representative of our own downturns
in life anytime we find ourselves running from God. These downturns
are an inevitable result of running from God.

The difficulty seems to be that running is hardwired into us. There
seems to be a natural impulse to flee. The key, however, is direction.
Instead of running from God, we need to run to Him, to run toward
what He has for us in life. Any other direction ultimately is going
down—away from Him. Let us learn from Jonah lest we, too, find ourselves going down. –Karch

Morning: 2 Chr 32; Rev 18 — *Evening:* Zech 14; John 17

UNCOMMON SENSE

"Seek good, and not evil, that you may live; and so the LORD,
the God of hosts, will be with you, as you have said. Hate
evil, and love good, and establish justice in the gate;"
AMOS 5:14–15A

D ayrooms, rec-yards, chow halls, or hallways, it doesn't matter where you go; the prevailing wisdom around here seems to be one of foolishness. It's almost as if guys intentionally go looking for trouble. Whether it is frivolous confrontations with officers or prideful altercations with other inmates, some guys just don't know when to quit. Peace is a meaningless word in many prisoners' vocabularies, and occasionally, those of us who aren't looking to do our time the hard way get caught in the cross-fire. Officers and inmates alike usually know who the troublemakers are, but it's still too easy to get caught up in the shenanigans of those clucks.

Interestingly, the Bible gives us some pretty sound instructions concerning making the right decisions. What's even more interesting is that it would seem like common sense to most people: "Seek good and not evil," and "Hate evil, and love good." The question we must ask ourselves is twofold, "Are we living by these words?" And, if not, "Why?"

Prison affords us so many opportunities to get in trouble, but it's no different in the free-world. If we were making bad choices out there, coming to prison isn't going to magically stop you from continuing that pattern. Are you still finding yourself getting into trouble? Are your unwise actions affecting others around you? Eventually, you're going to need to do something different. Take a page from God's Word, and seek good and not evil. Try using a little "uncommon sense." –Blevins

Morning: 2 Chr 33; Rev 19 — *Evening:* Mal 1; John 18

FINISHING WELL

*"I have fought the good fight, I have finished
the race, I have kept the faith."*
2 TIMOTHY 4:7

Does your past sometimes weigh you down? Mine does. I believe Paul's past weighed him down, too. It is not hard to imagine that Paul struggled with the things he had done prior to his conversion. He stood there holding Stephen's clothes while the crowds stoned Stephen to death (Acts 7:58). He persecuted, imprisoned, and put to death the very people he would come to love so dearly. In his own words, Paul proclaimed himself to be the chief among sinners (1 Tim 1:15). Yet, in his last letter from a Roman prison, you can sense the passion Paul felt when he tells Timothy, his beloved son in the faith, that he finished well. He fought the good fight, and he kept the faith. In essence, what Paul is saying is that though he may have started bad, he finished well.

Like Paul, many of us have started bad. We have lived lives we really regret. More than anything, we wish we could change our pasts—take away some of the hurt and pain we have caused. Because of the destructive lives we have lived, it is so easy for us to allow our pasts to sit on our shoulders and weigh on us. However, the life of Paul teaches us a valuable lesson: Sometimes it is not how we start in life that matters, but rather, it is how we finish.

Let our hearts no longer be weighed down by the past. Instead, let our heart's desire be to say at the end of our road that we have fought the good fight, we have finished the race, and we have kept the faith—we have finished well. –Solley

Morning: 2 Chr 34; Rev 20 — *Evening:* Mal 2; John 19

HARD TIME

"Good sense wins favor, but the way of the treacherous is their ruin."
PROVERBS 13:15

At some point, we have all heard stories about hard time. Most of us in prison still tend to think of the more restricted custody levels as hard time. I look back and think about the times I spent on those restricted custody levels—particularly the years I spent in segregation—and have those same thoughts. In many ways, it was hard time; and compared to the time I am doing now, it was hard time.

Proverbs 13 is part of the collection of the proverbs of Solomon. In this verse, we see what it is that makes time hard. Other Bibles translate the last half of this verse as "the way of the treacherous is hard." Solomon lets us know that it isn't necessarily the custody level that makes time hard; it is the actions resulting in us getting to those restricted custody levels. What is in our hearts is what makes time hard. When our lives are defined by the treachery and sin within our hearts, we can expect our way to be hard. As this is the case, the only way to keep from doing hard time is to deal with the problem of treachery and sin in our hearts.

We know the good news of the gospel liberates us from the problem of treachery and sin in our lives. Knowing this good news is the best good sense we can ever have. Through the good news of the gospel, we have the favor of the Lord, and hard time becomes not so hard anymore. –Karch

Morning: 2 Chr 35; Rev 21 — *Evening:* Mal 3; John 20

FREE INDEED

". . . Truly, truly, I say to you, everyone who practices sin is a slave to sin . . . So if the Son sets you free, you will be free indeed."
JOHN 8:34–36

For those of us incarcerated, December 31 is bittersweet. As we mark this day off our calendars, we breathe a sigh of relief because we have survived another year of prison life and are one step closer to freedom. On the other hand, we grieve for having spent another year of our lives behind bars, which is difficult to accept. We rightly feel we have lost so much by being locked away.

Many of us have lost more than we ever thought we had to lose. However, as Christians, we can take comfort in the fact that we have gained one thing which far surpasses all we have lost—we have gained a true freedom that is only found in Christ. We have been set free from the chains of our pasts, liberated from the slavery of sin, and given new life—a life of eternal freedom. And the most beautiful thing about this gift of freedom is that it can never be taken away from us.

Yes, another year of being incarcerated has passed you by, and that is tough. But even though you are locked up, you have a freedom that many people in the free-world will never enjoy. As you end one year and begin another, thank God for the freedom He has given you in Christ because who the Son sets free is free indeed. –Solley

Morning: 2 Chr 36; Rev 22 — *Evening:* Mal 4; John 21

APPENDIX A: TOPICAL DEVOTIONS

GOOD FRIDAY

"And with him they crucified two robbers, one
on his right and one on his left."
MARK 15:27

O ver one-third of the content of the four gospel accounts focuses on the last few hours of Jesus' life. Why such detail about the suffering of Jesus? Why does Christianity traditionally refer to the Friday we reflect on the crucifixion of Christ as *good?* In view of the violence and brutality of crucifixion, how can we call such an event good? Ultimately, our understanding of the day we reflect on Jesus' crucifixion as good boils down to a matter of contrasts.

Think about the contrast between Jesus and the men crucified on each side of Him. Unlike Jesus, who was sinless and completely innocent of the charges against Him, the two robbers crucified with Jesus were both guilty criminals. For one of them, the one who mocked Jesus, there was nothing good about that day. But for the other, who looked upon Christ and asked to be remembered by Him, the most horrible day of his life provided redemption (Luke 23:39–43).

The crucifixion of Jesus stands between criminals still today. Each of us has committed crimes against God and is guilty. As we look upon the crucified Christ, He provides a point of contrast between all of us who are guilty of sin—prisoner and free people alike. Unfortunately, some will go on mocking; nothing good can be seen in the cross for them. However, for those of us who acknowledge our guilt and ask to be forgiven and remembered by Jesus, the darkest stain in human history becomes our brightest light. For us, it is *good* Friday indeed. –Solley

NOT HERE

"He is not here, for he has risen, as he said.
Come, see the place where he lay."
MATTHEW 28:6

I n the early church, the resurrection of Jesus was central to expressing and living out the Christian faith. Because of the resurrection of Jesus, early believers who had been changed by the power of the gospel always had the hope of their own resurrection in sight. They thought about it often. Today, however, the resurrection is often just treated as a cool story. Unfortunately, even Christians tend to think of the resurrection as a cool story, if they think of it all.

J. Gresham Machen, an early twentieth century biblical scholar who devoted his life to affirming the biblical witness of Jesus Christ, knew there was something about the resurrection because it turned a handful of Galilean fishermen into a force that turned the world upside down. What did they know that we don't? The answer is quite simple: nothing. So, why are we not impacted in the same way? The ramifications of the resurrection are the same for us as it was for them.

When was the last time you seriously thought about the resurrection of Jesus and what it means for you? The same Jesus that died for our sins was raised again for our justification. Thus, the resurrection demonstrates the glory of God through the vindication of the Son by the Father, and without it, our faith would be in vain. As Christians all over the world celebrate the resurrection of Jesus, don't lose sight of what it means for you. Because Jesus was raised, those of us who believe in Him have truly been forgiven our sins. Because of the resurrection, we have been declared righteous and made clean in the sight of Almighty God. –Karch

A MOTHER'S LOVE

*"but standing by the cross of Jesus were his
mother and his mother's sister, . . ."*
JOHN 19:25

J esus was dying. He hung from the cross, beaten and bloody, bearing the sins of the world. Yet, in the darkest moment He would ever face, He was not alone. His mother stood there at the foot of His cross. Displayed and shamed before the world, labeled a blasphemer and dissident, His mother did not forsake Him. Even when others abandoned and betrayed Jesus, Mary remained by her son's side and loved Him until the end like mother's do.

Mary's love for her son was a love that knew no end and counted no cost. Her love for Jesus is a vivid representation of many of our mothers' love for us. On any given weekend, you can walk into the visitation room of any prison in America and see the same thing: mothers coming to see their children, children who have been labeled criminals and rejected by society. Yet no matter how we have been labeled or how many others have abandoned us, our mothers are there, believing in us, supporting us, and loving us. Even when it pains them to see us locked up, they bear that pain for us because we are their children. Moms are the only ones who have truly stayed down with us until the end. A mother's love is amazing!

We owe a great debt of gratitude to our mothers. We can never repay them for all they have done for us over the years. This Mother's Day make sure your mother knows how much she means to you. Do not let another day go by without letting her know how much you love and appreciate her. –Solley

A FATHER'S COMPASSION

*"As a father shows compassion to his children, so the
LORD shows compassion to those who fear him."*
PSALM 103:13

O f the primary characteristics of a father, compassionate has to be the most important. Although parenting also entails tough love and a firm hand, the most effective form of parenting always centers on compassion. It is through our compassion that our children learn the depth and breadth of our love for them. Unfortunately, many of us in prison never experienced compassion from our fathers. Nevertheless, it is a characteristic of proper parenting, and one we would do well to display in our relationships with our children.

The author of Psalm 103 clearly portrays a relationship between a father and his child as being marked by compassion. He associates it with the type of compassion the Lord shows His own. God's compassion is defined by knowing our condition, being slow to anger, and forgiving our transgressions. Here, we are provided meaningful insight to what being a father entails. As fathers, we ought to remember the example provided by God and extend the same compassion to our children. By modeling compassion throughout the Bible, God has demonstrated what true fatherhood should look like.

With so many deadbeat dads in the world and so many fathers incarcerated, there is never a lack of children who need to experience a father's compassion. This Father's Day, whether you're a father or maybe just happen to be close to a child who needs a father, think about the example God has displayed in His Word, and ask yourself what you can do to show a little fatherly compassion. –Blevins

THANK GOD

"The LORD is good, a stronghold in the day of trouble;
he knows those who take refuge in him."
Nahum 1:7

As I pen this, thousands of Christian brothers and sisters are flee-
ing for their lives. Islamic militants have overrun several Iraqi
cities and are exterminating those who refuse to convert to Islam.
Leaving everything behind, these brave men and women are facing
death in order to remain true to their risen Lord Jesus Christ.

That type of persecution is foreign to most of us. We sit safely in
the confines of our cell or cubicle professing our faith with near im-
munity. We never have to worry about dying for what we believe in
because we're safe behind the shield of our Bibles and Sunday morning worship services. Yet, what happens when those shields become
bull's-eyes? Have you ever thought about what would happen if the
very name of Jesus was the deciding factor of whether you lived or
died? What if the name of Jesus became anathema to the American
people? What if being a true follower of Jesus meant constant ridicule,
harassment, or death? Could you stand up under that type of pressure? Would your faith be able to endure the harshest circumstances?
I'm not sure if you've looked at the direction our wonderful country
is headed, but it wouldn't surprise me if that day eventually arrived.
Thank God it's not here, yet.

Persecution is not something new for God's people. Dying for the
faith isn't a twenty-first century fad Christians must all of the sudden
figure out how to overcome. The answer to the torments experienced
by first century Christians as well as by contemporary Iraqi Christians is
to know that the Lord is good, a stronghold in the day of trouble. God
is our safe haven, and this Thanksgiving we should be thankful that in
whatever circumstance we find ourselves, we can rely on Him to get us
through. –Blevins

THE DEATH OF A LOVED ONE

SOMEDAY

"But now he is dead . . . Can I bring him back again?
I shall go to him, but he will not return to me."
2 SAMUEL 12:23

When my father was diagnosed with terminal lung cancer and given weeks to live, my prayer was to be able to say goodbye to him before he died. We were both incarcerated so it was not easy to get approval for an inter-unit phone call, but by the grace of God, my prayer was answered. I was able to talk to my father—I was able to say goodbye. Yet, as I hung up the phone after our brief conversation, I sat there knowing that I had not told him all I wanted to—there was so much left unsaid between us. I walked back to my cellblock with a heavy heart filled with words to my father that would never be spoken.

After talking to my father, I lay on my bunk thinking about him, our lives together, and all of the words left unspoken. My thoughts turned to my faith. Though I knew I would deeply mourn the loss of my father, it was a great comfort knowing that someday I would see him again. In heaven, I would be able to tell him all that has gone unspoken between us. King David took comfort in the same knowledge. Although his son had passed away, he knew that he would someday see his child again. Though we may have to say goodbye, it is only for a while. Someday we will be reunited in our home in heaven.

If you have experienced the loss of a loved one, rest assured that, in Christ, life for your loved one has just begun. Some day you will see them again. Some day you will be able to share with them all the words that have gone unspoken. –Solley

FACING FREEDOM

"Trust in the LORD with all your heart, and do not lean
on your own understanding. In all your ways acknowledge
him, and he will make straight your paths."
PROVERBS 3:5–6

Afterspending years incarcerated, facing freedom is almost unbelievable. You have done your time; your out-date is approaching. You are ready to walk out of here and make up for all of the lost years. You are focused, determined, and ready to show everyone how much you have changed.

Yet, with freedom comes many decisions and choices which will greatly test your faith and commitment to Christ. Satan will try to trip you up at every opportunity and lead you back down roads you no longer want to travel. He would love nothing more than for you to become another statistic where everyone can point their finger and say, "I told you so. He had jailhouse religion." Therefore, it is important when you walk out of prison to stay focused on God as you face the challenging tasks of restoring broken relationships, looking for employment, finding long-term housing, and becoming accustomed to your newfound freedom. Do not give in to the temptation to move too fast. Take life slowly, one day at a time, and trust in God to provide the things you need. And when times get rough, and you find yourself tempted to revert back to the old lifestyle of easy money or to escape by drowning your frustrations in drugs or alcohol, remember where God has brought you from and the price you paid to get to where you are.

Life out there never goes as you plan in here. Times will get hard, but if you keep your focus on Christ, you can make it. God loves you. You are His now, so trust Him to care for you and to direct your path. –Solley

BIBLIOGRAPHY

Lewis, C. S., Ed. *Essays Presented to Charles Williams.* Oxford: Oxford University Press, 1947.

Machiavelli, Niccoli, *The Prince.* 1532. Ed. & Trans. Robert M. Adams. Norton Critical Editions. New York: Norton, 1992.

Metaxas, Eric, Bohnoeffer: *Pastor, Martyr, Prophet, Spy.* Nashville: Thomas Nelson, 2010.

Strom, Linda, *Karla Faye Tucker Set Free: Life and Faith on Death Row.* Colorado Springs: WaterBrook Press, 2000.

Wiesel, Elie, *Night.* 1956. Trans. Marion Wiesel. New York: Hill and Wang, 2006.

TOPICAL INDEX

A

Abandonment: Apr 7; May 18; Sept 9

Acceptance: Apr 14

Accountability: Aug 28; Sept 7

Achievement: Apr 22; Dec 29

Addiction: Feb 22; Sept 30, Aug 31

Adversity: See: Conflict; Suffering; Trials

Affliction: See: Adversity; Conflict; Suffering; Trials

Alone: See: Loneliness

Anger: Apr 29; Jun 24; Oct 17; Dec 23

Anxiety: May 9; Sept 1; Oct 15

Appreciation: July 12, 17 (*see also: Gratitude; Thanksgiving*)

Ashamed: See: Shame

Assurance: Feb 13; Jul 13; Sept 5, 15; Oct 24; Dec 26 (*see also: confidence*)

Attitude: Oct 9

Authenticity: Sept 27; Oct 22 (*see also: Character; Integrity*)

Authority: Dec 4, 10, 14

B

Belief—Believe: See: Confidence; Faith; Trusting God

Blessings, God's: Jan 15, 31; Jun 23; Sept 2

Blessings: Jun 17

Body of Christ: See: Church

Brokenness: Jan 20

Brotherhood: See: Fellowship; Friendship

Burdens: Sept 30; Nov 29

C

Character: Feb 3; Mar 16; Oct 13; Nov 7

Charity: See: Loving Others

Choices: Jan 22; Jun 15; Aug 9; Sept 30; Nov 12; Dec 28; Getting Out of Prison

Christian Life: Feb 12, 19; Mar 20, 22; Apr 1, 3; May 17; Jun 6; Jul 6; Aug 14; Sept 22; Dec 2, 28, 29; Nov 30

Christian Walk: Feb 25; Jan 7; Feb 27; Nov 30

Christlikeness: Feb 3; Mar 1, 21; May 1; Sept 21 (*see also: Lifestyle*)

Church: Feb 21, 27; Mar 18; May 10; Aug 23; Sept 7

Comfort: Mar 4; Aug 8; Sept 30; Oct 15

Commitment: Jan 5; Feb 28; Jun 1; Aug 21

Community: See: Fellowship; Church; Body of Christ

Compassion: May 1; Sept 11; Father's Day (*see also: Loving Others*)

Condemnation: Feb 13; Mar 3

Confidence: Feb 7; Jun 20; Oct 15; Nov 20 (*see also; Trusting God*)

Conflict: Mar 7

Contentment: Jan 8

Courage: Feb 8

Creation: May 23; Jul 30; Aug 20

D

Darkness: Feb 17

Death: Mar 28: Jun 11; Nov 2; Dec 15; The Death of a Loved One, p. 374

Decisions: Jan 13, 22; Feb 9; Jul 16; Aug 9 (*see also: Wisdom*)

Defending the Faith: See: Evangelism

Dejection: See: Depression

Deliverance: Nov 28

Dependence on God: Feb 18; Mar 4; Jun 12, 26; Jul 10; Aug 17; Nov 1

Depression: Jan 31; Feb 5, 6; Apr 27; Jun 20; Nov 4

Despair: Apr 16; Sept 30; Nov 1 (*see also: Weariness*)

Devotion: Jan 10; May 30; Oct 5

Difficult Times: See: Suffering; Trials

Discipleship: Jan 22; Mar 22; Apr 1

Discipline: Jun 1, 10; Oct 5, 20

Discontentment: Feb 1; May 26

Discouragement: Jul 19; Dec 8

Doubt: See: Confidence; Faith; Trust; Trusting God

E

Endurance: See: Overcoming

Evangelism: Jan 19; Feb 4; Mar 15, 23; Apr 3, 15; May 2, 7, 12; Jul 25, 29; Aug 15, 16, 19; Sept 14; Oct 26; Nov 15, 23

Evil: May 28

F

Faith: Jan 28; Apr 9; Jun 6, 8, 22; Jul 20; Aug 5; Sept 22

Faithfulness: Apr 18

Fatherhood: Jun 16; Jul 13; Father's Day

Fear: Mar 4, 9; Apr 2; Oct 15, 21; Nov 13

Fellowship: Jan 24; Feb 11, 15; May 10; Aug 12, 23, 25; Sept 7; Oct 5, 20

Forgiveness, God's: Jan 20; Feb 13; Oct 3

Forgiveness: Jan 6; Mar 31; Apr 29; Jun 19; Aug 7

Freedom: Feb 22; Mar 31; Apr 1, 28; May 2; Jul 4; Dec 30, 31; Being Released, p. 375

Friendship: Jan 17, 24; Feb 15; Jul 23; Nov 9

Frustration: See: Struggles

Future: Jan 9, 19

G

Giving: Mar 23

God's Faithfulness: Feb 5, 22, 28; Jun 22; Jul 31

God's Love: Apr 7; Jun 16; Jul 13; Nov 21

God's Mercy: Apr 8; Sept 13; Oct 23

God's Sovereignty: Jan 23; Feb 6; Apr 24; Jul 20; Aug 6; Dec 24

God's Will: Jun 23; Aug 9

God-centeredness: Feb 23; Mar 12; Apr 15

Gospel: Jan 12; May 2, 12; Jun 27; Aug 2; Sep 11, 17; Dec 7, 11, 26, 30

Grace: Jan 27; Jul 7; Nov 14, 17

Gratitude: Mar 27; May 25; Jun 20 (*see also: Appreciation; Thanksgiving*)

Grief: Jan 21; Feb 28; Mar 10

Guidance: Feb 18; Aug11; Nov 25

Guilt: Jan 20; Mar 27; Jun 4; Oct 3, 6

H

Hard Times: Jan 30; Feb 6, 16; Mar 4, 12; Apr 17, May 24; Jul 10, 15, 20; Aug 3; Nov 3, 25;

Healing: Apr 12; Jun 12

Holiness: See: New Life in Christ; New Life

Honoring parents: Jan 4

H

Hope: Jan 9, 30; Apr 8, 11, 14, 20, 26; Jul 1, 2, 19, 31; Aug 4, 11, 16; Sept 10; Oct 25, 31; Nov 16, 19; Dec 12, 15

Humility: Jan 25; Feb 26; Mar 20; Sept 16; Dec 14

Hypocrisy: Jan 11

I

Identity: May 19; Jun 30; Jul 22; Aug 13, 22; Sept 29

Idolatry: Feb 23; Jul 12; Oct 1

Injustice: See: Justice

Integrity: May 29; Dec 22

Insecurity: See: Confidence; Identity; Trust

J

Jesus: Mar 2; May 3, 11, 26, 30; Jun 1, 22, 30; Aug 12, 21, Sept 6, 29; Oct 11, 12; Dec 31 **Joy:** Apr 4; Sept 22

Judgment: Apr 25; Sept 26; Oct 2

Justice: Sept 16; Dec 13, 16

K

Kindness: See: Loving Others

L

Lifestyle: Mar 1, 22, 26, 29; Apr 5; May 16, Jun 30; Sept 21

Loneliness: Apr 7; Mar 15; May 18, 25; Jul 6, 14; Aug 24; Sept 9

Made in the USA
Lexington, KY
13 November 2018